THE POLITICAL AND
CONSTITUTIONAL IDEAS OF THE
PHILIPPINE REVOLUTION

CESAR ADIB MAJUL

THE POLITICAL AND CONSTITUTIONAL IDEAS OF THE PHILIPPINE REVOLUTION

Revised Edition

WITH AN INTRODUCTION BY LEOPOLDO Y. YABES

New York

ORIOLE EDITIONS, INC.

PRINTED IN THE UNITED STATES OF AMERICA
by SENTRY PRESS, NEW YORK, N. Y. 10013

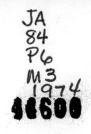
To Ricardo Pascual,
who originally suggested the possibility of a work along these lines,
this book is dedicated.

Introduction

OF THE GENERALLY recognized areas in the field of political science, political theory seems to have held the least attraction for Filipino political scientists in the twentieth century. The areas of government, political parties and public opinion, and international law and relations have attracted greater interest among local students. There seems to be a marked timidity to examine, assess, and evaluate systematically ideas that inspire and govern man's and society's political behavior.

And yet, when a well-known student of philosophy, Ricardo R. Pascual, ventured into the field of political theory some five years ago with his *Partyless Democracy,* the reception of his work among a number of our professional political scientists was rather cold, if not hostile. Whether they were cold to the work because they did not share his views or because they did not like the idea of a philosophy student encroaching upon what they believed to be their exclusive domain, I have not as yet been able to ascertain to my own satisfaction. But neither reason seems easy to understand, because Pascual did not expect immediate and uncritical indorsement of his views, or of the methods he employed in arriving at his conclusions, and because political theory, precisely, needs students who have had ample training in philosophy. Political theory is basic to the study of political science.

The present work is another attempt at political theory by another student whose basic discipline is philosophy. Cesar A. Majul is a member of the staffs of the Department of Philosophy and the Department of Political Science, College of Liberal Arts, University of the Philippines. *The Political and Constitutional Ideas of the Philippine Revolution* is an important attempt at examining and interpreting the ideas that brought about the Philippine Revolution, determined its conduct, and shaped its objectives. It is based on the doctoral dissertation which he presented recently to the Graduate Faculty of Cornell University. To my knowledge it is the first serious inquiry into and evaluation of the ideas of the Revolution, in the light of the development of Philippine political thought. In the author's desire to get at the truth, he does not show any attempt at evading issues which more timid students have evaded. He shows a firm although gentle hand in writing such issues.

Pascual's *Partyless Democracy,* Teodoro A. Agoncillo's *The Revolt of the Masses,* and Majul's *The Political and Constitutional Ideas of the Philippine Revolution* constitute a welcome departure from the undistinguished, uninspired works in Philippine history and political science on which two generations of Filipinos have been brought up. Where others, though Filipino citizens, have written, unconsciously maybe, from the point of view of some past or present foreign political, military, or spiritual mentors, Pascual, Majul, and Agoncillo have written as Filipinos and from the point of view of their own people. They are in the vanguard, as it were, of the movement, the need for which has been deeply felt since the recrudescence, not so long ago, of obscurantism and bigotry, to reassess our past from our perspective as a sovereign people, looking at the world and at ourselves as a free and independent nation, not as Spanish subjects or as American wards. It is hoped that other students with the competence and seriousness of Pascual, Majul, and Agoncillo will join in this movement to pave the way for a more enlightened understanding of our history and for a more healthy respect for our past and present struggle for intellectual freedom and political integrity.

Leopoldo Y. Yabes

Quezon City, May 25, 1957

Preface

THIS WORK IS essentially an attempt to present a history of ideas. It also represents an effort to relate historical data with the movement of ideas—more specially, ideas intimately connected with events of the Philippine Revolution. Thus the work covers many subjects, but there is no claim that all of them had been thoroughly investigated. However, it has analyzed to a great extent the contents of those ideas which our Revolutionary Fathers utilized to make the Filipinos more of a community with increasingly definite ideals and commitments. In brief, these were the ideas believed to have been conducive to the construction of *order* in Philippine society. Order—in the sense of uniting Filipinos by means of certain preconceived values and principles believed by their leaders to be most adequate for the happiness of the people; and order—in the sense of integrating Filipino society within a supreme coercive authority. It was the desire of the author to throw light on those fundamental aspirations that have contributed to the formation of our nation. The readers are given an opportunity to conclude as to whether or not the kind of community dreamt by our Revolutionary Fathers has been attained, or what amounts to the same question, whether or not the work of the Revolution has been terminated.

Since most of the primary sources for an understanding of the Revolution are still in Spanish, it was necessary to perform some translations. Every quotation whose corresponding footnote shows a title in the Spanish language has been a translation of the author. This covers all quotations from *La Solidaridad* and the *Epistolario Rizalino,* and most of those from the works of M. H. del Pilar, Graciano López-Jaena, Mariano Ponce, and Apolinario Mabini.

The bulk of the work constituted part of the author's doctoral dissertation in Cornell University. However, modifications in style and additional bibliographical data have been made. A whole new section (section 7) has been added to Chapter VI. Also, some additional observations in the last chapter were inserted. The author invites the readers to note his numerous digressions in his footnotes. These digressions contain important points for the understanding of the work.

Acknowledgment is due to the University of the Philippines which, in sending me abroad, gave me opportunities to consult a great number of documentary material. Dr. Tomás Fonacier's encouragement and providing of various kinds of facilities were indispensable. In my researches on the Revolution I had also received some financial aid from the Social Science Research Center of Cornell University. I wish to thank those who in various ways aided me in my work. Dr. Mario Einaudi's questions and subtle suggestions always challenged and inspired me. To him I owe a lot. My friends Dr. Rose Goldsen, Mr. Harry Holloway, Mr. Peter Woll and my colleagues Mr. Alejandro Fernandez, Mr. Armando Bonifacio, Mrs. Josefa Cabanos Lava, and especially Mr. Leopoldo Yabes have all given valuable suggestions and have aided me gather my thoughts together. However, none of them is responsible for whatever errors of fact or poor interpretations might have crept into the work. Above all, I want to thank my wife Wiene for her proof-reading, typing, patience, and encouragement.

—C.A.M.

Contents

THE POLITICAL AND
CONSTITUTIONAL IDEAS OF THE
PHILIPPINE REVOLUTION

CHAPTER ONE : *The Philippine Revolution*

WITH THEIR DYING gasps as they were garroted by order of the Spanish government on February 17, 1872, three Filipino priests grimly heralded the rise of Philippine nationalism. These executions brought to a head the acrimonious "secularization controversy" that marred nineteenth century Spanish rule in the Philippines. Above all else, this controversy centered on the demand on the part of Filipino priests to increase their opportunities to hold parishes. In this demand the Filipino clergy was combatted by the Spanish friars who controlled most of the parishes. With the growing sympathy of Filipinos for their own priests, the controversy gradually became a national issue.[1]

For their valiant struggles in defense of the rights of the Filipino clergy, these priests (José Burgos, Mariano Gómez, and Jacinto Zamora) had incurred the hatred of the Spanish friars but had become heroes in the eyes of Filipinos. It is therefore difficult to overestimate the demoralizing influence of their execution. The Spanish government claimed, in explanation, that these priests were largely responsible for a mutiny of Filipino soldiers that had occurred the month before. However, many people believed these priests to be innocent, and the radical measures meted out to them to be explicable on grounds of either racial discrimination or because these priests were the most vigorous proponents of the secularization movement. The fact that the archbishop of Manila refused to defrock these priests, in spite of the request of the

[1] Cf. James A LeRoy, *The Americans in the Philippines: A History of the Conquest and First Years of Occupation, with an Introductory Account of the Spanish Rule* (Boston: The Riverside Press, 1914), Vol. I, p. 60. LeRoy is considered to be the foremost American scholar on the history of the Philippine Revolution.

Spanish governor-general, confirmed the belief that these priests were innocent. Since it was well known that these priests were in continuous conflict with the friars, Filipinos tended to blame the whole affair on the machinations of the friars. And more than this: the civil government was believed to have become a tool to protect the vested interests of the friars.

At this time the most educated group of Filipinos were their priests. But with the opening of the Suez Canal in 1869 faster and more frequent communication with Spain and the rest of Europe ensued. With greater opportunities for education and with more chances for travel to Europe, there began to develop in the country a different group of educated men. These men, known as *ilustrados,* formed a social class easily recognized within Filipino society. They usually came from a rising middle class, more specifically from the lower middle class. Yet the *ilustrados* crossed economic lines, for many of them had parents who were peasants.

It was from the educated segment of the population that the demand for reforms came. Aside from the demand for political and social rights, it was noteworthy that many of the *ilustrados* utilized the secularization issue as one of the constant elements in the demand for reforms.

1. *The "Propaganda Movement."* From the 1870's to 1892, the most vocal Filipino demand was the granting of those political rights actually enjoyed by Spaniards. But this was to be done within the framework of the Spanish monarchy. There was no demand for any secession from Spain; on the contrary, the cry for "assimilation" was widespread. This movement has been called the "propaganda movement." Among the principal leaders of this movement were Marcelo H. del Pilar (1850-1896), Graciano López-Jaena (1856-1896), José Rizal (1861-1896), and Mariano Ponce (1863-1917). Del Pilar was a lawyer and journalist. López-Jaena was also a journalist. Mariano Ponce was a historian and physician. José Rizal, who is considered to be the greatest hero of the Philippines, was a physician, poet, and writer. The writings of all these men contributed to create a greater social and political awareness among Filipinos. Rizal's two

novels *Noli Me Tangere* and the *El Filibusterismo* are believed
to have contributed substantially to the germination of some of the
ideas of the Philippine revolution.[2] Most of the works of the
propagandists were not allowed to enter the Philippines. It was under the threat of imprisonment or exile that inhabitants of the
islands could read the novels of Rizal.

On February 15, 1889, a fortnightly newspaper was founded
in Barcelona by the propagandists. The aim of *La Solidaridad*
was to expose the political and social conditions of the Philippines.
Reforms asked for the Filipino people were voiced in this paper.
It asked for the curtailment of the power of the Spanish governor-general, the suppression of the *Guardia Civil,* the expulsion
of the friars, etc.

Not long after his second visit to the Philippines, Rizal founded
the *Liga Filipina* in Manila on July 3, 1892. The aim of this
organization was to inculcate moral and political principles among
the population in order to attain a greater unity. This organization did not last long. Four days after its establishment, Rizal
was arrested and exiled to Dapitan. However, in April 1893, the
organization was revived under a new leadership. Among the
original members of this revived *Liga,* there were two men destined
to play an important role in the development of Philippine politics, namely, Andrés Bonifacio (1863-1897) and Apolinario Mabini (1864-1903).

2. *The Katipunan.* On July 7, 1892, the very day of Rizal's
banishment, a secret society was founded by Bonifacio under the
name of *Katipunan.*[3] Its fundamental aims were to unite all
Filipinos in terms of a single ideology and to create an independent nation by means of revolution. Although originally most of
the members came from the humbler strata of society, later on
priests and members of the lower middle class joined it. A con-

---

[2] Rafael Palma (1874-1939), a biographer of Rizal, stated that *El Filibusterismo* was fundamentally "separatist"; that at least the men who read
it had this impression. Cf. *Biografia de Rizal* (Manila: Bureau of Printing, 1949), p. 199.

[3] The word "katipunan" is a Tagalog word meaning "association." The
full name of the society was *Kataastaasan Kagalanggalang Katipunan ng
mga Anak ng Bayan* (The Highest and Most Respectable Association of
the Sons of the People). In practice the society was simply called "Katipunan" or "K.K.K." Cf. Leandro H. Fernandez, *The Philippine Republic*
(New York, 1926), p. 13, footnote 4.

servative estimate of its members put them at 100,000.[4] Shortly after the establishment of the society Bonifacio wrote a credo for it (*Decalogue* or *Duties of the Sons of the People*). This credo was later set aside for the *Kartilla Ng Katipunan* which fully embodied the moral principles of the society. The *Kartilla* was written by Emilio Jacinto (1875-1899), who is known as the "brains of the Katipunan." The society had an organ called *Kalayaan* (Liberty). However, due to the early uncovering of the *Katipunan* by the authorities, not more than two issues were printed.

The existence of the *Katipunan* although suspected earlier was betrayed to a friar curate on August 19, 1896. Spanish officials arrested more than 500 of the most prominent Filipinos in Manila on the belief that the society was of their making. But the most important leaders of the society escaped from Manila in time. On August 26, in the vicinity of Manila at Balintawak about 100 *katipuneros* declared publicly that their objective was independence. Within a month the rebellion spread like wildfire to eight of the nearby provinces. The Revolution was on!

3. *The Rise of Aguinaldo.* Bonifacio and his men suffered many reverses in the attempts of the Spaniards to quell the rebellion. On the other hand, in the province of Cavite the revolt under Emilio Aguinaldo (1869-1963), a *katipunero,* was succeeding. Although Bonifacio was still the *Supremo* of the *Katipunan,* and Aguinaldo only a member, the prestige of the latter, due to his military exploits, was bound to bring about a contest for leadership. It was also clearly seen by many of the top leaders of the Revolution that the organization of the *Katipunan* was not only incapable of effecting a successful conclusion of the revolt but also ineffective in coping with problems on a national scale. The first apparent attempt to break away from the authority of the *Katipunan* occurred when Aguinaldo advocated the establishment of a revolutionary government to be constructed along republican lines. The rivalry between two provincial councils under Aguinaldo and Bonifacio, respectively, became so severe that a convention was held on December 31, 1896 to settle differences and form a more stable union. This convention succeeded only in agreeing to form

---

[4] Cf. James A. LeRoy, *op. cit.,* Volume I, p. 85.

another convention. On March 22, 1897, the Tejeros Convention was held, with a more representative character than the first. A revolutionary organization was formed to replace the Supreme Council of the *Katipunan*. In the election that ensued, Aguinaldo was chosen president, while Bonifacio was designated director of the interior. Although Bonifacio presided over the election and promised to abide by its decisions, he declared the elections invalid and dissolved the convention. He was then arrested by orders of the new president, charged with sedition, court-martialed, found guilty, and sentenced to be shot. Two counts against him were that he not only refused to recognize the new government but went so far as to name his own commander-in-chief. In any case, Bonifacio was shot on May 10, 1897 under circumstances that are controversial.[5] Aguinaldo thus became the undisputed military leader of the Revolution.

4. *Pact of Biak-na-Bató.* With the loss of Cavite to the Spaniards, in the height of General Primo de Rivera's campaign, Aguinaldo transferred his government to Biak-na-Bató, in the province of Bulacan. It was here that various proclamations as to the aims of the Revolution and the aspirations of the Filipino people were made public. On November 1, 1897, a provisional constitution declared to be valid for two years was signed and adopted by about 50 revolutionary leaders. Framed by Filipino lawyers, it is known as the *Biak-na-Bató Constitution*. This constitution declared the separation of the Philippines from Spain, presented a bill of rights, and established a government along republican lines.[6]

[5] There have been various versions of Bonifacio's death. The last version was that Aguinaldo changed the sentence of execution to life imprisonment for Bonifacio. However, he was prevailed upon to countermand this change by various generals of the army who believed that the discipline of the army was at stake. Cf. Jose P. Santos, "General Aguinaldo Unveils a Mystery," *The Evening News Saturday Magazine,* Manila, July 10, 1948. Also cf. Teodoro A. Agoncillo's *The Revolt of the Masses* (University of the Philippines, Quezon City, 1956), Chapters 14 and 15, pp. 236-275.

[6] Jaime de Veyra tried to demonstrate that a great part of the Constitution of Biak-na-Bató was copied from the Cuban Constitution of Jimaguayú. The similarity between these two constitutions is found in the administrative provisions; but what is noticeable is that the Cuban constitution has no parallel to the 4 articles of the bill of rights. This is significant insofar as they stress some of the things the Filipinos were fighting for. Cf. Jaime de Veyra, "Constitution of Biak-na-Bató," *Journal of the Philippine Historical Society,* I (July 1941).

The Spanish Governor-General Primo de Rivera himself commented that the capture of Biak-na-Bató would not crush the revolt and neither would it bring about the capture of its leaders. He perceived clearly that the revolt was only a symptom of a basic social and political disease in the Philippines. Thus he favored reconciliation rather than force to quell the rebellion. Among the various efforts at reconciliation, the successful one was that negotiated by a Filipino lawyer, Pedro Paterno (1858-1911). With the consent of the Governor-General, he went to Biak-na-Bató in August, 1897 to negotiate with Aguinaldo. Two things were discussed: money and reforms. The Filipino leaders originally asked for the sum of 3 million dollars (Mexican) as indemnity for those in arms and for those who on account of their common cause with the rebels suffered from the tribulations of war. However, the rebels settled for about half this amount. Most of the reforms asked were similar to those put forth by the propagandists. It was also understood that Aguinaldo and his men were to leave the Philippines. The rebels promised to cease fighting and guarantee peace for at least three years. The pact was ratified on December 16, 1897 and Aguinaldo left for Hongkong on December 27. The above conditions were never fulfilled. Not only was the whole sum not paid to the rebels, but repression on the part of the Spaniards continued. But the Spaniards were not alone to be blamed. It was believed that the bulk of the money collected by Aguinaldo was kept for the intended purchase of arms and ammunition from other countries to renew the struggle. Neither were all of the guns and arms given over to the Spaniards as promised, and there was evidence of a great number of arms in the hands of the rebels. Under such circumstances, the rebellion broke out again in different parts of the Philippines.[7]

5. *War between Spain and the United States.* When war broke out officially between Spain and the United States on April 24, 1898, the Filipino exiles in Hongkong took full cognizance of the possibilities of an understanding with United States Consular offi-

---

[7] These uprisings after the Pact of Biak-na-Bató were a continuation of the revolutionary movement. The Spanish historian Manuel Sastrón wrote that some of the uprisings were initiated by leaders who were not in agreement with those who accepted the Pact. Cf. *La Insurrección en Filipinas y Guerra Hispano-Americana* (Madrid: Imprenta de la Sucesora de M. Minuesa de los Ríos, 1901), p. 176.

cials. With the encouragement of American officials, the Filipino
exiles decided that Aguinaldo should go to the Philippines, organize an army, and put himself at the head of the Revolution.
On May 19, 1898, Aguinaldo and 13 other leaders arrived in
Cavite on board the American cutter "McCulloch." Already, Dewey
was master of Manila Bay, having decisively won the Battle of
Manila Bay on the first of May.

6. *Establishment of the Filipino Dictatorship* (*May 24, 1898–
June 23, 1898*). When Aguinaldo landed in Cavite, he brought
with him a constitution (*Constitución Provisional de Filipinas*)
drafted at his request by Mariano Ponce in April, 1898, at Hongkong. But his adviser Ambrosio Bautista suggested that he temporarily establish a dictatorial government until such time when
the country would be ready to be a constitutional republic. This
was not difficult for Aguinaldo to do as he was acknowledged
by many revolutionists as their leader.

The newly established government, by a series of decrees, attempted to organize a governmental machinery for the administration of those provinces and municipalities already controlled or
expected to be controlled by it. At around this time, Apolinario
Mabini began to emerge as Aguinaldo's chief adviser. It was the
decrees penned by Mabini and signed by Aguinaldo that became
the basis of the machinery of the new government on the local
level. It would be difficult to overestimate the role played by
Mabini in subsequent events. He became Aguinaldo's private adviser
on June 12, 1898. He was also prime minister of the first constitutional cabinet of the Philippine Republic from January, 1899
to May, 1899. He wrote nearly all the official proclamations,
messages, and communications signed by Aguinaldo during these
times.[8]

7. *The Revolutionary Government* (*June 23, 1898—January 21,
1899*). On June 23, Aguinaldo's title was changed to "President
of the Revolutionary Government"; and in three weeks he appointed
a cabinet to share executive functions with him. He also issued
an announcement with the promise that a Congress constructed
along republican lines was to be convened by his government.

---

[8] Cf. Apolinario Mabini, *La Revolución Filipina* (*con otros documentos de la Epoca*) (Manila: Bureau of Printing, 1931), Vol. I, pp. 93 and
167. Also cf. LeRoy, *op. cit.*, Vol. I, p. 283.

8. *The Resumption of Armed Conflict with Spain under Aguinaldo.* When Aguinaldo landed in Cavite and issued his proclamation to all revolutionary leaders for a resumption of activities
against Spain, his ranks were swelled by volunteers and the majority of Filipino militia men who were in service under the Spanish
government.

With the city of Manila surrounded by about 12,000 Filipino
troops and with the landing of about 11,000 American troops from
June 30 to July 31, 1898, the fall of Manila was inevitable.
Many of its educated inhabitants flocked to Aguinaldo's standard,
offering him whatever they could in terms of political or legal
advice. On August 14 the final act of the capitulation of the
city was signed by Spanish and American officers. This happened
without the representation of a single Filipino. The Filipino troops,
if armed, were neither allowed by the Americans to enter into the
city nor were they asked to join the formal entry of American
troops into the capital. Thus, resentment was aroused in the minds
of Filipinos. The establishment of the Military Government of the
United States in the Philippines on August 14, 1898, and the
refusal on the part of the American high command to allow
Filipino troops to share in the occupation of Manila, aroused fear
on the part of the Filipino leaders. These leaders believed that the
presence of American troops constituted a danger to the integrity
of the Revolutionary Government. They feared, in particular, that
the American troops intended to occupy indefinitely both the city
of Manila and part of its environs.

Filipino resourcefulness then attempted to meet the American
challenge by: (a) the extension of governmental authority to far-
away provinces; (b) transferring the Revolutionary capital to
Malolos (a town that was easier to defend as Dewey's guns could
not reach it and whose neighboring mountains made guerrilla warfare feasible); and (c) the convocation of a National Congress,
as promised by a decree of June 18, 1898—in order that the
Filipino government would be more representative and have the
loyalty of a greater number of inhabitants.

9. *The Malolos Congress.* On September 15, 1898, a Congress
was convened. One primary desire of Congress was to promulgate
a constitution. Although it was originally intended to have all members elected by town chiefs. at the beginning of the sessions only

13 were elected and about 35 were appointed by Aguinaldo, upon the recommendation of his advisers; but by the end of the sessions, of the 92 official representatives, 35 were elected. In some cases, many of those originally appointed by the President of the Revolutionary Government became official representatives when their appointments were confirmed by the town chiefs.[9] The chief reason the President had to appoint "provisional" representatives arose from the war conditions in distant provinces which prevented early elections. Aguinaldo's message announced that the object of the Congress was to form a constitution expressing the popular will. He also mentioned that the work of the Revolution was in the process of being terminated and the reconquest of Filipino territory completed. On September 29, the independence of the Philippines, previously proclaimed on June 12 by Aguinaldo, was ratified.

The most important legislation passed by Congress was a political constitution, called *Constitution of the Philippine Republic* (commonly known as the Malolos Constitution). The draft was presented by Felipe G. Calderón (1863-1908), a lawyer. It was presented to Congress on October 8, and voting by article commenced on October 28 and lasted until November 29. Most amendments presented were for purposes of clarification, and no fundamental change in principle took place except in reference to the relation between Church and State (Title III). On January 21, 1899, Aguinaldo proclaimed the Constitution to be in operation, and on the 23rd of the same month, the Philippine Republic was inaugurated with Aguinaldo as President.

10. *Expansion of the Authority of the Philippine Republic.* Excluding the city of Manila and the town of Cavite, which were occupied by American troops, and excluding the southern and western part of the island of Mindanao, and other lesser islands, the whole of the Philippine Archipelago was loyal to the Malolos government by January, 1899. It is possible that in some provinces the loyalty was doubtful; but it is important to note that the provinces with the heaviest populations, especially those in the

[9] Cf. Fernandez, *op. cit.,* pp. 95-96. Among the delegates were 43 lawyers, 18 physicians, 5 pharmacists, 7 businessmen, 4 agriculturists, 3 educators, 3 soldiers, 2 engineers, 2 painters, and 1 priest. Cf. Gregorio F. Zaide, *The Philippine Revolution* (Manila: Modern Book Company, 1954), p. 253.

central and southern provinces of Luzon, not only were loyal to the government, but they supplied the bulk of the troops that were later to fight the American army.[10]

11. *War with the United States.* With the issuance of McKinley's "Benevolent Assimilation Proclamation" in January, 1899, and with the attempts of United States forces to occupy territory that gave its allegiance to the Philippine government, a conflict between American troops and Filipino soldiers became imminent. The Philippine government refused to resign itself to the attempts of the United States government to impose American sovereignty upon the country. During this time, the governors of various provinces "sustained Aguinaldo and offered their unconditional allegiance to the Filipino republic, declaring that the people were willing to give up their lives and property in a struggle against the forcing of foreign domination upon them." [11]

There then developed a radical group of Filipino leaders who demanded war. In order to prevent these from gaining the upper hand and in order to prevent a possible rupture with American troops, Mabini on the request of Aguinaldo arranged a meeting between representatives of both opposing parties. A commission named by General E. Otis of the American forces and another one representing the Philippine Government held about six conferences from January 9 to January 29, 1899. The avowed purpose of these meetings was to create and secure an understanding between "the Filipino people and the people of the United States." Needless to say nothing came out of these meetings, except more bitterness. In the first place, the American officers refused to recognize the Philippine Republic; and they considered the Filipino commissioners as representatives of General Aguinaldo and not of any government. On the other hand the Filipino commissioners refused outright to accept American sovereignty and insisted that

10 That Aguinaldo did control the greater part of the Archipelago was attested by General Charles Whittier. Cf. *Senate Document No. 62,* 55th Congress, 3rd session, p. 500. In an article in the *North American Review,* General Thomas Anderson wrote: "We held Manila and Cavite. The rest of the island [Luzon] was held not by the Spaniards but by the Filipinos. On the other islands, the Spaniards were confined to two or three fortified towns." "Our Rule in the Philippines," CLXX (February, 1900), 281.

11 Henry Russell, *Our War with Spain and Our War with the Filipinos: Their Causes, Incidents, and Results* (Conn.: Hartford Pub. Co., 1899), p. 606.

the independence of the Philippines be recognized. The most that the American commissioners could say was that on the basis of American history and tradition a liberal form of government for the Philippines would be guaranteed within the framework of American sovereignty.[12]

On February 4, 1899, hostilities broke out between American and Filipino troops. From the very beginning the contest was decidedly unequal. Naval forces of the United States controlled all major towns and areas around Manila Bay; and the American infantry was well provided with modern weapons, especially artillery. By March 31, 1899, Malolos, the capital of the Republic, had fallen to American arms.[13]

In the meantime, a Philippine Commission (Schurman Commission) appointed by President McKinley arrived in Manila on March 4 with conciliatory gestures. Its proclamation declared that since

> . . . the United States [was] striving earnestly for the welfare and advancement of the inhabitants of the Philippine Islands, there can be no real conflict between American sovereignty and the rights and liberties of the Philippine People.

It also proclaimed that the Commission

> . . . emphatically asserts that the United States is not only willing, but anxious, to establish . . . an enlightened system of government under which the Philippine people may enjoy the largest measure of home rule and the amplest liberty consonant with the supreme ends of government and compatible with those obligations which the United States has assumed towards the civilized nations of the world.[14]

On April 29, 1899, Mabini, noting the conciliatory element in the Commission, attempted to request a three-month armistice, in

---

[12] Details of these conferences can be found in *Senate Document No. 331*, pt. iii, 57th Congress, 1st session, pp. 2709-2744. Also cf. *Senate Document No. 208*, 56th Congress, 1st session, pp. 60-64.

[13] Colonel Funston's account of the capture of Malolos is found in *House Document No. 2*, 56th Congress, 1st session, Vol. 6, p. 393.
By the end of August, 1899, the American Army numbered 31.000 men, of which 3,000 were state volunteers ready to go back to the United States. In October the army increased to 35,000, and by November it rose to 41,000 men. By August, the Filipino Army is believed to have possessed at least 35,000 rifles, 25,000 of which were in Central Luzon.

[14] *Report of the Philippine Commission (Schurman Report)*, Vol. I, p. 4. The Schurman Commission was composed of Jacob Gould Schurman. Major General Elwell Otis, Rear Admiral George Dewey, Charles Denby. and Dean C. Worcester.

order that he and his cabinet might have time to find out the general opinion of the people with reference to what was to be done. But this request was not granted, since the commission demanded that the Filipinos lay down their arms—a condition unacceptable to the Filipinos. Eventually, in May 1899, Mabini's cabinet gave way to Pedro Paterno's cabinet in the belief that the new one would be more able to secure peace; but negotiations seemed fruitless and the Paterno government decided to continue the struggle.

Filipino military reverses continued at a rapid pace. In spite of fierce resistance, the American offensive in Central and northwest Luzon was successful. After holding a council of officers, Aguinaldo on November 12, 1899 disbanded the troops of the Republic, instructing that they be converted into guerrilla units under their respective commanders. By the 24th of November, General Otis could report to Washington: "Claim to government by insurgents can be made no longer under any fiction." [15]

But the savagery of the war had only begun. Guerrilla warfare became so widespread that General Arthur MacArthur, who succeeded General Otis on May 5, 1900, had to resort to repressive measures against the inhabitants of the towns supporting the guerrillas. However, Filipino troops fighting with inferior weapons and without a proper war strategy had by this time come to see the inevitable end. If they persisted in their struggle it was not so much to defeat the American troops as to show that they had a national personality and a definite set of principles and aspirations. On practical grounds, the struggle continued in the belief that American concessions would be proportional to the severity of Filipino resistance. According to MacArthur, if the Filipinos had a chance to voice and to formulate their opinions, they would run thus: "We are not fighting to drive America from the Islands, but to convince them . . . that we have ideals, aspirations, and hopes which must be recognized by giving us a government generally acceptable, and in the construction of which we must be consulted." [16]

---

[15] The optimism of General Otis led him to believe that the war would end soon. However, on December 5, 1899, President McKinley had to send an additional 80,000 soldiers to the Philippines.

[16] MacArthur's Report for 1900. Quoted from *Philippine Information Series*, Vol. I, No. 9, pp. 66-67.

On March 23, 1901, General Aguinaldo was captured, and on April 1, he took the oath of allegiance to the United States. On April 16, 1902, the last major guerrilla force under General Miguel Malvar (1865-1911) surrendered. On the 19th Aguinaldo issued a manifesto advising all who were still armed to accept peace. The first Philippine Republic was thus gone. Henceforth the struggle for independence and the realization of the hopes and aspirations of the Filipino were to be sought within the political framework established by the United States.

12. *Conclusions and the Problem.* The Philippine Revolution was primarily a national movement. Before 1896 all revolts were local and regional in character; and they were due chiefly to abuses of local officials, and to racial and social discrimination. They were also due to the particular character of the "feudal" system found in large agricultural areas. There is no evidence that these revolts represented a concerted effort to form a Filipino state in which all the inhabitants were to be united by means of a common government. Among the major conclusions of Leandro H. Fernandez in his work *The Philippine Republic* was that

> . . . the Filipinos' struggle for liberation, far from being an isolated episode forced by Aguinaldo and his associates on an unwilling populace, appears to have been the natural outcome of a growing determination on the part of the Filipinos to obtain improvements for their country. The movement was conducted at first solely in behalf of certain reforms considered by the leaders essential to the general welfare, and only became revolutionary as the conviction grew among them that their efforts not only went unheeded but were even wrongly interpreted. In the beginning, as is generally the case with any movement at its inception, it was alike local and partisan in character; then gradually extended over an ever-widening area and culminated in the establishment of the Philippine Republic.[17]

The very conditions that caused the above-mentioned local revolts helped in the long run to stimulate formation of common aspirations among the people in general. It was the tyranny of the government as experienced by the masses, and the realization on the part of a few Filipino leaders that the purposes of govern-

---

[17] Fernandez, *op. cit.,* p. 187. Leandro H. Fernandez (1889-1948) was for many years Professor of History and Dean of the College of Liberal Arts, University of the Philippines.

ment were being perverted by the interests of a small class, that were directly responsible for the birth and growth of the *Katipunan*. Mabini wrote that many Filipinos joined the *Katipunan* and subsequently the Revolution, either out of sheer desperation, or to identify themselves with a movement that appeared to be popular.

In general, the notion of independence was not as widespread in the Philippines in 1896 as it was in 1898; for, in 1896 this desire was confined to the *Katipunan* and to its sympathizers, and many Filipinos were not associated with it. But as the notion of independence began to permeate Filipino society and the people gained courage in the expression of their ideas, then nationalism became a more universally felt sentiment. With the universalization of this common idea, an additional element tending to form a Filipino community or nation appeared. Naturally, the birth of the Filipino nation had not been effected overnight. The formation of common aspirations and aims and the slow realization of a sense of community was the result of a long process; and this process also had social, political and economic roots. The formation, therefore, of the *Katipunan* with its wide membership was the end of a long historic process; and by 1896 and 1898 a unity among the different classes in the struggle for independence was manifest—something that simply did not exist fifty years before. LeRoy wrote of Filipino unity: "Never before had the Filipino been united in a common cause in anything like the same degree or in their movement against Spain in 1898 and in their resultant movement against the sovereignty of the United States in 1899 and in subsequent years." [18] He further added that there "was sincere patriotism evinced during this struggle, and that to some extent an ideal of nationality has been attained even by the masses, is beyond question." [19]

The political and moral ideals of Bonifacio and Jacinto had their bases on those already laid down by previous thinkers like José Rizal and M. H. del Pilar. The ideas of these two reformers, and others, were already widespread when Bonifacio organized the *Katipunan*. Some of the people who joined the *Katipunan* found it quite easy to identify their moral and social beliefs with

---

[18] LeRoy, *Philippine Life in Town and Country* (New York and London: G. P. Putnam's Sons, 1905), p. 257.
[19] *Ibid.*, p. 144.

those of the founder and other organizers of the *Katipunan*: for
these were verbalizing what they had already accepted in principle and in fact. Mabini claimed that Rizal, del Pilar, and others
had already instructed their people in their rights and liberties;
the aspirations of the people, vague in principle, had acquired
a determinate form. The impact of Spanish tyranny added to
the formation of these aspirations. Mabini added that, even though
the masses could not clearly verbalize their aspirations and desires,
the very fact they formed the bulk of the revolutionary forces
was itself evidence of the existence of such aspirations and
desires.[20]

Yet, in spite of a similarity and continuity of ideas between the
"assimilists" (J. Rizal, M. H. del Pilar, and other reformers) and
those who were founders and organizers of the *Katipunan*, it may
be pointed out that the latter were "separatists." Now, this does
not show a contradiction or opposition of fundamental principles.
The "assimilists" believed that the aspirations of the people could
be realized within the framework of Spanish rule; but the latter
believed that this was a condition Spain would never accept nor
grant. Therefore it was necessary to separate from Spain. Thus
the difference between the "assimilists" and the "separatists" lies
in the method or means to be utilized in order that similar aspirations could best be realized. The fundamental principles taken
as goals were similar in both cases.

The political aspect of the Philippine Revolution was clearly
evident in so far as the majority of the Filipinos desired independence and were willing to fight for it. But to view the Revolution solely as a political movement is to ignore its very life and
movement. Its social aspect is of greater importance. This aspect
was indicated by the steps taken to secularize the parishes; the
attempt to erect a Filipino ecclesiastical hierarchy; the denial of
the traditionally privileged position of the Church; the formation
of elaborate plans for improving educational opportunities for the
whole population; and the desire to improve the economic conditions of the country. Even during the propaganda days, the
demand of Filipinos for equal political and social rights as Spaniards, the demand for educational reforms and the chance and right

[20] "Cuestionario de Wheeler," *La Revolución Filipina,* Vol. II, p. 126.

to speak and write Spanish in practice, within the framework of the Spanish Monarchy, demonstrate that social emancipation was a primary aim.

That a revolution like that of the Philippines should have more than simply political aspects is to be expected. In most cases, political techniques and details are tools utilized to satisfy pre-conceived social and economic decisions. Also, in the course of political upheavals, many aspirations and sentiments become liberated from a vague and passive system found among men. Politics and life are so intertwined that it is difficult to anticipate what social elements are bound to accompany an apparently "pure" political movement like that for independence. It is expected that men will seize political transformations as occasions to liberate and realize social ideals. Also, when there are institutions that are so much part and parcel of the old social fabric, it is almost certain that the revolution will seriously alter the relations between such institutions and the people. The Philippine Revolution was to be used not only to free Filipinos from foreign domination but also to achieve a transformation of Philippine society and government.[21]

As the Revolution progressed to armed conflict in 1899 with the United States, there were men who both rationalized the actions and aspirations of the Revolution and sought to channel them to certain desired ends. It was these men who sought to formulate various constitutional systems believed to be the best for their people. Thus the constitutional systems devised were thought to reflect the people's aspirations and also to be means for realizing these aspirations. Notable among these men were Apolinario Mabini and Felipe Calderón. What Rizal was to the social and political events prior to 1896, Mabini was from 1898 to 1900. Rafael Palma wrote:

> In Mabini and Rizal is elevated the Filipino race that produced them. Their works and writings had the virtue of germinating and producing in the popular conscience those great moral movements, which are landmarks in the history of a nation.[22]

[21] Cf. *ibid.,* "Cuál es la Verdadera Misión de la Revolución Filipina?" (6 de Septiembre de 1899), Vol. II, p. 57.

[22] Rafael Palma, *Apolinario Mabini: Estudio Biográfico* (Manila: Bureau of Printing, 1931), p. 91.

The Philippine Revolution, both as a movement for ultimate independence and as a forerunner of political and social changes, would not have been a popular movement except for the belief on the greater part of the population and the revolutionary leaders that the purposes of the government were perverted and inadequate to Filipino aspirations. When a group of people believe that a government is tyrannical such that they try to destroy it, and hope to form another government, then they must have a system of values—either expressed by them or by their leaders. In general, it would be difficult to establish a complete identity between the leaders' ideas and those of the masses. But the situation in the Philippines was of a peculiar sort. The ignorant masses admitted the intellectual primacy of the leaders and were willing to listen to them. They accepted the principle that their leaders would not deceive them and that these men, on account of their superior training, knew what was good for them. The Revolution had shown that those of the masses who fought were loyal to their leaders, so much so that unswerving faith in the ideas and orders of the leaders was the universal rule. From this point of view, the political ideas of the Revolution may be conceived as a set of principles whose origin was restricted to the articulate leaders of the Revolution itself and to those who prepared the way for that revolution. This set of principles led Filipino leaders and their followers to withhold their loyalty to Spain, to resist American sovereignty, and to render allegiance to their own government. This Filipino government was believed to be most adequate to the security and order of Filipino society and to the well-being of its members.

The above-mentioned principles may be viewed as a system of political ideas that transformed Filipino society into a community with increasingly definite feelings and aspirations. At the same time, these values laid the foundations for the principles of political obligation and the necessary limitations on coercive authority. These foundations in turn were associated with traditional problems and political concepts as to the nature of man and society, the notion of state or government and its relation to the individual, and the relation of the state to institutions within society. Since the Philippine Revolution was a social movement, concepts of social change crept into it.

The problem is twofold. The first is to determine in what manner the political concepts of the Philippine Revolution took form; the second is to relate these concepts to the actual historical events. In relating these concepts to actual events, several possible relations will be examined. The first is how these concepts were instrumental as propaganda in bringing about the revolutionary uprising. The second is the extent to which these ideas were *ad hoc* rationalizations which arose after the upheavals. The third is the extent to which revolutionary leaders consciously used these ideas to channel the course of the Revolution. Since the Revolution set out a governmental system to secure the aspirations of the people, a study of the different proposed governmental techniques will also be undertaken. This will involve the analysis of different constitutional ideas and programs.

CHAPTER TWO : *On Man and*
Society

*Liberty is the attribute of man from the moment he is born;
thanks to it, he thinks and does as he pleases, provided he
does no harm to another. Liberty comes from Heaven and no
power on earth is entitled to appropriate it, nor have we a right
to consent to its being done . . . . Yet the majority of the peoples
bear the heavy chains of servitude.*[1]—EMILIO JACINTO

AMONG THE FILIPINO thinkers who had definite ideas on man
and society three stand out prominently—José Rizal, Emilio Jacinto,
and Apolinario Mabini. Rizal viewed man primarily as a moral
being and society therefore as a system of moral relations. While
Jacinto and Mabini viewed man and society along lines similar to
those taken by Rizal, they added an economic element to their
idea of society. Yet in spite of some difference in technique or
emphasis, the development and the limitations of the concepts of
these men aimed at the derivation of certain political consequences
from them. In the case of Rizal, his theory of man and society
aimed at two things. First he wanted to instill and develop in his
countrymen a sense of moral dignity. Second he desired to present
an appeal to Spain to grant basic recognition of certain rights to
Filipinos. He maintained that the development of moral dignity
among Filipinos was a prerequisite to the establishment of certain
basic reforms and to the recognition of their rights, both of which
were being demanded from Spain. In the case of Jacinto and
Mabini, their particular conceptions of man and society served
as a basis for the justification of both "authority" and "revolution," yet they never abandoned Rizal's first moral aim.

These men, having been reared since their infancy under the
jealous and protective shade of the Mother Church, and having

[1] From the article, "On Liberty." Quoted from Epifanio de los Santos
y Cristobal's "Emilio Jacinto," *The Philippine Review*, III (June, 1918),
423.

imbibed a basically Christian education, conceived man as a being in whom certain indelible elements were implanted by his Creator. They also assumed that man was "naturally" good. Not only was man capable of developing his intellectual and moral potentialities but he was also redeemable from whatever pitfalls he might have fallen into. Yet they were living in a society where general discontent was prevalent, where the corruption and rapacity of Spanish officialdom were rampant and where the existence of friars was considered inimical to the welfare of the people. Such a situation could only lead sensitive men to conclude on empirical grounds that in Filipino society there were members who took advantage of others to further their own interests, and who were able to maintain their position and power by actually refusing to recognize the rights of others. Thus these three Filipinos were faced by two mutually opposed principles: the first was an *a priori* principle that asserted that man was "naturally" good and possessed by nature a tendency for progress; the other was a generalization based on the empirical conclusion that the society they were living in was fraught with injustice and therefore immoral. Their problem was to create a social condition where justice and morality would be the rule. The methods by which they attempted to deal with their problem will be taken up separately.

1. *Rizal's Concept of "Man" and "Society."* Three general principles guided Rizal's concept of "man" and "society." The first, in common with Scholastic tradition, was that man by creation (or nature) possessed certain intellectual and moral potentialities. It is probable that it was his belief in these qualities that led Rizal to claim that man had in him the divine as a "small spark conceded to humanity." The second principle was that these potentialities had a natural tendency towards progress, progress meaning the full development or perfection of man's intellectual and moral faculties. Also, in spite of man's past errors, both experience and an intellect granted by the Divine make him better prepared for the future.[2]

The third principle held that any attempt to stifle or repress man's potentialities or his natural inclination to progress moral-

---

[2] "Letter from Rizal to Pastells, S.J." (November 11, 1892), Letter No. 575, *Epistolario Rizalino* (Manila: Bureau of Printing), Vol. IV, p. 66.

ly disfigures him. In a letter to one of his Jesuit friends, Rizal wrote:

> I view man as a masterpiece of creation, and perfect within the conditions under which he was created, to the extent that it would not be possible to deprive him of any of those component conditions, whether moral or physical, without disfiguring him or making him unhappy.[3]

Here Rizal is essentially claiming that there is an intrinsic value in man which must be either left unmolested or allowed to develop. This implies that man should be looked upon as an end and never as a means.

> Deprive a man . . . of his dignity, and you not only deprive him of his moral strength but you also make him useless even for those who wish to make use of him. Every creation has its stimulus, its mainspring: man's is his self-respect.[4]

To Rizal, at this stage, "freedom" means that condition in which man is allowed the full development of both his intellectual and moral faculties, and where he is allowed to keep his self-respect. At a later stage, as will be pointed out, there is a shift in meaning in Rizal's concept of "freedom."

Rizal's writings suggest both that man's natural inclinations tended toward self-development and progress and that it was a duty of man to further these. This duty is significant only in relation to Rizal's assumption that man is by nature good and that his natural inclinations are therefore good. This would be consistent with his assertion that man has a spark of the divine in him. It thus appears that evil is an element that is found either when men do not do their duties, such as perfecting themselves, or in that state of society where there are men who prevent others from perfecting themselves, that is, when they deny others their freedom. Yet Rizal's optimism led him to believe that the denial of freedom was not an inevitable pattern of society. On the contrary, he maintained that the repres-

---

[3] *Ibid.*, "Letter from Rizal to Pastels, S.J." (Sept. 1, 1892), Letter No. 566, p. 37.

[4] "The Indolence of the Filipinos," *Rizal's Political Writings*, ed. Austin Craig (Manila: Oriental Commercial Company, 1933), p. 198.

sion of what is innate in man could lead to a stronger desire
to have it expressed.

> Besides the duty of every one to seek his own perfection, there is
> the desire innate in man to cultivate his intellect, a desire the more
> powerful here [in the Philippines] in that it is repressed.[5]

Rizal attempted to deduce various consequences that would
result if man's natural inclinations (or rights) were tampered
with. Among these was that "to make a people criminal, there's
nothing more needed than to doubt its virtue." [6] In accordance
with this principle, he maintained that no man could be held
accountable to society for his actions, unless society was first of
all willing to recognize in him moral responsibility, which means
nothing more than allowing him his freedom.

> You must take into account the truth that society can be severe with
> individuals only when it has provided them with the means neces-
> sary for their moral perfection. In our country, where there is no
> society, since there is no unity between the people and the govern-
> ment, the latter should be indulgent, not only because indulgence is
> necessary but because the individual, abandoned and uncared for by
> it has less responsibility, for the reason that he has received less
> guidance.[7]

Another consequence is that in a society where the people are
not allowed freedom or granted moral responsibility, all the ills
found in it can ultimately be blamed on the governing powers,
or more specifically, upon those people in power who do not
allow the element of freedom to exist. Rizal wrote:

> We admit that in the Philippines, there is much immorality, great
> disorder, and a lot of intrigues and misgovernment.   But let us not
> blame the people for these, and make them shoulder the responsi-
> bilities that properly belong to others . . . . The misery of a people

---

[5] Said by Isagani to Padre Fernandez in *The Reign of Greed*, tr. Charles
E. Derbyshire (Manila: Philippine Education Co., 1912), p. 270. In this
work, with regards to Rizal's two novels, it is assumed that Rizal spoke
through his characters. As long as the ideas represented the general trend
of European Liberalism, the ideas can be asserted as reflecting those of
Rizal.

[6] *Ibid.,* p. 268.

[7] *The Social Cancer,* tr. Charles E. Derbyshire (Manila: Philippine
Education Co., 1912), p. 377.

who are without liberty must be blamed on the rulers and not on the people. For a man to be responsible it is necessary that he be the master of his actions—and the Filipinos are neither the masters of their actions nor those of their thoughts.[8]

Besides appealing to the Spanish government to grant the Filipinos more freedom, what Rizal was actually doing was to point out to the government its responsibilities. In so doing, the impression may be gathered that Rizal, like Rousseau, believed that the people were what the government made them. But he never intended to blame the Spanish government entirely for all the ills of the country. His argument mainly emphasized that the Spanish government did not have the moral right to blame the Filipinos for all the ills of the country. Actually he placed part of the blame on the Filipinos themselves:

> . . . when a house becomes disturbed and disordered, we should not accuse the youngest child or the servants, but the head of it, especially if his authority is unlimited. He who does not act freely is not responsible for his actions; and the Filipino people, not being master of its liberty, is not responsible for either its misfortunes or its woes. We say this, it is true, but . . . we also have a large part in the continuation of such a disorder.[9]

This digression cannot be understood unless the term "responsibility" is assumed to have been used in two different senses or levels. In so far as the Filipinos were not granted freedom under Spanish rule, the Spaniards could not blame them for all the ills of the country. From this point of view the Filipinos could be regarded as not fully responsible for their actions. But in so far as the Filipinos were viewed *qua* man, as having duties to themselves, and as having permitted themselves to arrive at that stage where the Spaniards were allowed to tyrannize over them and make them lose their freedom, they were responsible. To put it more briefly, the Filipinos were blamed for having lost their freedom by allowing themselves to be ruled by a government that would not recognize moral responsibility in them.

This, then, implies that to Rizal a people deserved a government which they permitted to rule. According to him, if the moral

[8] "La Verdad Para Todos," *La Solidaridad*, I, No. 8 (May 31, 1889).
[9] "The Indolence of the Filipinos," *op. cit.*, p. 185.

fiber of the people is strong, and if they had attempted to educate themselves to a high level and had refused to submit themselves to tyranny and oppression, then they would not have been reduced to the state in which they found themselves. In Rizal's words, "he loves tyranny who submits to it."

> An immoral government presupposes a demoralized people a conscienceless administration, greedy and servile citizens in the settled parts, outlaws and brigands in the mountains. Like master, like slave! Like government, like country! [10]

And also:

> People and governments are correlated and complementary: a fatuous government would be an anomaly among righteous people, just as a corrupt people cannot exist under just rulers and wise laws. Like people, like government . . . . [11]

In summary, Rizal's theory was that no corrupt government could survive for long if the people themselves were not corrupt. He did not place much emphasis upon the principle that wise and good laws could radically change a corrupt people overnight, for he believed that a corrupt people would produce a corrupt government. Consistent with this theory he blamed the Spaniards for the encouragement of gambling habits and the fostering of superstitious beliefs among the Filipinos; but he also blamed the Filipinos for having accepted them. From a more positive point of view, however, he believed that in a society where both the government and the people were corrupt, such a situation need not exist indefinitely. This belief was based primarily on his original theory of man's innate goodness and his inclination for progress, and leads back to his principle that if a people are morally developed they will eventually have a moral government.

Keeping these principles in mind, what Rizal tried to do for the Filipinos becomes clear. He wanted to instill in them at least two things: first, the need to develop the intellectual virtues, like the love of study and of what is just and noble; second, the cultivation of the moral virtues like love of fellowmen, temperance, etc., and the possession of a sense of dignity that was both personal and racial. In brief, he wanted Filipinos to

10 *The Reign of Greed*, p. 359.
11 "The Indolence of the Filipinos," *op. cit.,* pp. 200-201.

hate tyranny and possess those qualities that would make a corrupt government an anomaly with them. Rizal's ideas on these
qualities are found widely scattered among his works, but they
can be summarized in the words of Padre Florentino to the dying
Simoun, in his novel *El Filibusterismo*:

> I do not mean to say that our liberty will be secured at the sword's
> point . . . but that we must secure it by making ourselves worthy
> of it by exalting the intelligence and the dignity of the individual,
> by loving justice, right and greatness, even to the extent of dying
> for them,—and when a people reaches that height God will provide
> a weapon, the idols will be shattered, the tyranny will crumble like
> a house of cards and liberty will shine out like the first dawn.[12]

The second thing that Rizal wanted to instill in the minds of
his countrymen was that liberty had to be deserved. They should
be willing to make sacrifices to the extent of giving their lives
in its defense. The Filipinos were blamed for having tolerated
tyranny.

> Our ills we owe to ourselves alone, so let us blame no one. If Spain
> should see that we were less complaisant with tyranny and more
> disposed to struggle and suffer for our rights, Spain would be the
> first to grant us liberty . . . .[13]

In a letter to his masonic colleagues, Rizal wrote along similar
lines: "If Filipinos are willing to show firmness and valor to gain
their freedom, in spite of all odds, it can be said that they deserve liberty . . . ."[14]

Rizal's notion of "freedom" thus acquires a more complex
character. A man is said to be "free" if and only if he has
reached that stage of personal discipline, intellectual integrity and
moral uplift which, combined with a love of country and a refusal
to submit to tyranny, results in a willingness to give his life in
defense of all these qualities. Thus it becomes clear that there is
a shift in the meaning of "freedom" in the manner in which
Rizal utilized it. Formerly the term "freedom" signified a social
condition in which man was allowed to develop his natural inclinations and self-respect. Now it is a term that refers to the

---

[12] *The Reign of Greed*, p. 360.
[13] *Ibid.*
[14] "De Rizal a los Sol:s," *Epistolario Rizalino*, Vol. II, Letter No. 250,
pp. 157-158.

qualities of a man who has actually developed his natural inclinations. This second meaning becomes more significant in the light
of Rizal's assumption that in a society of "free" men, no form
of tyranny or oppressive government could exist.

Rizal carefully emphasized before his countrymen that under
no condition did he intend to equate "freedom" with "independence." Since his concept of "freedom" was essentially a moral
one, to his mind an independent Philippines with a tyrannical
government would not constitute freedom for the people. On the
contrary, he maintained that the condition of the people might
be worse with independence than under Spanish rule. His warning was clear:

> So, while the Filipino people has not sufficient energy to proclaim,
> with head erect and bosom bared, its right to social life, and to
> guarantee it with its sacrifices, with its own blood; while we see
> our countrymen in private life ashamed within themselves, hear the
> voice of conscience roar in rebellion and protest, yet in public life
> keep silent or even echo the words of him who abuses them in order
> to mock the abused; while we see them wrap themselves up in their
> egotism and with a forced smile praise the most iniquitous actions,
> begging with their eyes a portion of the booty—why grant them liberty?
> With Spain or without Spain they would always be the same, and
> perhaps worse! Why independence, if the slaves of today will be
> the tyrants of tomorrow? And that they will be such is not to be
> doubted, for he who submits to tyranny loves it.[15]

It seems as if Rizal was already anticipating that a revolution
against Spain would take place sooner or later, and that he
feared not all of his countrymen were morally prepared for it.
Yet, he had an implicit faith that the Filipinos had within themselves the energies to uplift themselves, both intellectually and
morally. This faith was based on his principle that man possesses
a natural inclination for progress. Rizal's social function could
therefore be viewed as an attempt to hasten this progress, or at
least to prepare his people for its proper enjoyment. His faith
was such that he appealed to Spain to adapt herself to what
would probably take place:

---

[15] *The Reign of Greed*, pp. 360-361. These were part of the words of
Padre Florentino to the dying Simoun. In a letter to Mariano Ponce,
Rizal wrote along a similar vein: "Suponed que lo libremos [Filipinas]
ahora de la tiranía del fraile, bien; mañana caerá bajo la tiranía de los
empleados." Letter No. 254, *Epistolario Rizalino*, Vol. II, p. 167.

Since some day or another he [the Filipino] will become enlightened, whether the government wishes it or not, let his enlightenment be as a gift received and not as a conquered plunder.[16]

With the above notion of "liberty" and the contention that in the Philippines there was no "society" (*sociedad*) because there was "no unity between the people and the government," a formulation of what an ideal society would consist of in accordance with Rizal's general principles would take the following form: An ideal society consists of a group of "free" men, where the interests of both the government and the people are identical.

Rizal insisted that education was a prerequisite to being "free." He personally tried to set himself as an example and decided to begin with his family, instructing his brothers and sisters to serve in turn as examples to their children, nephews and nieces.[17] In order to congratulate and also to encourage some women of the town of Malolos who, in spite of opposition from certain quarters, decided to form and join classes for the instruction of the Spanish language, he wrote an article designed to increase social awareness among Filipino women.[18] He appealed to them to be more dignified and more virtuous, detaching themselves

[16] "The Indolence of the Filipinos," *op. cit.,* p. 207.

[17] Rizal's versatility in the various social and physical sciences and in the different branches of art plus his knowledge of more than a dozen languages all represented conscious attempts to inspire his countrymen by demonstrating to them what they could make out of themselves. He followed his teachings and continually admonished those countrymen of his in Europe who were not models of temperance and virtue. Referring to the gambling habits of some of his countrymen in Europe, he wrote to M. H. del Pilar:
"I appeal to the patriotism of all Filipinos to give to the Spanish people a proof that we are superior to our misfortunes, that we refuse to be imprisoned by the planned inculcation of vices, and that our noble sentiments cannot be dulled by those corrupting influences that have crept into the customs of society." ("Letter from Rizal to del Pilar," May 28, 1890, Letter No. 373, *Epistolario Rizalino,* Vol. III, p. 40.)
Rizal's novels and other writings were designed to instruct his countrymen how to be "free," and his very life up to the time of his execution in the field of Bagumbayan represented this very conscious effort and plan to set himself as an example of his own teachings. Years before he had gone to Europe and while still a young man, in a walk with some of his friends in Bagumbayan field, he had mentioned to them that it was on this field he would be shot by orders of Spanish authorities. True to his idea of being "free," Rizal gladly gave his life for his ideas and love of country. It would be difficult to find a more deliberate attempt to make oneself a model and therefore to provide a legacy to one's people.

[18] *A Letter to the Young Women of Malolos* (Manila: National Library, Bureau of Printing, 1932).

from both the power of the friars and superstitious beliefs, and to rear and instruct their children in deep patriotism.

When Rizal was imprisoned on the charge of rebellion, and he desired to deny publicly that he was the author of the rebellion, he wrote a message on December 15, 1896, intended for the Filipino people. Besides stating his position with regard to the *Katipunan* uprising, he never for once retracted his desire to see the Filipinos "free." He was equally insistent that education was a necessary condition for such "freedom." His *Farewell Address* stated in part:

> My countrymen, I have given proofs that I am one most anxious for liberties for our country, and I am still desirous of them. *But I place as a prior condition the education of the people,* that by means of instruction and industry our country may have an individuality of its own and make itself worthy of these liberties. I have recommended in my writings the study of civic virtues, without which there is no redemption.[19]

This document is interesting, too, in that it reveals Rizal's attempt to make the Filipino people more of a community. In so doing he not only verbalized some of their aspirations, but by his teachings he created even more. His political novels and his newspaper articles were all directed to the formation of a distinct Filipino community.[20]

But Rizal went beyond mere writing, and in 1892 organized the *Liga Filipina*. This association aimed at instilling in Filipinos a greater social and national consciousness. Besides intending to serve as a medium for the political education of the people, it was intended to encourage economic projects.[21] The organization of the association was patterned along the Masonic system.

19 *The Philippines a Century Hence* [and other writings], ed. Austin Craig (Manila: Philippine Education Co., 1912), p. 116.

20 Rizal was aware that he was one of the first Filipinos who made the attempt to foster a greater unity of community ideals among the Filipino people, yet he modestly wrote that his attempts would be shared by others. In a letter to M. H. del Pilar in January, 1889, he wrote: "I wrote the *Noli Me Tangere* in order to awaken the sentiments of my countrymen, and I would be a happy man, indeed, to find more renowned champions among those whom I awoke." *Epistolario Rizalino,* Letter No. 218, Vol. II, p. 97.

21 Cf. "Constitution of the Liga Filipina," Blair and Robertson, *The Philippine Islands 1493-1898* (Cleveland: The Arthur H. Company, 1907), Vol. LII, p. 217.

An elaborate program for the administration of the *Liga* was made and among its rules were moral prescriptions such as "One shall not submit to any humiliation or treat anyone with contempt," etc., and economic provisions such as exhortations to mutual help and the lending of funds by the association to finance new economic enterprises of its members. The motto of the *Liga* was *Unus instar omnium* (One like all), indicating emphasis on the moral equality of the members. Rizal's moral prescriptions all meant to be instances of the maxim that no man can arrogate to himself that kind of moral responsibility which he is not ready to recognize in others.

The *Liga* did not survive long as an organization, for a few days after its inauguration Rizal was exiled to Dapitan. But the influence of its ideas on some of its members, when it was revived, like Andrés Bonifacio and Apolinario Mabini, was immense. It was the very death of the *Liga* in 1892 as an organization that stimulated the immediate formation of the *Katipunan*. In general, it may be maintained that the *Liga* represented a forward step in the attempts of Filipino intellectuals to prepare the Filipinos for their eventual emancipation. To use a phrase of Rizal, it was intended to make the people ready for "freedom."

2. *Jacinto and the Teachings of the Katipunan.* Emilio Jacinto, called the "brains of the Katipunan," was one of Rizal's ardent admirers, and many of Rizal's ideas took root and flowered in his mind. Jacinto postulated in his moral and political theories that there were certain qualities such as "liberty" and "equality" which by nature belonged to man *qua* man. Jacinto did not elaborate on his conception of "freedom," but a study of his writings shows that he understood by it a situation where no tyrant restrained man's actions and where these actions were guided by what was reasonable. What was meant by the "equality of all men" was that "the origin of all is the same."[22] It also connoted that regardless of race or different talents, there was no "difference . . . between them as man to man."[23]

According to Jacinto there are at least two ways by which freedom may be lost and equality not recognized. First, some

[22] From the article "All Men Are Equal." Quoted from Epifanio de los Santos y Cristobal, "Emilio Jacinto," *op. cit.,* p. 424.
[23] From Emilio Jacinto's *Kartilla.* Quoted from Teodoro M. Kalaw, *The Philippine Revolution* (Manila: Manila Book Co., 1925), p. 6.

individuals deliberately instigate discord among their fellowmen, in order to perpetuate their self-interests:

> But love for the fellow-creature does not always prevail in the people: sometimes they are assailed by selfishness and deprivation, and when this is the case, the fishers in troubled waters profit by the occasion and sow discord . . . because such internal divisions are necessary for their criminal egoism.[24]

Second, freedom is lost because of the attempts of government officials to perpetuate their power. It is also to the interests of these agents to perpetuate certain habits of mind and traditions to keep the people under their power:

> The sons of the people are generally despoiled of the fruit of their labor, which goes to increase the power and tyranny of the directors and of the government . . . . There are instances when Liberty is smothered by errors, by the blind worship of ancient bad practices and laws suggested by crafty henchmen.[25]

Jacinto's concepts concerning the loss of freedom suggest a tacit recognition that "evil" is a situation developed and found only in society, and that it might have come about when a group of men used government as a tool to further their own interests. The problem of taking into account of how evil arises in society when men are by nature "good" is a problem to which Jacinto, like Rizal, did not contribute much. It was sufficient for him to state that evil existed in society and assumed the form of the loss of "freedom." Actually, this theory of society was a technique used to impress Filipinos that their freedom was lost on account of the tyranny of the Spanish government, which had intentionally fostered differences among the people to keep itself in power.

Now, according to Jacinto, the state of "freedom" and "equality" can be recaptured by the development of *reason* in the people, for it impels men to love and help mankind; and at the same time it makes them hate and fight tyranny. *Reason* therefore becomes identified with respect and with love of God.[26] But

---

[24] From the article "Love." Quoted from Epifanio de los Santos y Cristobal, "Emilio Jacinto," *op. cit.,* p. 425.
[25] From the article "Liberty," quoted from E. de los Santos y Cristobal, *op. cit.,* p. 424.
[26] Cf. E. Jacinto's article, "False Belief," *ibid.,* p. 428.

from a more practical point of view, it is identified with education, and this means nothing else but what Rizal understood by the full development of man's intellectual and moral faculties, and a proper balance between them. By education, tyranny could be banished and the state of freedom recaptured; it was a powerful tool against the abuses of government: "The most efficient lever against these evils [governmental abuses] is the education of the people and a change in their customs." [27]

But Jacinto did not desire a return to "nature" in the recapturing of "freedom." He was interested in the formation of a society with a definite governmental form in which "freedom" could still be maintained. In this respect, Jacinto belonged to the tradition of Rousseau—at least in the formulation of the fundamental problem in the *Social Contract* as to what political philosophy should propose.

On the assumption that tyranny could not survive in a society where the people were morally well developed, Jacinto appealed to his countrymen to develop civic virtues. As a fundamental belief, he stated that

> . . . the prosperity of a people lies with the people itself. A people that knows and esteems right and has as a rule of conduct kindness and dignity in all its acts, will not place itself at the mercy of any tyrant, nor submit to force and fraud, nor become the accomplice of the exalted and abominable prevaricator who rules on the height of power.[28]

When the *Katipunan* was organized with the expressed purpose of creating among Filipinos "the unification of all wills and a unity of ideas," it fell upon Jacinto to provide those moral prescriptions intended to serve as a cohesive bond among Filipinos, in order to make them more of a community. These prescriptions were formulated in his *Kartilla* which all *katipuneros* swore to uphold as their moral code.

The *Kartilla*, besides presenting rules for the behavior of the members of the *Katipunan*, also laid down definitions as to what constituted nobility of character in relation to one's attitude towards his society and country. A sample is:

[27] "The People and the Government," *ibid.*, p. 427.
[28] *Ibid.*, p. 426.

Man is great and truly noble . . . if his manners are under proper restraint, if his character, dignity, and honor are unsullied; and he is equally great and noble who neither tyrannizes over nor helps those who oppress others; whose feelings flower into love of country, whose vigils are kept that her welfare be safeguarded.[29]

Other rules asked that actions of Filipinos be dedicated to what is just and noble; that their actions should aim at virtue for its own sake, and not for the furthering of purely personal interests; and that charity should be considered important and men should love each other. Also asked for was the elevation of the concept of womanhood. But considered of great importance was the demand that one should defend the oppressed, fight the oppressor of one's country, not tolerate tyranny, and above all, love one's country. The *Kartilla* ends up with the promise that when its teachings become propagated and freedom finally attained, all the sacrifices of the *katipuneros* would have been worthwhile.[30]

That the *Katipunan* took its moral teaching seriously was evidenced by the fact that one of its rules provided that anyone who joined the organization had to pledge to abandon immediately any morally irregular life that he might be leading, to the extent that the member had to allow an investigation of his private life in order that the organization might find out whether or not it was contrary "to dignity and to morality."

Historians had pointed out that Andrés Bonifacio had written his *Decalogue* (Duties of the Sons of the People) intending to present it as the official code of the *Katipunan*, but when he noted the more adequate character of Jacinto's *Kartilla*, he allowed this to be the official Code.[31] In any case, the moral and patriotic maxims of Bonifacio were similar to those of Jacinto, with the difference that Bonifacio laid greater emphasis on love of God, adding that the moral rules of the *Katipunan* were to be assumed as being God's commandments. In all probability, this was to present a stronger sanction for the maxims.[32]

[29] Quoted from Teodoro M. Kalaw, *The Philippine Revolution*, p. 7.
[30] *Ibid.*
[31] Cf. Maximo Kalaw, *The Development of Philippine Politics*, p. 72.
[32] Cf. "Duties of the Sons of the People." This is found in *ibid.*, p. 73. It may also be found in Teodoro M. Kalaw, *The Philippine Revolution*, p. 22, and E. de los Santos y Cristobal, "Andrés Bonifacio," *The Philippine Reviewer*, Vol. II, Nos. 1-2 (January-February, 1918), p. 38.

In brief, it can be stated that the *Katipunan* under the inspiration of both Jacinto and Bonifacio, desired first of all to develop among the Filipinos a greater sense of self-respect and dignity, and secondly to create a community where mutual aid and love would be a major bond among the members. In this manner, the people would be better prepared for an eventual separation from Spain.

Isabelo de los Reyes, a Filipino writer and journalist who was very friendly with some members of the *Katipunan,* wrote his reflections on the society:

> What was admirable among the *katipuneros* was their great faith in their eventual triumph and the manner in which they commonly shared their goods . . . . The miseries of the poorer members disappeared before the wealth of the more fortunate ones, in an atmosphere of liberty and good-will, which flourished with the honest toil of everyone.[33]

3. *Mabini's Concept of "Man" and "Society."* Of all the political thinkers of the Revolution, Mabini was the one who had a more developed concept of "society" and, as further analysis will show, he developed the ideas of Rizal and Jacinto to their logical conclusions. He presented the following principle as a self-evident truth—a principle which was a summarized presentation of some of Rizal's ideas:

> . . . all men have been given life by God . . . to preserve and employ in terms of a preordained mission, which is to proclaim God's glory in doing what is good and just.[34]

From this axiom, he concluded that since God gave man his life, it was both a right and a duty to preserve it in accordance

---

[33] *La Religión del Katipunan* (2nd edition: Madrid, 1900), p. 37.

On July 15, 1898, Aguinaldo as president of the Revolutionary government formally disbanded the *Katipunan,* on the basis of the claim that the Filipinos were already united under common aspirations, thereby implying that the sectarian character of the *Katipunan,* which had been justified under the Spanish regime, had become unnecessary. Cf. John R. Taylor, *Philippine Insurgent Records,* Vol. II, Exhibit 60, and *ibid.,* Vol. IV, Exhibit 595. These records consist of a historical resumé and the English translation of more than a thousand revolutionary documents captured by the American Army in the Philippines. John R. Taylor, who made the collection, was a U.S. Army officer. The work is still in galley proof because Taft, then Secretary of War, ordered the work suppressed.

[34] "Protesta Americana Contra la Guerra en Filipinas," July 5, 1899, *La Revolución Filipina,* Vol. II, p. 22.

with one's ability and natural strength. Now, man's nature was such that all the means he might call upon to maintain his life ought to be in accordance with what was reasonable. Happiness was then defined as the enjoyment or just satisfaction of the honest necessities of rational man.

At this point Mabini presented what might be considered his first concept of "freedom." This essentially consisted of the right to acquire all the means to preserve life, provided that the actions involved were in accordance with what was reasonable. Such freedom was indispensable to man and prior to all human law.[35] Since all men possessed this right by the mere fact of possessing life, they were all said to be "equal," regardless of race, color, or accidental circumstances of birth. Mabini further asserted that the right to life, the equality of all men, and the right to happiness, were all inalienable, having God as the ultimate source.

When Mabini maintained that freedom was limited to actions that were reasonable, he probably meant that it was to be used only for good and not for evil acts. This assumes that he had definite ideas as to what was "good" and what was "evil," and considering his scholastic background these concepts could not have been much different from what is found in the general stream of the Hebraic-Christian tradition. This is what was understood by "true liberty":

> Many believe that to have liberty is to act without full restraint, for good or for evil . . . . True liberty is only for what is good and never for what is evil; it is always in consonance with Reason and the upright and honest conscience of the individual. The thief is not free when he steals for he allows himself to be led by evil and becomes a slave to his passions; when he is punished. it is precisely because he did not use true liberty.[36]

According to Mabini, society came about when men entered into economic relations with one another in order that their talents and different products might be used more effectively to satisfy their varied necessities. Because of man's varied and complex wants it was impossible for him to live alone.[37] In

[35] *Ibid.*
[36] "A Mis Compatriotas," April, 1898, *La Revolución Filipina*, Vol. I, p. 104.
[37] Cf. "Protesta Americana Contra la Guerra en Filipinas," *op. cit.*, pp. 22-23.

general, society may be viewed as a system designed for mutual help:

> Society is an association of men who gather together for mutual help, in order that each may enjoy the greatest possible well-being, which would not be possible if men were isolated.[38]

It was in society that men came to lose those rights given to them by Nature. This loss came about through the attempts of some men who either by force or by guile began to live at the expense of the work of others, reducing them to servitude or to slavery, disregarding those rights which belong to everyone by Nature.[39] This is repeating the famous theme of Rousseau that man is born free, but in society he is reduced to servitude.

A general assertion of Filipinos was that the loss of their "natural liberty" was due to the sovereignty of another nation being imposed upon them. Rizal suggested that the Filipinos' loss of freedom was due to their tolerance of Spanish tyranny. In the case of Jacinto his theory of society was an appeal to Filipinos to recover their rights by separating from Spain. With Mabini, his theory was to justify the revolution against Spain and to exhort the Filipinos to resist the imposition of American sovereignty.[40]

Like Rizal and Jacinto, Mabini undertook to present a set of moral rules to make the Filipino people a more compact unit. Unlike the other two who wrote before the actual revolution against Spain in 1896, Mabini wrote when he was in the throes of a revolutionary movement; therefore his writing would normally be expected to have a more practical political import. In 1898 he presented to the people two of his famous works: the *True Decalogue* and the *Constitutional Program for the Philippine Republic*. The former consisted of many moral maxims

---

[38] "La Trinidad Política," September 20, 1899, *ibid.*, p. 68.

[39] Mabini, "Protesta Americana Contra la Guerra en Filipinas," *op. cit.*, p. 23.

[40] The Colonial policy of Spain and the general discontent found in the Philippines made the propagandists point to the Spanish government as an exploiter of the Filipinos. They noted that Filipino society was divided into two classes: the exploiters and the exploited. López-Jaena, in one of his orations, stated that all colonial policy was one of sheer exploitation and that the policy in the Philippines was the "synthesis of all the causes that was reducing the Philippines into frightful decadence." *Discursos y Artículos Varios* (Manila: Bureau of Printing, 1951), p. 15.

having a political aim, while the latter presented a definite constitutional program for a future Republic. To Mabini these two
works presented principles indispensable for the successful conclusion of the Revolution. In a brief work where he presented
his ideas as to the most efficient methods to be utilized in order
that the Revolution might be successfully completed, two rules
were inserted:

> Make available to the masses the truths found in the True Decalogue,
> as a solid base and fundamental principle for the moral education
> of the Filipino, as man and citizen.
>
> Implant in the country a constitutional regime as provided for in
> the Constitutional Program for the Philippine Republic, after the Re-
> volution had triumphed.[41]

In general, the *True Decalogue* asked Filipinos to develop virtues like truthfulness and industry. It exhorted the love of God
and country. It maintained that all authority not sanctioned by
the people should not be recognized. It was a duty to strive
for the independence of the country. Filipinos who were bound
by the same aspirations and interests were asked to love each
other as brothers and comrades, in order that the struggle for
independence might be successful.[42]

Mabini's motive in presenting a Decalogue which contained
many moral elements was primarily to "draw therein the fundamental lines of . . . political education" for Filipinos—an education which, he maintained, was intentionally withheld from
them by Spain. To most Filipino political thinkers there was no
sharp dividing line between "morality" and "politics," since the
function of politics was primarily a moral one. Mabini was continuing the work of Rizal in the attempt to change radically
some of the Filipino ways of thinking in order to either bring
about or at least prepare for their eventual emancipation. In
an article he wrote that:

> . . . . in order to build the proper edifice of our social regeneration,
> it is imperative that we change radically not only our institutions,
> but also our ways of thinking and behaving. It is necessary to have

41 "Ordenanzas de la Revolución," *La Revolución Filipina*, Vol. I, p. 109.
42 Cf. "The True Decalogue of Mabini," *Philippine Social Science Review*, IV (October, 1932), p. 313.

both an internal and external revolution, establishing our moral education on a more solid foundation and purging ourselves of those vices, the majority of which had been inherited from Spain.[43]

What is significant here is the reference to a radical change of "institutions." Whereas Rizal did not have a definite plan for a system of political administration of the Philippines and contented himself with preparing his countrymen to be able to control their own political machinery, Mabini wrote during the Revolution and had an immediate problem at hand. Although he wrote the *True Decalogue* and the *Constitutional Program* before he ever met Aguinaldo in 1898, his ability was so clearly recognized by some of his countrymen that it became a social duty for him to present to them a system of governmental administration. It was with pride that in a *Message* directed to the Spaniards on June 30, 1898, he claimed that although the Filipinos did not have a definite political program at the beginning of the Revolution, they now had one. And Mabini knew what he was writing, for it was he who planned the system of local government that went into effect on June 18, 1898, and drafted the plan for the administration of the Revolutionary government on June 23, 1898.

It is not difficult to understand that there should have existed in the Philippine scene a group of men who took it upon themselves to be the spokesmen of Filipino aspirations and who deliberately laid down plans for the creation of new ideals. During the last quarter of the nineteenth century very few Filipinos were able to be educated to the extent that they could be called *ilustrados*. These men formed an elite in the Philippines and their membership crossed economic lines. It is important to note that, as a rule, these men were held in very high regard by the people, because Filipino society had always placed a high premium on education. It was used as a tool to improve family social status and to rise to a par with the colonial administrators and immigrants. In any case, whatever may have been the motives involved, the Filipino masses had (and still have) always looked to the educated segment of the population to lead them. Their confidence in the leaders, their faith that they would not be de-

[43] "A Mis Compatriotas," April, 1898, *La Revolución Filipina*, Vol. I, p. 105.

ceived by them and the assumption that their leaders knew what
was best for them, had always been part and parcel of their
mental makeup. Rizal and Mabini knew this. This primacy of
the intellect of the elite was clearly evident when Mabini claimed
that his ideas were the articulate expression of the inarticulate
thoughts of the people. This was also assumed by Rizal when he
disclaimed any connection with the uprising of the *Katipunan* in
his *Farewell Address,* a few days before he was executed:

> I have written likewise (and repeat my words) that reforms, to be
> beneficial, must come from *above,* that those that come from below
> are irregularly gained and uncertain.

That these men should also present moral rules to their countrymen should be understood in terms of the situation in which
Filipinos were living during their times—different linguistic groups
and different regional loyalties, without any definite conception
of nationality. These men tried to inculcate a social and national
consciousness in order to unite the Filipinos, to the extent that
a leader was to be considered not as a Tagalog or a Visayan
or an Ilocano, but as a Filipino. From this point of view moral
ties had deliberately been utilized to serve political ends. How
effective these teachings were in uniting the Filipinos in their
Revolution against Spain is difficult to estimate. But it is, at the
very least, evident that what began as a Tagalog revolution was
transformed in time into a Filipino revolution; and in many
cases different regional groups did not hesitate to fight under
the leadership of a commander who belonged to another regional
and linguistic group. In any case, these men even while alive
were already looked up to as both intellectual leaders and models
of inspiration and disinterestedness by the country as a whole.
Their teachings were widely disseminated among the literate element of the population at the same time that they advanced their
ideas by the process of persuasion.

What is of interest is that the moral teachings of Rizal,
Jacinto, the *Katipunan* and Mabini, which attempted to weld the
Filipinos into more of a community, were secular rules not logically derived from the teachings of the Catholic Church—the
church of the majority of the Filipinos. This in effect, while
demonstrating that the Church was believed to be an institution

not needed as a bond for social order and cohesion, showed that radical attitudes toward the Church had been developed. It may be maintained that the moral rules given by these Filipino leaders were rules of expediency, but in some manner they might have been considered to possess intrinsic values because they were claimed to be ultimately based on God's sanction.[44] In any case, the particular attempt to present these moral rules and the form in which these moral ideals appeared showed a basically Western European influence. But what is important to note is that the presentation of the above moral rules demonstrates the peculiar conception of the above-mentioned Filipino political thinkers concerning the form of government they planned for their countrymen.

---

[44] Even when rights were asserted to be based on Nature, God was their ultimate source as He was assumed to be the Author of Nature. Rizal and Mabini may be considered to have been mainly "deists."

CHAPTER THREE: *On the Origin,* *Necessity, and Function of* *Government*

> *The perfection of humanity is not possible without freedom for the individual. Thus, the existence of social institutions and all political organizations and relationships is justified insofar as they have for their primary aim the defense and protection of freedom.*[1]—M. H. DEL PILAR

1. THE FUNCTION OF *the Institution of Authority or Government in Maintaining "Freedom" and Producing "Order" in Society.* Mabini held the theory that society was a system of relations between various individuals, who originally associated in order to satisfy their multiple needs by the mutual exchange of their individual products. Now, according to Mabini, some individuals begin to appropriate the products of the work of others, by means of either force or deceit. The net result is both the loss of freedom for some members of society and a general lack of order.

> Among those who are united into a society, there are some who desire to live at the expense of others . . . . They are either the strongest or the most shrewd. Forgetting how they ought to act . . . they begin by either force or deceit, to appropriate the means of the livelihood of others. In so doing they mock the rights which others have by nature. These, being reduced into slavery, are forced to labor for the increase of the personal interests of others.[2]

Very likely, Mabini never intended to create the impression that such an act of appropriation was historical fact. Neither did he intend to make his theory valid as an explanation for

1 From one of the speeches of M. H. del Pilar before a Masonic meeting. Quoted from Teodoro M. Kalaw, *La Masonería Filipina: Su Origen, Desarrollo y Vicisitudes hasta la Epoca Presente* (Manila: Bureau of Printing, 1920), p. 31.
2 "Protesta Americana Contra la Guerra en Filipinas," *op. cit.,* Vol. II, p. 23.

the development of all societies. His theory may be interpreted as a technique to illustrate that Spain used both force and guile in attempting to establish her sovereignty over the Philippines and that the United States, in turn, was following Spain's footsteps. As such, the contention of Mabini was that all colonies were held for the sole interest of the colonial power. But there was another important aspect of the utility of the above theory as a technique. This was the attempt made by Mabini to inquire into both the legitimacy of authority and the proper limits of political obligation.

Mabini assumed that the right to the products of one's labor was a natural right; therefore the loss of this right involved a loss of freedom. It was to prevent the loss of this freedom, or rather, to regain it that Mabini argued for the necessity of an authority in the person of an executive.

> Thus the necessity of having a person, who by superior force and intelligence, will prevent some individuals from usurping the rights of others, and who will allow everyone to work in accordance with their respective specializations.[3]

The problem was to find out:

> Who shall be that power who will order others and to whom obedience is necessary . . . and who will mediate on the clash of interests—that chronic disease of society.[4]

First of all Mabini eliminated the suggestion that the physically strongest man should be this power, for he maintained that this man might be brutish and stupid. The most educated member of a society was also rejected as he might use his intelligence for evil ends. The richest might utilize his power to increase his wealth, while the most honorable and virtuous might be such a dreamer as to be judged a fool. Since it is unlikely that a single individual may have all the above combined characteristics, another alternative system for choice must be considered. This is the election into power of a man who is believed by society to be the one most able to direct them, and who will

---

3 *Ibid.*
4 *Ibid.*

be charged with the protection of freedom and the administration of justice as God's representative on earth. The elected one

> . . . although equal to all others, has the right to direct others, because his associates (*consocios*) have conferred upon him this power. Thus, the associates are obliged by their own free will to obey him in all that is just, offering him all their strength and resources that might be needed in order that he may administer justice and repress what is evil.[5]

At this point Mabini raised the problem of what guarantee there would be that the elected one, being a human being, would not utilize the power granted to him to serve and further his own personal interests. He suggested an agency that would serve not only to check a possible tyranny but also, as a representative of the people, see to it that the power of the elected leader is used in accordance with the desires of the people.

> It is necessary that the members of society should nominate a group of men that will represent them before this authority, with the expressed purpose of determining the limitations of the power of this authority and the extent of how much force and resources the authority needs in order to fulfill his mission. This group of men should also see to it that the maintenance of this public power should be done with the greatest possible equality and in proportion to the individual capacity of each member of society. This is the only method by which the elected one will be prevented from abusing his power.[6]

Thus Mabini laid down a theoretical basis for the distinction of at least two powers of government: the executive and the legislative. The executive to him was always a person with power derived from the people. The legislative organ, however, was composed of a group of persons whose function was to see to it that this power was used in accordance with the mandate of the people. Thus the power of the executive was justified only in direct proportion to the degree of identity or overlap that existed between the executive and the people. Mabini also introduced the notion of a judiciary as a power that determined the kind of punishment for evil in society. The executive, legislative,

[5] *Ibid.*, p. 24.
[6] *Ibid.*

and judicial powers constituted what Mabini called "authority" or "government." This was the institution by which certain persons exercised their political functions. At times, "government" referred to the group of people who exercised the highest political functions.

The function of Authority was not confined solely to the elimination of what "brutish" elements may creep into society. It had a more positive aspect, and this was to coordinate the work of the members of society into a harmonious system for the general good. The purpose of Authority was both to "order" the community by the use of coercion in the elimination of disruptive elements and to construct a better planned society.

> Whenever men join together to perform a certain activity . . . there should be someone who apportions to each the specific work. Otherwise, they would not know what the other is doing and nothing will be accomplished . . . . If society is nothing else but a mere agglomerate of persons moving without direction, order, or coordination, then it is truly a corpse; for whatever one member might do, the other may undo. It would not be long before the members would be fighting and the society dissolved . . . . It is thus necessary to have a Soul that will give life to society and this soul is Authority.[7]

Jacinto's belief in the necessity of Authority or government in order that society achieves what it believes to bè for its good may have been one of the sources of inspiration for some of Mabini's views. Jacinto, in spite of his belief that government officials had in the past utilized their positions to tyrannize people, always believed in the necessity of government to serve the aims of society:

> . . . in every community and society there is need of a head, of one who has power over the rest for direction and good example, and for the maintenance of unity among members and associates, and who will guide them to the desired goal, just as a vessel that is not guided by a skillful navigator runs the risk of losing its course and suffer dreadful shipwreck in midocean, without hope of ever reaching the shores of the happy land of promise for which it was bound . . . . This head is called the government, and he who is called upon to exercise its power, the governor . . . .[8]

---

[7] "La Trinidad Política," *La Revolución Filipina,* Vol. II, p. 68.

[8] From an article by Emilio Jacinto, "The People and the Government," quoted from Epifanio de los Santos y Cristobal, "Emilio Jacinto," *op. cit.,* p. 425.

Jacinto's writings also show that he had a notion of a "congress" elected by the people which, besides being a law-making body, would also serve as a form of "intermediary" between the people and the "governor." [9] However, he did not present an elaboration of his views on the matter.[10]

Jacinto used the term "head" in the same sense that Mabini sometimes used the term "authority." The highest political official (governor) was not considered as the "head." Thus, to both men, "government" sometimes meant the institution by which a group of men were charged with the political administration of society.

2. *The "Welfare of the People" as an Aim of Government.* The theories of Rizal, Jacinto and Mabini on man and society as discussed in the last chapter, all asserted that man had a certain intrinsic value and possessed certain intellectual and moral capacities which ought to be allowed to develop unhampered. Essentially, freedom was the necessary condition for this uninterrupted development. It had been further asserted that freedom was explained as a natural right, having God as its final source.

Accepting all these assumptions, it may be suggested that to the above three men, a "State" was partially viewed as a society where there was a recognition of certain natural rights among men, and where a government existed whose function was to protect these rights. Whatever coercive powers government might have, it existed precisely to preserve these rights. It also appears that to Filipino political thinkers it was not enough for government to recognize these natural rights. It has to provide the favorable conditions under which such rights can exist. Actually these conditions were all conceived as forming part of what was called the "welfare of the people," a fundamental aim of government.

In his novel *El Filibusterismo* Rizal wrote that "Governments are established for the welfare of the peoples . . . ." [11] Jacinto also wrote:

[9] *Ibid.,* p. 426.

[10] Mabini, who recognized the value of Jacinto to the Revolutionary Movement, wanted Jacinto to serve with him in the Revolutionary government. Mabini wrote him a letter on November 17, 1898, inviting him to come to Malolos, but Jacinto never made it, for he died on April 16, 1899, on account of a malignant fever. Cf. G. F. Zaide, *op. cit.,* p. 82.

[11] Said by Isagani to Señor Pasta in *The Reign of Greed,* p. 142.

The welfare of the people is the sole purpose of all governments on earth . . . . The welfare of the people, and nothing else, is the real reason and object, the alpha and omega, the beginning and the end, of all the duties of those who govern 12

The phrase "welfare of the people" as such is quite general and ambiguous. Nevertheless it may be viewed as being equivalent to the "satisfaction of the desires of the people." This equivalence is suggested by Mabini: "To govern is to study the needs and interpret the desires of a people, in order to fulfill the one and to satisfy the other." 13

If the above equivalence is accepted as valid, it would appear that the "welfare of the people" means nothing else but the satisfaction of what the people believe is good for them or for society in general—in other words, the satisfaction of the aspirations of the people. Since the masses of the Philippines were generally voiceless, the problem is to discover how their political thinkers verbalized their aspirations.

Apparently propagandists such as Rizal, M. H. del Pilar, Mariano Ponce and López-Jaena did not define "welfare of the people" in exactly the same way as Jacinto or Mabini did. It may be maintained as a reason for this suspicion that the propagandists were thinking of granting rights to Filipinos within the framework of Spanish sovereignty. On the other hand, Jacinto was thinking of an imminent revolution while Mabini was charged with the actual formation of an administrative system that was to all intents and purposes independent of both Spain and the United States. Yet an investigation of the aspirations of these different leaders demonstrates that they all agreed in their general principles, and that whatever differences may have existed concerned solely the means of satisfying these aspirations. What follows will be an analysis of the nature of the aspirations of the Filipino people as presented by some Filipino political thinkers.

a) *Aspirations during the "Propaganda Period"*

On theoretical and moral grounds Rizal asked Spain to recognize "that the right to life is inherent in every individual like

12 "The People and the Government," *op. cit.*, p. 427.
13 "Consideraciones al Congreso Norte-Americano," *La Revolución Filipina*, Vol. II, p. 129.

the right to liberty and light." [14] By the right to light Rizal meant not only that Filipinos should have the right to educate themselves but that the government should provide the opportunities for them to do so. By right to life Rizal meant, most probably, that a person had not only the right to be protected from what was arbitrary in the actions of colonial officials but that the government also had to provide opportunities for his social and economic well-being. His demand that government should allow man his personal dignity meant in effect that he should never be used as a tool by the colonial powers for their own selfish interests. To Rizal, the absence of freedom was identical with a state of tyranny—a condition stifling the expression of the native energies of the Filipino people to the extent that they were prevented from thinking the way they should. As such, a man cannot properly be said to be a member of a nation.[15] Neither would it be morally just to punish an individual who had not been granted these rights, for it is

> . . . an abuse on the part of governments to punish in a culprit the faults and crimes to which they have driven him by their own negligence and stupidity . . . .[16]

In the *Noli Me Tangere*, the aspirations Rizal believed to be those of his countrymen, or at least the reforms from Spain that he asked for them may be briefly summarized: the Filipinos' "right to dignity" was to be recognized, that is, they were not to be exposed to unnecessary humiliations. The Spanish government had to provide for greater personal security for the people and develop a better system for the administration of justice. The abuses and power of the armed forces in the country had to be curtailed. The government was asked to better the economic and educational status of the people. Filipino priests were to be given better opportunities to hold parishes from which the friars were to be excluded.[17]

---

[14] This is Rizal's reflection as to what Basilio should have told Simoun. Cf. *The Reign of Greed*, pp. 317-318.

[15] This is the central theme of Rizal's essay, "The Indolence of the Filipinos."

[16] *The Reign of Greed*, p. 318.

[17] Cf. *The Social Cancer*, pp. 376-385.

When Rizal was exiled to Dapitan in 1892, the specific reforms he demanded from Spain, according to the Spanish military officer Carnicero, were that the Philippines should be represented in the Spanish Cortes and the administration in the country be revamped. These were in order to end the abuses of many Spanish officials. The secularization of the parishes was further asked. So was the encouragement of primary education without any intervention on the part of the friars.[18] Two minimum political rights asked were the freedom of the press and the freedom of religion.[19] Rizal himself summarized all his basic demands in a letter to the Spanish governor-general when he wanted to be relieved of his exile:

> . . . my crime consists solely in having desired for my equals [Filipinos] the exercise of political rights, a most just aspiration which any man possessing self-respect should have . . . .[20]

Rizal also believed that to know the aspirations of the people they should be consulted, for they are the most capable of stating what they desire.

> Governments are established for the welfare of the people, and in order to accomplish this purpose they have to follow the suggestions of the citizens, who are the ones best qualified to understand their own needs.[21]

The plea that a government should consult or at least be amenable to the suggestions of the people should be understood within the context of Rizal's position in Filipino society. In all probability he did not believe that there should be direct consultation with the masses, but rather with the educated elite, to which he belonged. Actually, Rizal during his lifetime was acclaimed as an intellectual leader and competent to voice the aspirations of a great part of the inarticulate masses.

The voicing of Filipino aspirations by other members of the Propaganda Movement was similar to that of Rizal. M. H.

---

[18] "De Ricardo Carnicero al Gral. Despujol," Letter No. 565, August 30, 1892, *Epistolario Rizalino*, Vol. IV, p. 29.

[19] "De Ricardo Carnicero al Gral. Despujol," Letter No. 568, September 21, 1892, *ibid.*, p. 41.

[20] "De Rizal al Gobernador General," Letter No. 620, February, 1894, *ibid.*, Vol. IV, p. 191.

[21] *The Reign of Greed*, p. 142.

del Pilar explained that part of their movement was to entreat from Spain a condition in the Philippines where "there are rights guaranteeing the security of the individual and the recognition that men are possessed of the element of responsibility, and where one's conscience is inviolable." [22] Other aims of the movement were:

> To entreat also, that all civil and religious institutions be subject to the prescriptions of Law and to the demands of Morality. To obtain by legal methods, ways and means by which the government is prevented from being arbitrary, thus insuring harmony between the principle of authority and the liberties of the people.[23]

López-Jaena tirelessly attempted to convince officials in Spain that with the granting of more political rights for Filipinos, the Philippines would become progressive and more useful to Spain. Besides asking for the freedom of the press and the chance to choose one's trade, what he demanded was the "liberty of conscience and association, instead of religious communities which humiliated the spirit." [24] The repeated demand for "liberty of conscience" is significant when it is considered that Church and State were united in the Philippines. Not only were non-Catholic religious missions not allowed, but Catholic priests had to be mainly Spaniards or Filipinos. It may be mentioned that the demand for "the security of the individual" in general meant the absence of arbitrary arrest and protection from the abuses of the *Guardia Civil*. It included, too, the elimination of what was believed to be arbitrary detention and exile to other islands—a most common occurrence during the Spanish regime in the Philippines.

This is, then, a general view of Filipino aspirations during the Propaganda Movement. It was the demand for the satisfaction of the above aspirations by the Spanish government that most probably led Mariano Ponce to assert that there must be an identity between the interests of the Spanish government in the Philippines with those of the Filipino people, and that the failure to satisfy these aspirations was the actual cause of antagonism between government and people.[25] In general, Filipino leaders

---

[22] "Tampoco," *La Solidaridad*, January 31, 1894, No. 120.
[23] *Ibid.*
[24] *Discursos y Artículos Varios*, p. 37.
[25] Cf. "Carta a Blumentritt (May 11, 1897), *Cartas Sobre la Revolución, 1897-1900* (Manila: Bureau of Printing, 1932), p. 12.

asserted that it was the friars, who, in preventing the government from satisfying the major aspirations of the people, had succeeded in separating the people from the government.

b) *Aspirations voiced by the "Katipunan"*

According to Isabelo de los Reyes, the *Katipunan* had at least three objectives: political, social, and moral. The first involved the separation from Spain, if political rights were not granted; the second was to encourage mutual help among the members; and the third was to work for the greater education of the people and the lessening of religious fanaticism in the country. In general, according to De los Reyes, the *Katipunan* wished "to perfect the race by a good and vigorous education and by the possession of a good political institution." [26] It is safe to assume that the specific reforms and aspirations desired were virtually identical to those stated by the propagandists, with the difference that whereas the propagandists for a long time maintained the illusion that Spain would listen to their demands, the *katipuneros* were preparing to secure the satisfaction of their aspirations by means of revolution. The leaders of the *Katipunan* were, if not personally acquainted with the propagandists, well-read on the issues of *La Solidaridad*. Since the *Katipunan* began as a movement where the majority of the members belonged to the uneducated masses, they must have looked toward the intellectual leadership of the propagandists. Actually, there were attempts to ask Rizal to lead the movement after it was already established.[27]

It is doubtful if the *Katipunan* had a planned program for either the recognition or the granting of rights for Filipinos, or

---

[26] *La Religión del Katipunan*, p. 34.

[27] It may be speculated as to why Rizal who was aware of the humble character of the majority of the members of the *Katipunan* and who did not believe that political ideas or reforms should originate from "below," to use his own word, should have refused to lead the movement and indoctrinate it from "above." It may be suggested that he believed that the time for revolution was not yet ripe. To be considered also was his word of honor to the Spanish governor-general not to indulge in political agitation, and the fear that his parents and other members of the family would have to undergo more suffering than what they had already endured by continuous persecution by Spanish authorities. It is important to note that Rizal's suspicions of the reforms from "below" were unfounded, for many of the ideals of the most educated organizers and leaders of the *Katipunan* were his. In this sense, Rizal helped to bring about the Revolution.

whether they had an elaborate system of administration for the country, when independence was to be secured. Its organization was designed for an immediate end, that is, to ensure a unity among Filipinos within a highly secretive organization in order to assure them eventual emancipation from Spain.

Jacinto, who may be considered among the most educated of the members of the *Katipunan* and who formulated most of the fundamental rules and maxims of the society, did not give a comprehensive theory as to the function of government. He contented himself with stating that "the object of government is the people, and the security and welfare of the people must be the aim of all its laws and acts." Another example of his generalities was that "the happiness of all is the only duty of the ruler." [28] But just what he understood by "welfare and security of the people" and "happiness of the people," is difficult to determine. It may be suggested that he understood these in the same sense as Rizal and the other propagandists understood them. Actually some of the writings of Jacinto paraphrased or restated those of Rizal.

c) *Aspirations expressed by the "Hongkong Junta"*

One of the most lengthy documents in which the aspirations of Filipinos and their specific grievances against Spain's rule in the Philippines are elaborated is the *First Manifesto of the Hongkong Junta,* dated April, 1898. The Junta was composed of a group of exiled Filipinos and their sympathizers in Hongkong. It included many men who were later to play an important part in the affairs of both the Philippine Revolutionary government and the later Philippine Republic. When the Spanish-American War ensued after the "Cuban Affair," and there was hope that Aguinaldo would be able to go back to the Philippines under the protection of American naval forces and assume the leadership of the resumption of the Revolution against Spain, the Junta published a manifesto. After mentioning the bad faith of the Spanish government in the Philippines with regard to the Pact of Biak-na-Bató, and after a specification of grievances against Spain, the document stated the main aspirations of the Filipinos. With regard to the rights of the individual, what were

---

[28] "The Government and the People," *op. cit.,* pp. 424-426.

specified were freedoms of thought, press, association and religion. The right to property was also to be recognized. The "Guardia Civil" was to be suppressed. With regard to the government, what was asked was that it should not grant privileges to any special group in society. The people were also to participate to a greater extent in the election of government officials, and were to be consulted on taxes affecting them. Government had to encourage and protect industries. It was to develop a system of primary and higher education in the trades, arts and sciences—without the interference of religious institutions. Regarding institutions within the state, what was demanded was that all religious communities were to be subject to Law. The Church in the Philippines was to be under the control of a Filipino hierarchy.[29]

d) *Mabini's concept of the functions of government*

The major function of government, according to Mabini, was to grant citizens the following: (1) personal security and the greatest number of liberties; (2) the maximum satisfaction of economic wants; and (3) the best possible education.[30] These were claimed to be the major aspirations of the people, the satisfaction of which were held to be the first duty of government. In answer to a question by General Joseph Wheeler as to why Filipinos revolted against Spain and were still continuing the struggle against the forces of the United States, Mabini replied:

> The reasons can be condensed into the following: the popular desire to have a government which will assure the Filipinos the freedom of thought, conscience, and association; the right to life, the inviolability of the home and the freedom of communication; a popular assembly that will make the laws of the country and decide the nature of taxation; equality of opportunity to hold public offices and equality in the share of public benefits; respect for laws and property; and the progressive development of the country by modern methods.[31]

---

[29] Cf. Murat Halstead, *The Story of the Philippines* (Chicago: Our Possessions Publishing Co., 1898), pp. 294-303, for the complete text of the *Manifesto*. An abridged version is found in *The Philippine Social Science Review*, III (November, 1930), 204-221.

[30] Mabini succinctly stated: "Para procurar la mayor suma de libertades, conocimientos, bienes y seguridades para los ciudadanos." "La Trinidad Política," *La Revolución Filipina*, Vol. II, p. 69.

[31] "Cuestionario de Wheeler," *La Revolución Filipina*, Volume II, p. 125.

Mabini's political ideas can be further developed from an analysis of his proposed *Constitutional Program*. Its bill of rights and educational provisions demonstrate an attempt to put into practice some of the theoretical ideas as to the three functions of government. With regard to personal security and granting of liberties, the proposed constitution provided for the protection of the individual from arbitrary arrest and unlawful detention. The domicile of the individual could not be subject to entry or search without authority of a judicial official acting under provisions of law. Detainment and censorship of correspondence were prohibited. No Filipino was to be compelled to change his dwelling or residence except by virtue of a sentence issued by competent authority. No person could be deprived of his property unless the property was needed for the public benefit and there was just compensation. Capital punishment for civil cases was not allowed. There were provisions for freedom of thought, press, association, religion, and choice of profession. Filipinos were to have the right to petition the highest governmental authorities for redress.[32]

The above provisions were so elaborately stated that it can immediately be guessed that they were meant to do away with the situation that existed in the Philippines under the Spanish rule. This was the combination of a police and theocratic state. It was a common occurrence for the Spanish government to deport persons or exile whole families to distant islands or other colonies—hence, the prohibition for arbitrary change of residence. That the right of petition should be explicit is understandable due to the fact that petitioners for reforms or those who demanded that certain friars be taken out of their parishes, etc., were persecuted, imprisoned or exiled.

Since, to Mabini, education was "one of the most powerful factors of social progress," his constitutional program provided for free elementary education. Although private institutions of learning were to be allowed, they were to adopt "analogous systems" of instruction to those sponsored by the State. In general, it may be stated that education, to Mabini, was a major responsibility of the State. Considering that during the Spanish re-

[32] Cf. "The Constitutional Program of Mabini," *Philippine Social Science Review*, IV (October, 1932), 315-316.

gime, especially on the lower levels, education was practically a monopoly of the religious orders, this view on education may be considered a relatively radical one.

Although Mabini felt that government should provide maximum economic satisfaction to the citizens, his proposed constitution did not present any provisions for the creation of a definite economic plan. However, it did provide for some measures designed to prevent the economic exploitation of the inhabitants by the government. Oppressive taxes were to be absolutely eliminated.

The aspirations of Filipino leaders from the "Propaganda Period" up to the time of armed conflict with United States forces did not present any radical differences. A revolution against Spain was not an aspiration. It was only resorted to by the *Katipunan* when other means to attain the wishes of the people were believed to have been fruitless. Mabini and his sympathizers looked to the independence of the country as the *sine qua non* for the realization of aspirations. This was because it was believed for a long time that the Americans were the inheritors of the mantle of Spanish government. American sovereignty became immediately tolerable when part of the former Filipino demands on Spain were attained. Relevant to this discussion, the Schurman Commission sympathetically noted in 1899 that

> The more one studies the recent history of the Philippines and the more one studies by conversation and intercourse with the Filipinos to understand and appreciate their political aims and ideals the more profound becomes one's conviction that what the people want, above every other thing, is a guarantee of those fundamental human rights which Americans hold to be natural and inalienable birthright of the individual but which under Spanish domination in the Philippines were shamefully invaded and ruthlessly trampled upon. Every scheme of government devised by the Filipinos is, in its primary intent. a means to secure that end.[33]

---

[33] *Report of the Philippine Commission to the President, 1900* (Washington: Government Printing Office, 1900), Vol. I, p. 84.

CHAPTER FOUR: *On Obedience*
to Law

> *When a people is muzzled and its dignity, honor, and lib-*
> *erties are trampled upon; when it has no legal resources against*
> *the tyranny of its oppressors; when its complaints, supplica-*
> *tions and laments are not listened to; when its last hopes are*
> *even uprooted from the heart and it is not even allowed to*
> *cry—then, and only then, is there no other remedy left but*
> *to wield the bloody and suicidal dagger of Revolution.*[1]

IT HAS BEEN shown that Filipino political thinkers defined the main function of government as that of satisfying the aspirations of the people. And more than this, they also believed that the government not only had to recognize certain natural rights of men but also it had to provide the conditions under which these rights could be best maintained. As Mabini suggested, one cannot have liberty unless first assured of the conditions that will preserve it.[2] All of these demands on government meant that "society" was conceived as something distinct from "state" and that government had a moral task. Yet, government was not expected to work directly to make men good. Since men by nature possessed a moral personality, government should not impede the development of this personality. Further, it should provide for those conditions under which men could more easily be good.

That government should not impede the development of man's moral personality may partially explain the negative character of many of the provisions in the bills of rights of the various constitutional projects framed during the Revolution. The demand that government should provide conditions to develop this personality

[1] From a document signed by "Los Filipinos" (October 19, 1889), and whose authorship is questionably attributed to Rizal by Retana. Cf. W. E. Retana, *Vida y Escritos del Dr. José Rial,* p. 182.
[2] Cf. "La Corte Suprema de Justicia" (August 28, 1899), *La Revolución Filipina,* Vol. II, pp. 47-48.

necessitated the existence of positive laws. In either case law was necessary. Filipino political thinkers may not have explicitly stated the above implications, but it was clear to both Jacinto and Mabini that without law neither morality nor order could exist in society. It is for this very reason that both maintained that in a society, authority or government was essential. It was justified because it was an efficient tool for the coordination of society and aided the achievement of the "welfare of the people." Finally, and of great importance, it prevented some individuals from usurping the rights of others.

Now, interpreting both Jacinto and Mabini as having assumed that authority acted through law, what follows will be a brief analysis of what they considered to be some of the major characteristics of law.

1. *The Ideas of Jacinto and Mabini Concerning "Obedience to Law."* Jacinto wrote that law was to be obeyed in so far as it was an expression of the popular will and not simply the will of those individual men in control of the administrative functions of government:

> The laws must therefore be obeyed and respected, as the expression of the popular will, and not the will of those who govern, as they are merely charged with carrying out those same laws . . . .[3]

This assertion must be interpreted as a rule specifying a condition under which law is to be obeyed; for having written this while the Philippines was still under Spanish rule, Jacinto could not possibly have meant that the laws of the existing regime had to be obeyed.

With regards to obedience to law, Mabini wrote:

> Conscience obliges us to obey the mandates of the authority which we have recognized and to whom we have promised obedience, for this authority is the power that had been charged with the governance of the country. Nevertheless, we have to be ever watchful as to the justice of the laws, for if this is not done, then we fail in defending our society . . . .[4]

---

[3] "The People and the Government," *op. cit.,* p. 427.
[4] "La Trinidad Política," *op. cit.,* p. 66.

It thus appears that Mabini considered the possibility that government might not live up to the purposes for which it had been instituted. In such a case, when laws might not be just, and government might be abusing its power, the interests of government become opposed to those of the members of society. This implies that obedience to government is in direct proportion to its ability to protect the interests of society or the community. This basis for political obligation is further borne out in a message of Mabini to the Philippine Congress on January 2, 1899:

> The Cabinet will never deviate from this principle: "In a society of men equal by nature, if anyone leads, it is because all others have decided to obey him as that power charged with the protection of the interests of the community." [5]

Mabini was quite vehement in his assertion that ultimately all governmental power originated from the people. He wrote that he had his own religion which guided both his conscience and his actions, and that this religion taught him "that all authority belonged to the people by natural right." [6] However, in his *Decalogue,* he considered God as the ultimate source of all "true" authority. The seventh rule of this work presents a guide for the recognition of authority:

> Thou shalt not recognize in thy country the authority of any person who has not been elected by thee and by thy countrymen; for authority emanates from God, and as God speaks in the conscience of every man, the person designated and proclaimed by the conscience of a whole people is the only one who can use true authority.[7]

Jacinto, like Mabini, also held that all power belonged to the people, and his reasons were as follows:

> The people is all: blood and life, wealth and strength, all is of the people. The army raised for the defense of the lives of all is formed by the sons of the people; the wealth of the government comes from the sons of the people; the greatness and the strength of the government are due to the loyalty and obedience of the sons of the people, and all that is useful to life, is the product of the industry of the

---

[5] "Mensaje del Gabinete al Congreso," January 2, 1899, *La Revolución Filipina,* Vol. I, pp. 241-242.

[6] *La Revolución Filipina,* Vol. II, p. 270.

[7] " 'The True Decalogue' of Mabini," *op. cit.,* p. 313.

sons of the people who till the fields, breed and keep the cattle, and make the things and utensils necessary for life.[8]

It is evident that Jacinto was writing in such concrete terms in order to be better understood by the *katipuneros,* the majority of whom were of the humbler strata of society. Yet it brings home the point that the strength of a government is ultimately based on the consent of the governed.

The theory that all powers of government derive ultimately from the governed was utilized mainly as a theoretical technique for a justification of the Revolution; nevertheless it was part of the tradition of the propagandists. In a letter written by Edilberto Evangelista to Rizal on April 29, 1892, the former reminded the latter that in a gathering Rizal had told the group that: "Power belongs not to the government, but to the people." [9] Now, according to Rizal, any government whose power did not originate from the people was a power that imposed itself on the people. Thus, the Spanish government having an authority not granted by or derived from the people had to utilize its coercive powers "with much morality," for the contrary would mean that the government was at war with the people.[10] Rizal's veiled allusion to the fact that the Spanish government did not have the full consent of the Filipino people was by implication a plea for a government by consent. This plea of Rizal was a principle also assumed by other Filipino thinkers. Among them, it was Jacinto who wrote:

> The power of those who govern depends upon the love and esteem of the governed, and these are obtained only by a just and prudent conduct . . . . Those make a great mistake who believe they can maintain their power by means of force and the gun: they are near-sighted and do not understand the lesson taught by terrible events recorded in History.[11]

It was from the theoretical basis of the idea of "consent of the people" that both Jacinto and Mabini inferred that no taxation of the people was valid without consent. The former wrote:

8 "The People and the Government," *op. cit.,* p. 427.
9 *Epistolario Rizalino,* Letter No. 538, Vol. III. E. Evangelista (1862-1897) was one of Rizal's friends. He became both Director General of the Engineering Corps and Lieutenant General in the Revolutionary Army.
10 Suggested by Elias in *The Social Cancer,* p. 381.
11 "The People and the Government," *op. cit.,* p. 426.

We have seen that the people, in order to exist and progress, need a head or government whom it is the duty of the people to grant, for its maintenance, subsidies or taxes which must be imposed and invested only with the manifest consent of the taxpayers.[12]

When the Taft Commission in August, 1900 asked Mabini (after his capture by the American Army) to give some advice or suggestions in its study of taxes to be levied on the Filipino people, Mabini answered that he was unable to help in the study without the mandate of the people because "all taxes imposed without the consent (or intervention) of the people who have to pay them, are unjust." [13] That Mabini devoted a whole "Title" to taxation with at least eight subsections in his proposed Constitution was symptomatic of the widespread fear that government may impose excessive taxes on the people.

Another fear that carefully reflected some characteristics of Spanish rule was found in the demand of Jacinto that everyone in society should be subject to Law. This included the very judges who administered the laws:

> The ancient custom of considering the judge as above the law has serious consequences, because law and right are both undermined by it . . . . This custom must, therefore, be abandoned and it must be proclaimed that the laws are above all human consideration, because they are the expression of the will of the people, and that if the judges desire to retain their positions, they must necessarily comply with the dictates of justice; otherwise they must be removed.[14]

That Jacinto also intended to include high governmental officials, especially the highest authority of the land, to be subject to law is evidenced by his assertion that "the representative of the authority, as a man, is a man like the rest." But it was not enough that everyone should be subject to law; it must not be utilized for the benefit of a special class or a single individual in society. This is what Mabini had in mind when he characterized a "patriotic government" as one that attempted to . . . "secure the general well-being, and not just the well-being of a particular individual or a privileged class." [15]

12 *Ibid.*, p. 427.
13 "Conferencia con la Comisión Taft," *La Revolución Filipina*, Vol. II, p. 191.
14 "The People and the Government," *op. cit.*, p. 427.
15 "Cual es la Verdadera Misión de la Revolución Filipina?" *La Revolución Filipina*, Vol. II, p. 57.

Mabini, more than any other Filipino political thinker, was more explicit in the contention that a government in no way must associate itself with the particular interest of a definite group in society. He maintained that one of the functions of government was to balance the different (and possibly opposing) interests that may be found in the various institutions within the State. Mabini's contention is partially evidenced in his Message to the Malolos Congress on January 2, 1899, where he stated:

> The Council [*Gabinete*] belongs to no party, nor does it desire to form one; it stands for nothing save the interests of the fatherland. . . . It is convinced that the health of a country depends upon the balance of its live forces. It shall see to the interests of all, neglecting none; it shall harmonize and adjust them to the level of perfect equality, to the national aspiration of independence.[16]

The fear that government may be utilized in order to further serve the interests of a particular group in society was based on the past experiences of Filipinos who lived in a society where at least two elements were clearly noticeable. The first was the belief that the Spanish government either sided with or took the part of the friars in their conflicts with the people, or was utilized as a tool that served to perpetuate their power. The second element was the existence of a privileged group, the *cacique* class, in Filipino society.

2. *Attitude toward the "Cacique."* The existence of a group of men who by virtue of wealth and prestige not only claimed the prerogative of guiding the affairs of the community, but were also the very persons whom Spanish officialdom dealt with as the intermediary between them and the generality of the people, was found to be intolerable by many of the propagandists and leaders of the Revolution. These men called "caciques," were usually owners of large tracts of agricultural lands. Out of their group came the local tax-collectors and administrators of justice chosen by the Spaniards. According to James LeRoy, the campaign of the propagandists "was not only a protest against ecclesiastical domination, but also against economic and administrative caciquism . . . ."[17]

[16] Taylor, *Philippine Insurgent Records,* Vol. III, Exhibit 354.
[17] *Philippine Home and Country Life,* p. 181.

Rizal made fun of the caciques in the person of Capitán Tiago in the *Noli Me Tangere*. Here he also objected to the sale of office or appointments to private persons, presumably belonging to this group. López-Jaena was probably attacking this group when he criticized the administrative system of the Philippines, which he believed was under the control of a few.[18] It is likely that a major fear that Rizal had, if independence was wrested from Spain, was that the country might fall under the power of the "caciques." This is what he might have meant when he warned that independence may not necessarily imply freedom, but may produce a worse form of tyranny. Some Filipinos opposed the granting of certain reforms from Spain which might inadvertently give more power to this group, which was actually a distinct economic class. Foremost among the men who were afraid of reforms was Felipe Buencamino, who later on became one of Aguinaldo's advisers. With regard to the granting of the above-mentioned reforms Buencamino wrote on August 24, 1889, that these

. . . would give rise to the creation for the few, of privileges which would enable them to dominate the masses, which would be equivalent to the establishment of a most infamous tyranny, because it would mean the subjection of the majority of citizens to the minority, producing as an immediate consequence a most odious regime of political tyrants (caciquismo).[19]

During the Revolution, the "cacique" class was believed to have been antagonistic to the masses, but some writers believed (erroneously) that it was disappearing. This belief probably came about on account of greater participation of the people in the elections and in the government, and primarily because the armed Revolution was initiated as a movement by the masses.

18 Cf. *op. cit.*, p. 111.
19 Taylor, *Philippine Insurgent Records*, Vol. I, Exhibit 4, 59-60 FZ. Buencamino failed to note that the "cacique" system was perpetuated by Spain herself. He did not consider, too, that greater reforms from Spain, especially on the local levels where the masses would have great participation in the management of their own affairs, would tend to decrease, rather than increase the power of the "caciques." In any case, as long as the caciques were the most relatively opulent part of the population, with or without Spain, they would always have had a controlling influence in the affairs of their districts.

An unsigned article in a local paper during the Revolution throws light on a prevailing attitude towards the "cacique":

> One of the phenomena which prevents the present social situation from normalizing is "caciquism." This is a form of combination between quixotism and feudalism. The "cacique" in a town is both a deceiver and whip-master of the masses . . . . In all the details of public life, you will see him interfering, either directly or indirectly, by means of his agents, in order to further his own personal interests and swell his pockets. During election time, he does a great deal of manipulating, making justice conform ' to his personal whims . . . . Fortunately, this class is diminishing, with the result that the people are becoming more sovereign . . . .[20]

The belief that the "cacique" class was disappearing was a pure case of wishful thinking. The fact is that the Revolutionary government could not dispense with this class when it had need for the aid and loyalty of all the different social classes in the Philippines. By virtue of their economic position and their social preeminence the "caciques" were needed by the government to provide help in the resistance against the American army in the Philippines. How the members of this class were able to provide part of the leadership in the struggle against the United States may be partially observed in the report of Wilcox and Sargent:

> There is a marked line between these two classes (the rich and the poor), and this has been broadened by the insurrection, for the reason that military officers must equip themselves without pay, and that civil officers have numerous expenses for which they received no return. All officers, civil and military, have therefore been chosen from the richer class; and the political and military power of the provinces is in the hands of that class.[21]

The patriotism of many of the "caciques" was unquestionable in view of the fact that many of them risked their lives in battle. But they were also determined to get both political and economic power into their hands. In other words, they planned

[20] In *Columnas Volantes,* I, No. 21, August 23, 1899.
[21] "Report of Tour through the Island of Luzon," *Senate Document No. 66,* 56th Congress, 1st session, p. 41. Wilcox and Sargent were two American naval men who travelled 600 miles and visited 40 towns in seven provinces controlled by the Revolutionary government.

to step into the shoes of the former Spanish officialdom. It would have been expected that if the Revolution had triumphed, there might have been a conflict between them and those who contributed to the bulk of the Revolutionary army. Those few members of the *ilustrados* who acted disinterestedly in attempting to make the Revolution a success, did not sympathize with the "cacique"; but neither were they ready to give way to all the demands of the masses, in case these were believed to be getting out of hand.[22] The Malolos Constitution was intentionally designed to put the country under the rule or control of an "intellectual oligarchy," to use the term of Felipe Calderón, its principal author.

3. *Notion of a "Moral Government."* The demand that government should express the popular will and have the consent of the governed, and should, therefore, never pervert the purposes for which it was established for the benefit of a privileged class in society, was only one of the conditions by which Mabini characterized a so-called "moral government." Other conditions were that government "had to obey all the laws, and not act on deceit but do everything that it had promised the people." [23] Government also ought to do only what was "right." When Mabini became head of the first cabinet of the Republic he needed the full support of Aguinaldo and in order to do what was believed to be for the benefit of the country, he wrote Aguinaldo on January 29, 1899:

> You are undoubtedly aware of the fact that you have clothed the government with authority to do what is right; and if you will not give us your support in performing our duties, nothing can be attained by us.[24]

---

[22] That the masses might misinterpret or abuse its newly-found freedom was a fear found among both the intellectual leaders and the "caciques," for different reasons. In the long run, with more participation of the people in elections, and a more equitable distribution of land, it was expected that the "caciques" would lose their former influence. A note written by Mabini says in part that while he was serving the Malolos government, "the complaint was made to the writer by certain individuals that this talk of liberties had caused to germinate in the mind of the masses certain socialistic or communistic ideas, which forbode no good for the future of certain properties of doubtful origin . . . ." John Taylor, *Philippine Insurgent Records,* Vol. I, 24 FZ.
[23] "Cual es la Verdadera Misión de la Revolución?" *op. cit.,* p. 57.
[24] Taylor, *Philippine Insurgent Records,* Vol. III, Exhibit 419.

Now, the demand that government should do that which is "right" or act morally assumed the existence of the absolute principles of natural law. Thus, success in government was to a large extent based on its adherence or adjustment to the tenets of natural law. Mabini's reflections on this point, which, incidentally, illuminate some of the intellectual influences upon him, are as follows:

> The success of governing is based on those practices that are the results of the adjustment between the necessities of actual affairs with the natural and immutable order of things, and this adjustment is to be effected by a combination of both theoretical knowledge and practical experiences. It is not theory but the practical actions of government that may be disorganized by passion or ignorance, that is the source of bad government. If the government of the United States had been able to guide the Union through the road of prosperity and grandeur, it was because its actions had not deviated from those theoretical elements contained in the Declaration of Independence and the Rights of Man. These are an exposition of the principles of human rights, the knowledge of which had come about by the introduction of scientific method into the sphere of politics.[25]

It may be suggested that to Mabini, a moral government essentially meant a government guided by natural law. Aguinaldo's Proclamation of June 18, 1898, appealing to the Filipino soldiers to treat all Spanish prisoners with "humanitarian sentiments" may be interpreted as an instance of the attempt to adhere to natural law.

4. *Mabini's Second Notion of "Freedom."* On the presupposition that a government is moral in the above sense, Mabini presented a definition of "freedom" in a civil society. Whereas in a state of society (without government) freedom consisted mainly in doing what was right, in a civil society, it consisted in obeying the laws, provided that government was legitimate in the sense that it expressed the will of the people. This was "true freedom." It may be suggested, too, that Mabini considered freedom to consist of doing actions that tended to produce "order" or "unity of action" in society, in order to attain the general well-being:

---

[25] *La Revolución Filipina,* Vol. II, p. 271.

Liberty does not mean that we should not obey anyone. On the contrary, it demands that we adjust our conduct and actions to what Reason directs and justice regulates. Liberty does not provide that we should obey everyone, but it demands that we should always obey that power which we have elected and recognized as the most competent to direct us. In such a situation, one is only obeying his own Reason . . . .

An army that refuses to obey its authorities does not have true liberty, for in its act of disobedience it threatens that order and discipline which they by their reason had imposed upon themselves. In brief, without unity of action or an end in mind, nothing can be accomplished.26

Mabini's statement that obedience to law or authority, with certain qualifications, was equivalent to obeying one's own reason, was stated earlier in an equivalent fashion by Jacinto who wrote:

. . . he who obeys the power conferred by the people obeys the people and identifies himself with the will of all the citizens that compose the people, which identification or accord is necessary for the very life of the people.27

Whereas Mabini asserted that obedience to authority was obedience to oneself, and Jacinto asserted that obedience to authority was obedience to the will of the people, in the final analysis they both expressed the same principle. This is because obedience to the will of the people was held to be equivalent to obedience to oneself or one's reason.

One of the motives that Mabini might have had when he wrote of "true freedom" was to secure a justification for more obedience to a future revolutionary government or planned Republic. The same may be said of Jacinto in so far as a government to be planned along lines laid down by the *Katipunan* was concerned.

5. *Attempts to Let the People Have Active Participation in the Government. Basis for the Legitimacy of Aguinaldo's Authority.* In order to have a government that reflected the popular will and at the same time prevent it from representing the interests of a single class—in brief, to have a "moral" government—a system for elections was devised by Mabini. On a more practical

---

26 "A Mis Compatriotas," *La Revolución Filipina*, Vol. I, p. 104.
27 "The People and the Government," *op. cit.,* p. 426.

aspect, the electoral system aimed at the creation of a revolutionary Congress that could serve as a visible sanction for the government. It also made provisions for the establishment of local government. The electoral system was officially declared in the Decrees of June 18, 1898 and June 23, 1898, proclaimed by Aguinaldo. In spite of the approval of the Malolos Constitution on January 21, 1899, there is no evidence that the electoral provisions of the two above-mentioned decrees were ever changed.[28]

Mabini believed that the strength of a democracy rested on a municipal basis. His electoral system thus laid emphasis on local government. Briefly, the system of local government was as follows: Whenever a town was freed from Spanish domination, those inhabitants "distinguished for high character, social position, and honorable conduct, both in the center of the community and in the suburbs" were asked to gather in a meeting and, by majority vote, elect the chief of the town (*jefe de pueblo*) and the headmen for each *barrio*. The same voters also elected three officials: one for the office of police and internal order, one for justice and civil registry, and another for taxes and property. The chief of the town, the headmen of the *barrios,* and the above-mentioned three officials constituted the "popular assembly." The chief of the town was the president of the assembly; the headman for the center of the community was the vice president; and the official on justice was the secretary of the assembly.

Now, the different chiefs of the various towns that composed a province, after consulting their respective popular assemblies, would meet together and by majority vote elect the chief of the province (*jefe de provincia*), and three councilors, whose duties correspond to the three offices found in the local level. The provincial council was composed of the chief of the province, as its president; the chief of the town that was the capital of the province; and the three above-mentioned councilors. The chiefs of the towns, by majority vote, elected the representatives of the provinces in the Revolutionary Congress.[29]

---

[28] Cf. J. Taylor, *Report on the Organization for the Administration of Civil Government Instituted by Emilio Aguinaldo and His Followers in the Philippine Archipelago: Compilation and Report* (Washington: Government Printing Office, 1903), p. 15.

[29] Cf. *ibid.,* Exhibit B, p. 20.

The powers of the Revolutionary Congress which are stated in the Decree of June 23, 1898, characterize it mainly as an advisory body. Since Aguinaldo was dictator before June 23, 1898, the transformation of the Dictatorship to the Revolutionary government established him as President of the Government. The Revolutionary Congress did not elect him. The Decree of June 23 provided, however, that his office should continue until the Revolution triumphed, and only under the event of his resignation was Congress given the power to elect his successor.[30] It was not until the promulgation of the Malolos Constitution on January 21, 1899, that the Revolutionary Congress, now to be called conveniently the Malolos Congress, could by virtue of the new Constitution (Temporary Provisions: Article 97) proclaim Aguinaldo on January 23, 1899, as President of the Republic. This article provided that the President of the Revolutionary government would at once assume office as President of the Republic.

That Aguinaldo could proclaim himself as Dictator on May 24, 1898, and be accepted as such by the bulk of the revolutionaries, was based on the fact that he was the recognized leader of the Revolution, after the *Katipunan* society became transformed into a revolutionary government in the Tejeros Convention which met on March 22, 1897. This Convention, by majority, elected Aguinaldo President, instead of Bonifacio who, it will be recalled, founded the *Katipunan*. The Biak-na-Bató Assembly. on the basis of its constitution, formally recognized in Aguinaldo a position which he already enjoyed. After Aguinaldo's voluntary exile to Hongkong (in accordance with the Pact of Biak-na-Bató made between the Spanish government and the leaders of the Revolution), he came back to the Philippines to resume the leadership of the Revolution, and immediately proclaimed himself Dictator. From then on his leadership was never seriously questioned—at least, he never gave anyone a chance to question it.

That Aguinaldo could have maintained his leadership under so many changes of decrees and constitutions reflected the deep

---

[30] Cf. Chapter I, Article X of the Decree of June 23, 1898. M. Kalaw. *The Development of Philippine Politics,* p. 425.

need that Filipinos had for a leader to guide them. At the same time the need for a single individual to take the role of leadership may reflect ingrained habits of the Filipino people due to the only political system that they had been exposed to, that is, the Spanish system of a highly centralized government, under the Spanish governors-general. However, some form of reaction to the "cult of leadership" became evident in the Malolos Congress. For the present it suffices to state that the electoral system designed by Mabini did not in any way affect the position of the highest political authority of the land. It can therefore be questioned how much the decrees of Aguinaldo or the laws passed by the Revolutionary Congress (whether pre-Republic or not) truly expressed the "will of the people." It should also be considered that due to war conditions normally about half of the delegates or deputies to these congresses were appointed by Aguinaldo—waiting to be confirmed by those electorates as provided for by law. It may be maintained, however, that the bulk of the revolutionary forces and, presumably, the majority of the inhabitants of the area governed by the Revolutionary government supported the Revolution. This suggests that the majority of the people, at one time, did give their consent to a government which they always considered to be their own.

6. *Evaluation of Mabini's System for Local Government.* There is no doubt that Mabini's system for local government gave the people a relatively greater amount of participation in government than could ever have been dreamt of during the Spanish regime. During this regime the electors of the *gobernadorcillos,* who governed the town, never exceeded thirteen; while during the Revolution the head of the town was intended to be elected by the majority of the inhabitants of the towns, provided that they satisfy certain requirements.[31] The governors of the provinces (*alcaldes mayores*) were, during the Spanish regime, appointed by the Spanish governor-general, while in the case of

---

[31] For actual elections of municipal and provincial authorities, cf. Exhibits E and F, respectively, of Taylor's *Report on Organization.* In the province of Isabela, to take a particular example, records of the elections show in part the following:

Town of Gamu (pop. 6,101) cast on October 5, 1898—72 votes

Town of Echague (pop. 5,400) cast on October 7, 1898—54 votes

Town of Cabagan (pop. 6,240) cast on October 2, 1898—111 votes.

The system of voting and the number of people voting must have prethe Revolutionary government the provincial governor was elected by the majority of all the chiefs of the towns.

The electoral provision that stated that the citizens who were distinguished on account of social position, etc., were the ones to meet and elect their local officials meant that the "caciques" were still to be considered as a power. For those people who had been used to guiding or greatly influencing the economic affairs of the community would not easily have given up what they considered their birthright. The other people, who may have been victims of habit, would no doubt follow the election suggestions laid down by those whom they always looked upon to manage their affairs. It was precisely to prevent the voters from being controlled by a few of the leading citizens of a town that Mabini and other dedicated men undertook to educate their countrymen along political lines by means of articles, pamphlets, and oratory.

There was another method by which the "caciques" could be checked in their activities, and this was by a close supervision of the elections by the electoral commissioners appointed by the central government. However, these commissioners being military men in most cases, would have liked to see elected men closely identified or very sympathetic to the government which was headed by Aguinaldo, a military man. In some cases these commissioners possibly suggested who the candidates were to be.[32] All elections to be valid had to have the final approval of either Aguinaldo or his government thus securing an administration that was loyal to Aguinaldo and his regime.[33]

All these undesirable features, however, have to be judged relative to the troubled conditions of the time. A war against Spain was being waged, and the preparation for a probable war with the United States also had to be considered. Apart from these considerations, a whole population had to be instructed in the process of an unfamiliar political system. Mabini, who more than anybody else vehemently believed in basing democracy upon

sented a novel and unique experience for the people. It was definitely their first attempt to experiment, however limited, with democratic procedures. For the above figures, cf. *ibid.*, p. 12.

[32] Cf. *ibid.*, pp. 10-11.

[33] *Ibid.*

a local or municipal foundation, was later on the first to insist
on a highly centralized and authoritative government during
those days when "the ship of state was imperiled by terrible
storms."

It must be admitted that irregularities during elections took
place in more than one instance, but the mere fact that there
was complaint in the form of petitions to Aguinaldo or the
government may mean that the Filipinos for the first time in
their history had come to feel that the Revolutionary government
was their own government and that they could look to it as an
agent that would redress any wrong done to them. The complaints usually referred to interference in the elections, either by
the commissioners or by military officers, but they substantially
showed that there was a group of people in each town that
understood fully the provisions of the law that could be used on
their behalf. It was significant that these complaints were signed
by dozens of individuals—demonstrating that there was no fear
of retaliation on the part of either government or military officers. No doubt an awareness as to their part and function in
the political system of their country was spreading—at least, in
a segment of the Filipino population.

Mabini's electoral system may be viewed as an attempt to
establish a government that had the consent of the people. One
of the conditions for a "moral" government was precisely the
consent of the governed. That a government should be moral
was a fundamental requirement laid down by Filipino political
thinkers. The major justification of revolution was based on the
absence of this morality in government.

I die without seeing the Day dawning on my country . . . .
You who will see it, greet it . . . and forget not those who
fell during the night.—JOSE RIZAL [1]

1. DEFINITION OF "REVOLUTION." Of all the Filipino political thinkers, Mabini, more than any other, was the one who presented an elaborate justification of revolution. In April, 1898, he wrote:

> A revolution is the violent means utilized by the people, in the employment of the right to sovereignty that properly belongs to them, to destroy a duly constituted government, substituting for it another that is more in consonance with Reason and Justice.[2]

Aguinaldo, in his Message of June 23, 1898, as president of the newly organized Revolutionary government, similarly proclaimed:

> Political revolutions, properly understood, are the violent means which people employ to recover the sovereignty which naturally belongs to them, usurped and trampled upon by a tyrannical and arbitrary government . . . .[3]

"Sovereignty," as asserted in the above definitions to be a natural right of a people, might be said to mean the right to control or monopolize the coercive powers in society. In other instances, however, Mabini used the term "sovereignty" in a sense identical with "independence." From this point of view, revolution can be interpreted to mean a tool used by a people to gain its independence and control its own government. In the historical context of the Philippine Revolution, since the Spanish government was considered a foreign government, a revolution against Spain was considered to be the recovery of "sovereignty" —this term connoting simultaneously all the above senses.

---

[1] From *El Filibusterismo,* translated in *Rizal's Political Writings,* p. 303.
[2] "Ordenanzas de la Revolución," *La Revolución Filipina,* Vol. I, p. 108.
[3] *Senate Document No. 62,* part ii, 56th Congress, 3rd session, p. 437. This Message was penned by Mabini.

The recourse to revolution in order to attain independence was considered by Mabini as a mere substitute for what was termed "evolution." [4] This, according to M. H. del Pilar, meant a peaceful struggle for reforms in order to gain the "sovereignty of law" and "social equilibrium." But both have the same ends:

> A powerful movement for reform and a revolution aiming at independence have the same ends. These are the sovereignty of law (*imperio del derecho*) and the elimination of social disequilibrium. Thus, if a reform movement can be successful, a revolution becomes both impractical and unnecessary.[5]

To the propagandists, whose movement antedated the Revolution for more than a decade, a "movement for reform" did not imply independence. The cry in the early days was assimilation with Spain; but this implied that there should be "social equality" between Spaniards and Filipinos; and there should also be "the sovereignty of law," which meant the absence of what was arbitrary in government and that the law held equally for both Filipinos and Spaniards.

2. *Revolution as a Movement for Independence: Historical Digression.* The propagandists had the hope, for some time at least, that the major aspirations of the Filipino people could be satisfied within the framework of a Spanish government. It was only when the propagandists became convinced that such aspirations could not be satisfied within the framework of Spanish sovereignty, that some of them came to the sad conclusion that revolution was the only recourse left. It has been said that M. H. del Pilar arrived at this conclusion not long before he succumbed to a fatal sickness. Two years before his death in 1896, he anticipated the future by writing the following:

> A revolution does not and cannot constitute an aspiration or an end. It is an extreme means or recourse. A people victimized by tyranny finds recourse to revolution when by successive deceptions on the part of government, they arrive at the sad conviction that all peaceful negotiations to redress their wrongs are useless.[6]

---

[4] Cf. *La Revolución Filipina,* Vol. II, p. 275.
[5] "Tampoco," *La Solidaridad,* No. 120, January 31, 1894.
[6] *Ibid.*

López Jaena, who loved to talk of Spain in admiring terms, also showed his disillusionment in a letter written to Rizal on October 15, 1891. Referring to himself in a hypothetical situation as a representative for a district in Spain, he wrote:

> As a deputy in Spain . . . I do not have any pretensions about being able to give to the Philippines her rights and liberties. These she must conquer with her own blood, in the same manner as her independence. . . . I believe that the Philippines can only separate from Spain by means of revolution.[7]

Now, whether or not Rizal favored a revolution as the only alternative to satisfy the aspirations of the people has been quite a controversial issue. But that he anticipated the inevitability of a revolution, was more likely. From this point of view, it may be surmised that Rizal undertook to prepare his people to be "free," in the event that they should gain their independence. In a very important sense, Rizal paved the way for the Revolution, or at least hastened its coming. This is a conclusion that may be derived from his attempts to instill among the Filipinos racial pride, an awareness of their past history, a sense of national consciousness, and a hatred of tyranny. This last-mentioned sentiment involved pointing out all that was objectionable in the political, social and moral life in the Philippines. A revealing letter to his brother, sometime before he was executed, stated in part:

> I assure you, my brother, that I die innocent of this crime of rebellion. That my past writing may have contributed something to bring it about, I do not absolutely deny. But since then, I believe that this fault had been expiated by my deportation.[8]

In 1898, when the Revolution against Spain showed signs of being successful, independence was then considered to be the only tool for the attainment of what the people aspired to have. Mabini, who was committed to the independence of the country, rationalized:

---

[7] Letter No. 492, *Epistolario Rizalino,* Vol. III, p. 254.
[8] Letter No. 701, *Epistolario Rizalino,* Vol. IV, p. 298, Dec. 29, 1896. Writing about Rizal, Miguel de Unamuno said: "He was a soul fearing revolution but deeply longing for it . . . . Regardless of his fear, he possibly desired it in spite of himself." Cf. Epilogue of Retana's *Vida y Escritos del Dr. José Rizal,* p. 479.

We desire independence, not as an end, but as a means. It is the condition *sine qua non* for the attainment of what is desired, for without it, we will not be able to attain anything that we desire.[9]

In a proclamation made during the Dictatorial government, on June 18, 1898, Aguinaldo declared that independence also meant the entrance of the Philippines "into the concert of civilized nations," as well as freedom from tyranny and the regaining of liberties. A great part of the Filipino population became so deeply imbued with the idea and desire of independence, that even when the Republic was defeated and American sovereignty established, Mabini could maintain with good reason that the Filipino people could no longer be happy without their national liberty. On this basis, he advised that Filipinos should not petition the United States for statehood (a chimerical demand, he stated), but that they should rather use political means to make the United States government so conciliatory to the extent of promising the Filipinos eventual independence.[10]

In consonance with his belief in natural law and natural rights, Mabini considered independence as a right that belonged to a people. This followed since liberty was a natural right, and the only method of achieving it was by revolution and independence. This belief assumed, naturally, that Spanish sovereignty and liberty for Filipinos were incompatible. It was this belief in natural law and natural rights that might have embarrassed Mr. W. H. Taft in an interview granted to Mabini. When the Taft Commission informed Mabini that it was setting up a popular government in the Philippines, the latter bluntly told the Commission:

. . . the principles upon which the American Constitution rests declare that sovereignty belongs to the nations by natural right; that the American Government, in not remaining contented with limiting the sovereignty of the Filipino people but annulling it completely, commits an injustice which, sooner or later, will demand retribution; that there can be no popular government when the people are denied real and effective participation in the organization and administration of that government.[11]

---

[9] "Cual es la Verdadera Misión de la Revolución?" *La Revolución Filipina*, Vol. II, p. 57.
[10] Cf. *La Revolución Filipina*, Vol. II, pp. 324-325.
[11] Quoted from Teodoro Kalaw, *The Philippine Revolution*, p. 246.

3. *On the Justification of Revolution.* Among the many reasons given as justifications for revolution, three stand out prominently: the first is that it was always "right" or "legal" for a people to overthrow a government that was believed to have denied them their rights and liberties. Rizal's ideas on this point were:

> When a people is denied light, home, liberty, and justice—things that are essential to life, and therefore man's patrimony—that people has the right to treat him who so despoils it as we would do a robber who intercepts us on the highway.[12]

In a letter to M. H. del Pilar, Rizal denied being a revolutionary, yet stated conditions under which men must, in any case, fight. With the loss of liberty and other essential things to life, then, when one was forced to fight, it was a matter of self-defense; and since ". . . God gives the right to every being to defend himself to the best of his ability, we are under legality . . . ."[13]

Jacinto gave a reason for revolution that is close to Rizal's first condition, that of loss of liberty. Justifying the separatist aims of the *Katipunan,* he wrote:

> If there is right, it is because there is liberty: liberty is the column that sustains the edifice and the audacious one who tears it down in order to bring down the building must be annihilated.[14]

Mabini characterized this first reason as a resolution of a conflict between "natural right" and those human laws that violated these—a conflict that led the government to maintain itself by force and not consent.[15] On this principle, the war with the United States was still a revolutionary war, since the Filipinos were not yet successful in recovering those natural rights which the Americans prevented them from enjoying.[16]

Recalling Mabini's theory that authority was established in society in order to protect the liberties of the people, it can be

---

[12] Said by a high Spanish official to the Governor-General, *The Reign of Greed,* p. 304.

[13] Letter No. 273, *Epistolario Rizalino,* Vol. II, p. 201.

[14] "Liberty," *op. cit.,* p. 424.

[15] "La Verdad en su Lugar," Oct. 15, 1899, *La Revolución Filipina,* Vol. II, p. 93.

[16] Cf. *ibid.,* and also Mabini's "Cual es la Verdadera Misión de la Revolución?" *op. cit.,* pp. 53-54.

said that a revolution against this authority was justified when it abused the power that the people gave it. This in effect means that a revolution against a government that uses its authority arbitrarily is justified.

> A revolution may be conducted against a national government, if such a government has abused the power placed at its disposal by the people with the purpose of having justice administered, by using this power to drown out the public voice and at the same time to administer to its own convenience or caprice.[17]

The second reason justifying revolution is partially based on the above. Thus, a revolution is justified when the powers of government were utilized to maintain its own interests, that is, for the betterment of the officials controlling the reins of government; or when it was biased in its functions in favor of a special group or class in society. In Philippine history, with regard to the struggle against Spain, this class usually was understood to refer to the friars—a class believed to have either controlled the government at various times or whose interests the government had always protected. It is from this point of view that the Philippine Revolution was considered by many people to have been initially a war against the friars.

Mabini clearly perceived that a government which was clearly biased in favor of a special class in society, sooner or later had to face revolution.

> When a government produces a stagnation of a people in order that it may perpetuate its own interests or that of a definite class . . . a revolution is inevitable.[18]

It was for this very reason that Mabini declared that a justifiable revolution must be a popular movement. This involved, substantially, that it should not be motivated for the satisfaction of the interests of a special group in society.

> I say *popular movement* because I think it indispensable that the change anticipated should be a need felt by the majority of the citizens. All agitations fostered by a determined class in order that its particular interests be benefited, do not deserve the name.[19]

---

[17] "Ordenanzas de la Revolución," *La Revolución Filipina,* Vol. I, p. 108.
[18] *La Revolución Filipina,* Vol. II, p. 276.
[19] *Ibid.,* p. 275.

A "moral" government was, in the main, characterized by Mabini as one that both recognized the natural rights of individuals, and did not favor the interests of a special group in society. It followed that the above two reasons were justifications for any revolution against an "immoral government."

A third reason justifying a revolution concerned a government that was either foreign or a "usurper." According to Mabini, "a revolution is always just, if it attempts to destroy a foreign government or a foreign usurper." [20]

This probably aimed at rationalizing a revolution against Spain that was already on its way. Nevertheless, the same reason was later on used to justify resistance to the imposition of American sovereignty in the Philippines. In this light the United States government was viewed as the mere successor of the Spanish government.

4. *A "Compact" Theory to Justify Revolution.* It is interesting to note that the idea of Spanish rule in the Philippines being based on a historical "compact" was voiced by several Filipino leaders during the Revolution. It was further maintained that Spanish authorities broke the compact by not living up to its provisions. It appears that one of the first to write on this violation of the compact was Andrés Bonifacio. His article, "What the People Should Know," [21] in the *Kalayaan,* declared that the Spaniards came to the Islands on the pretense of peace. The Filipinos accepted their offer to guide them in both wisdom and prosperity, in return for material aid to the Spaniards. This pact was concluded between King Sikatuna and Don Miguel López de Legazpi, who represented the king of Spain, by means of the so-called "Blood Compact." [22] Bonifacio wrote that the Spaniards

---

[20] "Ordenanzas de la Revolución," *La Revolución Filipina,* Vol. I, p. 108.

[21] Found in Epifanio de los Santos y Cristobal, "Andrés Bonifacio," *The Philippine Review* (January-February, 1918), p. 39; and Wenceslao E. Retana, *Archivo del Bibliófilo Filipino* (Madrid: Imp. de M. Minuesa de los Rios, 1897), Vol. III, pp. 144-148.

[22] The "Blood Compact" was so-called because it took place in the following manner: "one from each party draws two or three drops of blood from his own arm or breast and mixes them in the same cup, with water or wine. Then the mixture must be divided equally between the two cups, and neither person may depart until both cups are alike drained." "Relation of the Voyage to the Filipinas Islands," Blair and Robertson, *op. cit.,*

violated this compact by forcing Filipinos to fight battles for Spanish colonial expansion; by making Filipinos fight one another in order that Spanish sovereignty be perpetuated; by leading the Filipinos to lose their native traditions and virtues; and by exiling Filipinos to various parts, etc. In brief, the Spaniards made the compact serve themselves alone.

This theory was echoed as late as February, 1900, in a message entitled, "To the Filipino People," which was attributed to Aguinaldo. This message said in part:

> Never have the Philippines been conquered by force of arms; if the Spaniards ruled it was by overthrowing the sacred compact of blood between Sikatuna and Legazpi, and abusing the good faith of our ancestors.[23]

This compact theory entered into an official communication of the Revolutionary government. In an official protest delivered to the signatory powers of the Paris Treaty, Felipe Agoncillo, the representative of the Revolutionary government, claimed one of the "historic facts in which the exclusive right of the Filipinos to decide their own destiny was implicitly recognized" was

> . . . the "Blood Treaty" (Pacto de Sangre) of the 12th of March, 1565, entered into between the General Don Miguel López de Legazpi and the Filipino sovereign Sikatuna, a compact which was ratified and confirmed on the one side, by the King of Spain, Philip II, and, on the other side, by the Monarchs of Mindanao, Bisayas and Luzon and by the Supreme Chief of that Confederation, the Sultan Lakandula; proclaiming as a consequence, the autonomous nationality of the Kingdom of "New Castille," formed by the Philippine Islands, under the sceptre of the King of Spain.[24]

Agoncillo probably mentioned the above compact in order to support the contention that the Philippines should participate or at least be consulted in a Conference in which its fate was being decided.

Vol. III, p. 201. It may be that such a compact was used mainly for purposes of friendship and mutual help. M. H. del Pilar in an article maintained that by means of the "Blood Compact" Spain committed herself to the political and social "assimilation" of the Philippines. Cf. "Asimilación de Filipinas," *La Solidaridad*, I, No. 15, September 15, 1889.

[23] Taylor, *Philippine Insurgent Records*, Vol. V, Exhibit 993.

[24] *Ibid.*, Vol. III, Exhibit 526. From the "Official Protest Against the Paris Treaty," December 12, 1898.

The assertion that the Philippines came under Spanish sovereignty on account of a compact, if meant to refer to historical fact, is inaccurate. The simple reason is that there was no such nation as the Philippines during the time the blood compact took place. Besides, Sikatuna was a local chief, and there is no evidence that he negotiated for the whole Archipelago. But in the mind of Bonifacio, the compact theory may only have been a technique to justify revolution against Spain. By suggesting to the *katipuneros* that, whereas their ancestors accepted the teachings of the Spanish missionaries in both religion and industry with the belief that these teachings were conducive to their progress, the later successors of these missionaries, the friars, were doing the very opposite. While credit was due to the early missionaries, the later ones had become a strongly entrenched political and economic class, with particular interests that clashed with those of the people. Thus in a certain sense a "compact" had been violated. The attempt to utilize the theory of the "Blood Compact" in order to convince the people that the Spanish government profited more than it ought to have profited from the Philippines is in a certain sense important. It assumed that a government in power should respect certain limitations based on a symbolic compact; and, when these limits were violated, they provided a cause for revolution.

5. *Revolution as a Tool Conducive to Progress.* A revolution was looked upon by Mabini as part of the natural evolution of a people who desired progress, but were obstructed by their government. When a government impeded the progress of the people, either the people had to submit to the government and therefore become stagnant; or they refused stagnation and revolted against the government. Thus, any people who aspired for progress and had an "immoral" government, had no choice but revolt.

> The Revolution is not the work of a mean ambition, but is the result of the necessities created by those natural laws which regulate both the life of a people and the progressive march of humanity.[25]

---

25 "Krueger y Aguinaldo" (October, 1900), *La Revolución Filipina,* Vol. II, p. 209.

The tendency for betterment or progress is a necessity or law found in all creatures, whether individually or collectively. Thus, a political revolution which is generally intended by a people to better their conditions, becomes an irresistible necessity . . . . A people that has not yet arrived at the fulness of life must grow and develop, otherwise its life would be paralyzed—which means its death. As it is unnatural that a being should resign itself to its own death, the people must employ all of its energies in order that a government that impedes its progressive development, be destroyed.[26]

Along similar lines, Aguinaldo's *Message to Foreign Government* on August 6, 1898, declared:

. . . . . this popular movement is the result of the laws which regulate the life of a people which aspires to progress and to perfection by the sole road of liberty.[27]

And when revolution was successfully used as a tool to gain freedom from Spain, and the Filipinos had their own Revolutionary government, independence was then stated to be a condition under which a people could contribute a share in the development of mankind in general. The *Statement of the Chiefs of Towns, Composing the Various Provinces* (August 1, 1898), said:

Filipinos are fully convinced that if individuals have need of material, moral and intellectual perfection in order to contribute to the welfare of their fellows, peoples require to have fulness of life; they need liberty and independence in order to contribute to the indefinite progress of mankind.[28]

The intellectual link between Mabini and the propagandists, especially Rizal, can be partially seen in Rizal's idea that individuals, like nations, have a natural impulse for progress. Although Rizal did not specifically advocate revolution, because of the historical conditions of the Philippines at the time when Spain was deaf to the pleas of the reformers, he did give some veiled suggestions as to its inevitability. For, if progress were natural and irresistible, to try to stop it would be fruitless. But since Spain was believed to be bent on preventing progress,

---

[26] *La Revolución Filipina*, Vol. II, pp. 275-276.
[27] *Senate Document No. 62*, 56th Congress, 3rd session, p. 438, part ii. This message was penned by Mabini.
[28] *Ibid.*, p. 439.

a revolution would follow as a consequence. The impulse of a people to progress was characterized by Rizal as follows:

> It is a known law, that nothing remains stationary, but that everything moves and tends to perfect itself. The colonies are subject to this law. To desire that a people maintains a stationary state, is more difficult than to prevent the flow of a river; for not inferior to the strength of waves is that of millions of people who think and feel.[29]

The belief that, in some way or another, a revolution was essential for the kind of change which signified progress led propagandists like López-Jaena to be enthusiastic about the French Revolution. In an article entitled, "The French Revolution," he wrote:

> Without the French Revolution, humanity would still be under the most loathsome obscurantism and still be dominated by the severe hands of old tyrannies. Without it, we would not be enjoying that wonderful spectacle of the new conquests of science, especially in physics and chemistry—conquests which have given the lie to those unwarranted assertions of truth which formerly were taken for revelations.[30]

6. *The Messianic Character of the Philippine Revolution.* Mabini intended that the Philippine Revolution should have more than a local character. He believed that it could serve as a model for the struggle for freedom among other Malay peoples. On this point he wrote:

> The Revolution has as a final aim, to maintain alive and resplendent the torch of liberty and civilization, in order to give light to the gloomy night in which the Malay race finds itself degraded, so that it may be led to the road of social emancipation . . . .[31]

Mabini well realized that it was not to the interest of the colonial powers of his time that the Philippine Revolution should be successful. For this success might serve as a bad example for those other people who were under the yoke of foreign governments. Speaking of Great Britain, Germany, France, Holland, etc., who were colonial powers interested in spreading their

---

[29] "Diferencias," *La Solidaridad,* I, No. 15 (September 15, 1889).
[30] *La Solidaridad,* I, No. 7 (May 15, 1889).
[31] "Cual es la Verdadera Misión de la Revolución?" *La Revolución Filipina,* Vol. II, p. 56.

spheres of influence on the southeastern part of Asia, he continued:

> They all know better than we do that the Philippine Revolution is very contagious, having within its womb the seeds of a disease that is mortal to their colonial interests—a dam to their overflowing ambitions, in the not far away future.[32]

It may be noted that this concern for the other Malay peoples was significant in the last century, when Filipinos were not usually called "Filipinos" but *"indios,"* and when they had a vague consciousness of belonging to a wider race. The word *"indio"* also referred to the other peoples inhabiting the other islands around the Philippine Archipelago.

Rizal's racial consciousness and his theory of race show that he considered himself a member of the Malay race. It was not just mere rhetoric that led others to refer to him as "the great Malayan." Spain had segmented what is now called the Philippine Archipelago from those other countries whose peoples were closely related to the Filipinos by race and culture. The division took place when Spain established a political entity in the Islands under a highly centralized form of government. The awareness of Filipinos as being part of a wider race, called the Malay race. became lesser with the development of a sense of nationalism accompanied by a greater loyalty to a central government recognized as distinctly "Filipino."

7. *On the Excesses of a Revolution, and a Condition Under Which Its Continuation Was Not Justified.* Mabini believed that there was a principle which served to prevent excesses in and the continuance of a revolution. This was the "instinct of preservation" (*instincto de conservación*) which served to

> . . . . moderate the impulses of the people, presenting before its eyes the black picture of the desolation and misery which all violent methods produce.[33]

Considering that Mabini wrote this after the Republic was defeated, and that he thought the war against the United States to be an extension of the Philippine Revolution, it may be surmised that he favored the discontinuance of the Revolution. He

[32] *Ibid.,* p. 57.
[33] *La Revolución Filipina,* Vol. II, p. 273.

feared to have a great part of the Islands laid waste and thousands of Filipinos killed in the struggle with the American troops.

Mabini, who was known as the *"intransigente"* and who would not compromise on the issue of independence of the Philippines, was finally forced to recognize that prolongation of the Revolution was unjustified. The moment the majority of the people preferred to accept American sovereignty, the Revolution lost its justification. On this point, he wrote:

> We fought under the condition that our duty and dignity demanded of us the sacrifice of defending while we could, our liberties, because without them social equality between the dominant caste and the native class would be practically an impossibility, and so we should not succeed in establishing perfect justice between us; but we knew that it would not be long before we shall exhaust our scanty resources and that our defeat was inevitable. War became, then, unjustified from the moment when the majority of the people preferred to submit to the conqueror and many of the revolutionists themselves passed to his ranks, because, not being able to enjoy their natural liberties while the American forces prevented it, and not having the resources for removing this obstacle, they deemed it prudent to yield and have hope in the promises of the people of the United States.[34]

These observations of Mabini are examples of his principle that a revolution *par excellence* must be a popular movement, that is, a movement instigated by the majority of the people. When the majority of the people preferred to submit to United States sovereignty on account of the destruction and miseries brought by war, the government of the Republic was unjustified in prolonging the Revolution or what amounted to the same thing, resistance to American forces. Incidentally, Mabini's observations also exemplify his principle that government had to reflect the popular will and ought not to follow a course that the majority of the people have abandoned.

8. *On the Morality of a Revolution.* Mabini, who was essentially a moralist, believed that for a revolution to be successful,

[34] This is part of Mabini's introduction to *La Revolución Filipina.* The translation is taken from "Apolinario Mabini on the Failure of the Philippine Revolution," Document No. 2, *The American Historical Review,* Vol. XI, 1906, p. 857. Mabini did not join the initial stage of the Revolution, fearing its consequences. However, according to him, when the majority of the people were believed to support the movement, he decided that it was his duty to join such a popular movement.

it had to satisfy at least two moral requirements: The first was that the rank and file of the revolutionary army were to avoid those excesses which usually accompany war; second, that the high officials of whatever government the revolution might establish, should be models of personal virtue. With the above conditions satisfied, he claimed the Filipino people would be an ideal people. "If the Philippine Revolution shall be kept free of stains, then we shall be an ideal people, superior to all those known in history." [35]

With regard to the first moral requirement he wrote:

> The revolutionists must understand that if they do not practice the virtues which the high ideals of the Revolution demand, they themselves are the ones who stand much to lose.[36]

No doubt because of the advice of Mabini, many of the messages and proclamations of Aguinaldo stressed the need for the development of moral virtues among the revolutionists. A few samples of these remonstrances are as follows:

> Remember that in order . . . that our ends may be gained, it is indispensable that we adjust our actions to the rules of war and of right, learning to triumph over our enemies and to conquer our own evil passions.[37]
>
> Let us display unimpeachable honor in social relations and refined manners towards our fellow beings.[38]

Considering that the majority, if not all, of the bulk of the revolutionary army belonged to the humbler classes, the need for instruction and moral exhortation is understandable. But of more importance to note is that the leaders of the Revolution had to make a conscious effort to show the world there were ways by which a revolution could be guided along civilized and honorable methods—giving the lie to the claim of some Spanish friars that without their instruction or the guidance of Spain, the Filipinos would "revert to savagery."

[35] "Testamento Político de Rizal" (December 4, 1900), *La Revolución Filipina*, Vol. II, p. 214.
[36] "Krueger y Aguinaldo," *op. cit.*, p. 209.
[37] *Senate Document No. 208*, 56th Congress, 1st session, p. 106.
[38] "Address to Local Presidents" (August 3, 1898), *Philippine Social Science Review*, VI (January, 1934), 51.

With regard to the second moral requirement, the essential demand was that the men guiding the Revolution ought not to utilize the government for their own personal ends. Consistent with the principle that a revolution had to be a popular movement, it also had to be "cautious" in order to prevent a special group with specific interests from seizing control. In all probability, Mabini had in mind the fear that the "cacique" class might infiltrate the revolutionary organization, assume its leadership, and then use the government as a tool to further its own interests. With this in mind he wrote:

> It must be taken into account the possibility that a powerful and unscrupulous class might exploit the ignorance or corruption of its compatriots, in order to further its own particular interests. In such a case, the revolution will worsen, rather than better conditions.[39]

The demand that a revolution be moral has its roots going back to Rizal's fundamental principle that before a people deserve their independence or more political rights, they should be "free." This meant they must acquire those virtues signifying moral development; for Rizal always assumed that increased virtue implied increased freedom. For this reason, excesses or abuses had to be eliminated in any venture aiming at freedom. Like Rizal, Mabini feared that independence, in which a special class controlled the reins of government, would not necessarily give the people more freedom. On the contrary, there might result a more pernicious form of tyranny than that of past masters. Since both men were primarily interested in developing the moral fiber of the Filipino people, it is evident why, to them, politics had to be guided by moral principles. Revolution, like government, was intended to serve moral ends.

As an idealist Mabini sincerely believed that if Filipinos were so well imbued with moral principles and were so well united by means of the cohesive forces of these principles, they were not likely to be defeated in their struggle for independence. On the

---

39 *La Revolución Filipina,* Vol. II, p. 275. Although Mabini had in mind the friars when he justified revolution on the ground that government had been perverted to serve the interests of this class, in the above quotation he could not have referred to them, as the power of the friars was believed to have been considerably weakened. In all probability, Mabini had the "caciques" in mind, for, unlike the friars, they were "compatriots."

other hand, if they were defeated by superior force of arms, the antagonists would be forced to grant concessions to them and thus, in this sense, the Revolution would not fail. It was on this point that Mabini wrote:

> When these giants of power and ambition have become convinced that we have here an organized and robust people who know how to defend their honor and the laws of justice, they will not only be obliged to restrain their ambitions but will also agree to compromise with us as the sole means by which they can get the best possible terms.[40]

When the Revolution ended and American sovereignty was firmly implanted in the Philippines, Mabini wrote his *La Revolución Filipina*. In logically applying his moral and political principles, he insisted that one of the reasons why the Revolution failed was because there was a general want of virtue in the rank and file of the revolutionary army. This lack was partially evident in cases of abuses on the part of soldiers. But the chief want of virtue was shown in the chief executive (*director*) of the Filipino government who governed in terms of personal interests. He mistook his own personal aggrandizement for that of his country, and judged men, not in terms of character, efficiency, or patriotism but rather in terms of the degree of friendship or family relations. Thus he failed to govern for the general interest of the people and country.[41]

Mabini's judgment as to the cause of the failure of the Revolution, in laying more emphasis on the moral shortcomings of the revolutionists rather than on the superior military power of

---

[40] "A Los Jefes Revolucionarios" (April, 1898), *La Revolución Filipina*, Vol. I, p. 101.

[41] For these reflections of Mabini, cf. *La Revolución Filipina*, Vol. II, pp. 318; 321-322. These remarks are actually a severe indictment of Aguinaldo and appear to be harsh and partially unjustified. In any case, the indictment reveals that in the Revolution, there was a clear distinction between two groups: one group, which sprang from the masses and had the loyalty and actual leadership of the masses, to which Aguinaldo belonged; and the other group, composed of *ilustrados*, among whom there were many inspired and disinterested men like Mabini, Calderón, the del Rosarios, *et al.*, who attempted to guide and direct the masses in the ways of morality, law, administration, and efficiency—for the successful termination of the Revolution.

It is regrettable that writers like Captain John Taylor, in carefully cataloguing the demerits of the Revolutionary government in order to cast aspersions on it and the leaders, forgot or ignored the important function of disinterested men like Mabini and Calderón in shaping the general trend of the Revolution.

the American army, appears to be unduly severe. Considering its magnitude, the number of Filipinos involved in it, and also the odds against its protagonists, the Philippine Revolution was less characterized by abuses and excesses than many other recorded revolutions. Rafael Palma, who was a contemporary to the events of the Revolution, wrote on the matter that:

> The Philippine Revolution was a notable one, not solely on account of the greatness of its ideals but also on account of the human and chivalrous spirit with which it was directed. Even if its followers were of the middle and lower classes of the country, it did not produce in the hour of victories those morbid manifestations of the lower passions, nor did it produce an insolent patriotism or that great overflow of blood which characterized terrible chapters of the French Revolution . . . . The Christian spirit had roots in its conscience of such extraordinary strength, that its humanitarian sentiments became second nature to the Filipino people.[42]

Along the same lines, Teodoro Kalaw, a contemporary Filipino political scientist, wrote that the separatist movement that began in 1896 and which culminated in the establishment of the Philippine Republic, was not a mere expression of ungovernable passions. It was above all an organized action that was conducted with an ideal of emancipation. Kalaw further added that:

> Whatever be the verdict of posterity, there remains the indisputable fact that the Philippine Revolution was not, as has been charged, a racial war, a licentious outburst of violent passions, but a war pledged to and determined by the ideals of liberty, democracy, and constitutionalism.[43]

In a very important sense, the Philippine Revolution was not a failure. For the first time in the history of the Philippines, the people began to experiment with a system of elections, however limited, with the result that about half of the men who administered the legislative function in the government of the Republic were elected. The existence of a Bill of Rights and of a group of men in the government who were determined to see to it that its provisions were respected indicates that a sense of ex-

---

[42] Rafael Palma, *Apolinario Mabini: Estudio Biográfico* (Manila: Bureau of Printing, 1931), pp. 72-73.
[43] "The Constitutional Plan of the Philippine Revolution," *Philippine Law Journal*, I (December, 1914), 204.

pectancy among the people along democratic lines had sooner or later to be satisfied. And Mabini himself played a large part in the development of this sense of expectancy among the people; for he actually guided the greater part of the Revolution, at least in its second stage. The idea of independence, which Mabini more than any one else helped to propagate, elaborate, and rationalize, became very widespread. And this even after the defeat of the Philippine Republic. Thus, Mabini could say with justification that the desire for independence had become so strong among the Filipinos that any idea opposed to this would make the people unhappy. It was then that he suggested that there should be a struggle for independence along legal techniques.

When the army of the Republic was scattered and Aguinaldo was for all practical purposes a fugitive struggling to keep himself alive, various groups were already being formed in Manila to lead the struggle for independence through peaceful methods. In 1901, these groups were prevented from becoming legal parties on account of the Sedition Law passed by the United States government. This law declared unlawful any attempt on the part of any person or group to advocate independence for the Philippines or separation from the United States, even by peaceful means, as long as the war or "insurrection" against the United States was not proclaimed officially at an end. In 1902 when President Theodore Roosevelt proclaimed peace in the Philippines, various parties were established with independence as a major aspiration. A movement was thus legally begun which culminated finally in the grant of full independence to the Philippines by the United States. It was the movement for independence which began with the Revolution which was the inspiration for all political agitation against the United States. In this important sense, the Revolution was not a failure.

9. *A Theological Basis for the Principle that the Revolution Should Be Based on Moral Principles.* One of the reasons why the Revolution had to be based on moral rules has already been given. This was the view that freedom increased in proportion to virtue. Therefore, if a change of masters were not to signify a greater tyranny, it was deemed important for Filipinos to possess those virtues that would not only gain the respect of their opponents but which would also be perpetuated, even after the Revolu-

tion was successfully ended. Another reason was based on a more abstract principle which involved the theory of God's intervention in historical events. In general, this meant that God designated certain nations to have certain ends, and He also provided them with the energies to fulfill these appointed ends—punishing nations or at least preventing them from reaching these ends if they did not utilize proper moral means. This was actually Mabini's theory. In one of his articles, he expounded instances of this theory, which may be briefly summarized as follows: Providence manifested itself in Christ to emancipate souls from the slavery of terrestrial passions; it manifested itself in France, in order that this nation could set the example for emancipation from the tyranny of kings and nobles; it also manifested itself in the United States, to demonstrate how the tyranny of nations can be eliminated. Providence manifested itself also in the Philippines, a country that presented an instance of near-slavery to a "continent." With regard to this last point, Mabini probably meant that the revolution in the Philippines signified the emancipation of peoples from the near-slavery to Europe. Taking into account that Mabini considered one of the aims of the Revolution to be the emancipation of all the Malay race from foreign domination, then he probably meant that Providence was manifesting itself in the Philippines, in order that by Filipino example, *all* the different Malay peoples could free themselves from their various European masters. At this time these included the British, the Dutch, and the Portuguese.[44] Providence punished, too; for, man being free in his will, man might abuse his mission.[45] Taking France as a particular example, Providence gave her enough strength to fight the armies of other kings attempting to invade her, in spite of the amount of blood shed during the French Revolution. It was Napoleon whom Providence used as a tool to achieve His purpose in France; but Napoleon, in the excesses of his despotism and in the use of his power to aggrandize himself and his family, failed in his mission. Napoleon ended in defeat and disgrace, while France

[44] "Cual es la Verdadera Misión de la Revolución?" *La Revolución Filipina*, Vol. II, p. 58.
[45] "Dos Palabras Sobre Una Carta Abierta" (November 3, 1899), *La Revolución Filipina*, Vol. II, p. 107.

suffered, besides other reversals, the additional misery of the Franco-Prussian War.[46]

Thus, in general, Mabini's theory was that the rise and fall of nations was not accidental but due to the intervention of Providence, though men had some say in it. Furthermore, if men were moral in their behavior and nations were founded upon this basis, Providence would protect these men and nations. It was upon this article of belief that Aguinaldo declared:

> Providence always had means in reserve and prompt help for the weak in order that they may not be annihilated by the strong; that justice may be done and humanity prosper . . . .[47]

The greatness of a people or nation was judged by the proportion of virtue that it or its citizens had. As such, the greatness of a nation was equivalent to its fulfilling the role laid down for it by Providence. Relevant to this point, in order to encourage the revolutionists in their work, Mabini wrote:

> Those nations chosen by Providence for certain ends grow in proportion to the amount of difficulties they are able to endure; and we do not doubt that our people will be able to give a good account of itself in the maintenance of high virtues (while in its process of growth).[48]

At this point, it is interesting to note that one of the messages of Aguinaldo claimed that the Filipinos had arrived at a certain height in the development of virtue deserving of both liberty and independence.

> A people that has given proofs that it is capable of suffering and valor in both tribulation and danger, and who has demonstrated hard work and study in peace, is not meant for slavery but greatness. Such a people is destined to be one of the firm tools for the fulfillment of that destiny which Providence had laid down for humanity.[49]

---

[46] "Cual es la Verdadera Misión de la Revolución?" *op. cit.,* p. 58. The similarity of Mabini's indictment of both Aguinaldo and Napoleon may be noted.

[47] *Senate Document No. 208,* 56th Congress, 1st session, p. 105. This proclamation of Aguinaldo of February 5, 1899, was penned by Mabini.

[48] "A 'Un Filipino Prudente'" (September 26, 1899), *La Revolución Filipina,* Vol. II, p. 85.

[49] "Mensaje del Presidente de la Revolución Filipina" (June 23, 1898), *La Revolución Filipina,* Vol. I, p. 185. This message which was penned by Mabini, is almost a paraphrase of an earlier work of his entitled "Primer Saludo al Pueblo Filipino" (April, 1898), cf. *ibid.* Vol. I, p. 97.

He also claimed that the Filipinos had within themselves the energies and resources to free themselves from those attempts of Spain to ruin them, and, at the same time, to claim "a modest place (but dignified) in the concert of free nations." [50] The *Statement of the Chiefs of Towns* stated in part:

> But what is most surprising in this people is that it goes on giving proofs that it knows how to frame laws, commensurate with the progress of the age, to respect them and obey them, demonstrating that its national customs are not repugnant to this progress . . . . [51]

This statement, besides trying to convince other nations that Filipinos could govern themselves, was also an effort by some Filipinos to assure themselves that the teachings of the propagandists had not been in vain. The Filipinos, according to this belief, had arrived at the stage where they deserved "freedom"—in the sense of Rizal.

The above discussion has shown that Rizal's theory of freedom is closely linked with Mabini's theory of Providence in historical events. Since virtues or morality led men to be free, and since a virtuous people fulfilled the plans of Providence, it followed that a people in the path of freedom was not only fulfilling the plans of Providence, but was also being protected by it. This would further imply that any nation which prevented a virtuous people from gaining its freedom would feel the retribution of Providence. It is on this last point that Mabini's appeal in an article to the American people is especially significant.

> The Filipino people are struggling in defense of their liberties and independence with the same tenacity and perseverance as they have shown in their sufferings. They are animated by an unalterable faith in the justice of their cause, and they know that if the American people will not grant them justice, there is a Providence which punishes the crimes of nations as well as of individuals. [52]

Although the assertion that Providence punishes nations follows logically from certain premises of Mabini's theory, there seems to be an element of despair or helplessness in its use. But since to Mabini, "virtue" consisted essentially in the harmony of action

---

50 *Ibid.*
51 *Senate Document No. 62,* part ii, 56th Congress, 3rd session, p. 439.
52 "A Filipino Appeal to the People of the United States," *North American Review,* CLXX (January, 1900), p. 60.

with the requirements of natural law, and since he believed that the principles of American government were fundamentally based on natural law, his appeal to Americans sprang from certain philosophical convictions.[53]

The assertion that the historic process is guided by Providence may be one of the few principles found in any Filipino political thinker that closely suggests a "philosophy of history." As such, there was nothing novel in this approach; for the above principle was part and parcel of the Scholastic tradition in the Thomistic line, that the affairs of men bear the mark of God's plan. Another principle suggestive of a "philosophy of history" is Rizal's and Mabini's idea that progress among peoples is natural and inevitable—a principle which was not fully developed by either man. In any case, the two above-mentioned principles were not so much attempts to describe or predict the historic processes of nations, as rules of action that were intentionally formulated to inspire Filipinos to support the Revolution and to try to build a better society. Considering the element of Providence in the first above-mentioned principle, it could have been used as a tool to convince Filipinos that supporting the Revolution was both a patriotic and moral duty. The second principle on the other hand served to portray to Filipinos a promise or hope of a better society.

[53] Mabini considered "virtue" to be the harmony between theory and practice, and when he used the term "theory" in this definition, he meant the "natural and immutable order of things." Cf. *La Revolución Filipina*, Vol. II, p. 271.

C H A P T E R   S I X :   *Church and State:*
Historical Introduction

I know too well that there are trees that can provide better shade than others; but in the midst of the darkness which reigns in my country, it is not shade that I search for—but light.
—FROM A LETTER OF JOSE RIZAL TO FATHER PASTELLS, S.J.[1]

1. HISTORICAL INTRODUCTION. Since the Philippine Revolution was essentially an attempt at social reformation, a critical attitude towards so fundamental an institution as the Catholic Church was inevitable. The Church was intimately associated with the political machinery of the Spanish administration of the Philippines and it had also intertwined itself closely with the social fabric of the Filipino people. Because of this connection between the Church and State, the writers of the Propaganda Movement and the Revolution undertook to reevaluate the functions of the Church and redefine its ties with the people in accordance with a new system of values. The prevailing attitudes towards the privileged position of the Church and towards ecclesiastical authority, coupled with habitual obedience to this authority, brought about radical transformation of values. The Spanish Church was disliked, not because the Filipinos had become irreligious or anti-Catholic, but because it stood as a symbol of the old order. Not only did the Church have among its servants men with decidedly political and civil functions, but in addition some of the orders within it represented a class of wealthy landlords.

In spite of their bitter hatred toward the monastic orders, the majority of Filipino leaders and followers professed their loyalty toward and love for the Catholic Church. United States Army officers and correspondents noted this and testified to it in their official communications. Major Frank S. Bourns (Chief Surgeon, U.S. Volunteers in the Philippines) testified on August 27, 1898, that

[1] Letter No. 575 (November 11, 1892), *Epistolario Rizalino*, Vol. IV, p. 65.

the feeling against the monastic orders is . . . not against the church itself, as they are all good Catholics and wish well toward the Catholic church. The bitterness is directed against all the members of the monastic orders . . . .[2]

Major-General F. V. Greene in a memorandum dated August 30, 1898, also stated that

the natives are all Roman Catholics, and devoted to the church, but have bitter hatred for the monastic orders—Dominicans, Franciscans and Recollects. They insist that these be sent out of the country or they will murder them. These friars own the greater part of the land and have grown rich by oppressing the native husbandmen.[3]

The *Schurman Report,* which painstakingly reproduces verbatim complaints of a dozen Filipinos on the matter, stated in the same vein that

the Filipinos do not antagonize the Church itself; they are faithful and loyal to it; their hostility is aimed at the religious orders; they demand that the parishes should be filled by priests who are not friars; they claim that this is a law of the Church and should be the practice in the Philippines.[4]

With regard to a report of an interview with Aguinaldo who was at the time president of the Revolutionary government, the American reporter Murat Halstead, quoting Aguinaldo's interpreter, wrote:

The General [Aguinaldo] says that the priests to whom objection is made, and with whom we have a mortal quarrel, are not our own priests, but the Spaniards' and those of the orders. We respect the Catholic Church. We respect our own priests, and, if they are friends of our country, will protect them. Our war is not against the Catholic Church, but upon the friars, who have been the most cruel enemies. We cannot have them here . . . . The Jesuits, too, must go.[5]

---

[2] *Senate Document No. 62,* part ii, 55th Congress, 3rd session, p. 378. It is significant that Bourns specifically excludes the Jesuits from the above-mentioned monastic orders. The term "friars" or "monastic orders" in the Philippines colloquially referred only to the Dominicans, Augustinians, Recollects and Franciscans.

[3] *Ibid.,* p. 734.

[4] *Report of the Philippine Commission,* Vol. I, p. 131.

[5] *The Story of the Philippines* (Chicago: Our Possessions Publishing Co., 1898), p. 58. Since the specific objections towards the friars were not levelled at the Jesuits, Aguinaldo's desire to see them go probably reflects his desire to see all Spaniards leave the Philippines. The desire to see the Jesuits go was not in any way a universal desire of the Filipinos, unlike the desire to see the friars go away for good.

The Spanish civil and ecclesiastical authorities not only took for granted Filipino loyalty to the Church but they also actually exploited it. When war broke out between Spain and the United States, the Spanish governor-general of the Philippines proclaimed to the Filipino people on April 23, 1898, that the Americans were attempting to substitute the Protestant faith for the Catholic one. On the twenty-sixth of the same month, the archbishop of Manila, B. Nozaleda, solemnly warned the Filipinos that the Americans had "all abject passions engendered by heresy." [6] It seemed as if the Spanish authorities were using loyalty to the Church as their last trump card in order to secure the aid and loyalty of the Filipinos in their conflict with the United States. It was Sinibaldo de Mas who, more than fifty years before, had reflected upon the strongest bond of union that could hold Spain and the Philippines together. This was their common Christian faith, a bond so strong that it might "induce the islanders to love and defend the Spanish domination as a duty." [7] The Spaniards relied on this bond as a matter of desperation; but as later historical events showed, the Christian ties between Spain and the Philippines were in no way a guarantee of Filipino support of Spain in her conflict with the United States. On the contrary, the Filipinos took advantage of the Spanish-American conflict to emancipate themselves from Spain.

It clearly appears that Filipino attitudes towards the Church presented a complex mixture of sentiments. It is, therefore, important to distinguish at least three elements: (a) the Catholic Church as a spiritual institution fostering a definite system of theology and morality; (b) the friars or monastic orders in the Philippines, the majority of whom were Spaniards—by the middle of the nineteenth century, no Filipino was permitted to join

[6] Cf. Teodoro M. Kalaw, *The Philippine Revolution*, pp. 84-85. During the days when American aid was seen as necessary for the defeat of Spain, especially during the time of Dewey's victory in Manila Bay, Filipino leaders took pains to explain to the Filipinos that the Americans did not come to destroy their faith.

[7] "Internal Political Conditions in the Philippines (1842)," Blair and Robertson, *op. cit.,* Volume LII, p. 45. Sinibaldo de Mas was a Spanish government official who visited the Philippines in the middle of the nineteenth century.

a monastic order; and (c) the Filipino clergy, the majority, if not all, of whom belonged to the secular clergy.

As will be seen later the monastic orders represented a class with definite political and economic interests, and it was this class that was hated by Filipinos and which they desired to see destroyed. However, it was still possible for individual Filipinos to maintain some form of friendship and even respect for individual Spanish friars during the Revolution. According to Wenceslao Retana, a one-time Spanish apologist for the friars, "the rebels themselves saved many of their parish priests, even when they rarely spared any white man who fell into their hands." [8] Rizal probably never harbored any personal grudge against any individual friar as such. And if one of the letters of the Military Commander R. Carnicero (who had many intimate conversations with Rizal when the latter was an exile under his charge) to Governor-General Despujol faithfully interprets Rizal's opinions, then it appears that Rizal was more interested in the secularization of the friars than in their expulsion. [9]

But in the eyes of Spanish authorities, especially when they were either influenced by or under the control of the friars, an attack against the monastic orders was viewed as an attack upon both the power of the Church and Spanish sovereignty in the Philippines. This apparently complex situation can be appreciated from the rationalizations found in the decree of Governor-General Despujol ordering the banishment of Rizal to Dapitan in 1892. The postulates and implications revealed by this interesting document clearly demonstrate that the official view of the Spanish government, at the time, was that an attack on the monastic orders was judged as a mere veiled attack on the Church itself. Furthermore, an attack on the Church was an attempt to denationalize the Philippines. By "denationalization" was meant that to destroy the Faith was to destroy the particular source of unity ("national integrity") of the Philippines, the Church itself. Any attempt to destroy the "national integrity" of the Philippines was treason,

[8] *Los Frailes Filipinos* (Madrid: Imprenta de la Viuda de M. Minuesa de los Ríos, 1898), p. 136.

[9] Cf. "De Ricardo Carnicero al Gral. Despujol," Letter No. 565 (August 30, 1892), *Epistolario Rizalino,* Vol. IV, p. 29.

and since Spain was the main Protector of the Catholic Church, then to combat the Church was to be disloyal to Spain.[10] It is noteworthy that in this document, Despujol called himself both "governor-general" and *"vicereal patrono,"* thereby emphasizing that he represented the royal prerogatives of the Spanish King with regard to affairs of the Church in Spanish territories. In order to maintain and spread the fiction that to combat the friars was consequently to be disloyal to Spain, the friars and their apologists in both Spain and the Philippines tried to prove that the friars were the most important guardians of Spanish sovereignty in the Philippines. Therefore, to do away with them was in effect an attempt to do away with Spain. The Filipino propagandists maintained, however, that this was not the case, and that the opposite was closer to the truth.

But before the respective merits of these arguments can be judiciously weighed, some historical events have to be discussed. It is also necessary to note how the members of the monastic orders rendered to the State certain civil and political services.

2. *Relation between Church and State during Spanish Rule.* That the Filipinos found themselves governed by both civil and ecclesiastical authorities up to the Revolution was due to the fact that from the onset of colonization, the Philippines was considered primarily a missionary territory. Thus both Spanish soldiers and priests undertook to establish Spanish authority. Although Spanish monarchs never intended to abandon their autocratic rule over the Islands by means of the appointed governors, they nevertheless conceded that the missionary character of the acquisition of the Philippines was of paramount importance. It has been reported that when Philip II was told that the holding of the Philippines would not involve any profit to the Throne, and would on the contrary serve as an additional expense, he said:

> That is not a matter of the moment. I am an instrument of Divine
> Providence; the main thing is the conversion of the kingdom of Luzon,

---

[10] Cf. "Decreto del Gobernador Despujol deportando a Rizal a Dapitan," *Epistolario Rizalino,* Vol. IV, pp. 12-15. Javier Gómez de la Serna, a Spanish writer, wrote that "En 1892 se destierra a Rizal por *antimonacal,* añadiendo que esto es ser antiespañol." Found in the prologue of Wenceslao E. Retana, *Vida y Escritos del Dr. José Rizal* (Madrid: Librería General de Victoriano Suárez, 1907), p. xv.

and God has predestined me for that end, having chosen me His king for that purpose, and since He has entrusted so glorious a work to me and my crown, I shall hold the islands of Luzon even so by doing I exhaust my treasury.[11]

In 1582, the first bishop of the Philippines, Domingo de Salazar, convened a council attended by about 90 clericals and laymen, with the express purpose of formulating a system of ecclesiastical government for the Islands. Although not all of the decisions of the council were fully accepted by the civil authorities, they provided a guide for the understanding of future claims of the Church for both the maintenance and extension of its authority.[12] An extract of the council's decisions stated:

> The captains, soldiers, governors, and judges have no right to these territories other than those which they receive from the King. And the King did not give them more than he has, except that he can direct that the Gospel be preached throughout the world, but he cannot take from anyone that which is his. This right belongs to the King, because in his execution of it he can send men for the protection of the ministers of the Gospel and their converts, and establish when necessary a temporal government for the accomplishment of the spiritual purpose of the free conversion of the natives and their preservation of the faith.[13]

With the coming of ambitious governors-general, not to say also ambitious archbishops, the struggle for power among these ruling figures was the rule in Philippine history. It also appears that there was an area in which the powers of both were not well defined. This was so far true as to lead the Schurman Commission

---

[11] John R. M. Taylor, *Philippine Insurgent Records,* Vol. I, 4 FZ.

[12] According to Captain Taylor, the "decisions of this council are interesting not only as showing the highly altruistic ideas of the early Spanish authorities, but because they served as the basis for the relations between the civil and ecclesiastical authorities. The civil authorities certainly never unconditionally accepted them, but it may be said that they express the ideal toward which the ecclesiastics labored. The sheltered and protected life, the condition of paternal tutelage contemplated is remote from the thoughts of the present century, but the methods of government, and, in a large measure, of thought, in those islands down to our time for good and for evil—the methods of medieval Spain. They lay dreaming dreams, remote from life, like the cities of a legend over which a magician had cast his spell." *Ibid.,* 8 FZ.

[13] *Ibid.*

to report that one of the "most prominent defects" of the Spanish scheme of government was the "confusion of the functions of the State and the functions of the Church and the religious orders." [14] In the nineteenth century, up to the time of the Revolution, the Archbishop of Manila and the other bishops of the Islands were members of the "Board of Authorities," an advisory body to the Governor-General, especially in times of crises. This board had the power to conduct investigations of the highest importance to the security of the state. The archbishops, bishops, and provincials of the religious orders also belonged to the "Council of Administration," which was likewise charged with advising the Governor-General. [15]

The Archbishop's Court and the Commission of the Inquisition (this, to which no Filipino but only Spaniards were subject) formed the judicial branch of the hierarchy. The ecclesiastical courts had jurisdiction over problems referring to marriages and ecclesiastical offenses. Priests "were exempt from trials for offenses, except the most heinous, in the ordinary civil courts of the islands under the Spanish rule, and were entitled to a hearing before an ecclesiastical court, and even in the excepted cases trials must first be had in the latter tribunal." [16] Since in some cases it was difficult to determine whether a crime was civil or ecclesiastical or both, there was sometimes not a little conflict between civil and ecclesiastical branches. The *Royal Patronage* of the Spanish King was exercised by the Governor-General.

Another institution was the *Royal Audiencia*. Consisting of royal appointees, it had advisory and judicial powers and was intended to moderate or check arbitrary governors. The *Audiencia* possessed disciplinary jurisdiction over prelates and other clericals. It was also empowered

. . . to banish or deport undesirable priests, and two archbishops were placed under such disciplinary measure for disobeying Royal de-

---

[14] *Report of the Philippine Commission,* Vol. I, pp. 81-82.

[15] Cf. *Senate Document No. 112,* 56th Congress, 2nd session, p. 26. This document compares the functions of the "board of authorities" to what a present Department of Interior does, and the "council of administration" to the Council of State of Spain at that time.

[16] *Ibid.,* p. 28. It was not until 1835 that priests who committed "atrocious crimes" could be brought under the jurisdiction of the civil courts. Cf. *ibid.,* pp. 227-228.

crees . . . . In the enforcement of such measures there were always troubles, the church authorities refusing to submit to the civil power.[17]

The *Audiencia,* jealously guarding the Royal prerogatives, also supervised ecclesiastical visitors from Spain, forbade the construction of churches and monasteries without permission from the King, and made regular reports to the King about ecclesiastical affairs. In some cases, the *Audiencia* was asked to settle disputes between the different orders with regard to privileges, land holdings, and parochial jurisdiction.[18]

The Church was also partially supported by the state. In the Insular Budget for 1894-1895, out of the total expenditures of $13,280,139.41 (Mexican dollars), $1,045,540.00 went for ecclesiastical maintenance, such as salaries of bishops, priests, supplies for missionaries, etc.[19]

According to John Foreman, an English resident in the Philippines during the Revolution, in the last quarter of the nineteenth century the Church was financially supported by the state to the extent of about three-fourths of a million pesos per annum.[20] The figures given for the Budget of 1888 are as follows:

Archbishop's salary	₱ 12,000.00
Cathedral expenses, including salaries	43,300.00
Salaries for 4 bishops @ ₱6,000.00	24,000.00
Court of Arches	5,000.00
For Sulu Mission, Mission House in Manila for Capuchins, Chaplain of Los Baños, 12 Capuchins for the Carolina Islands and Pelew Islands	7,620.00

[17] Gabriel F. Fabella, "Church Administration in the Philippines," *The Philippine Social Science Review,* IV (October, 1932), 268-269.

[18] Cf. *ibid.,* Chapters V and VI for details. For additional information as to the complex relations between the Spanish governor-general, the *Audiencia* and the Church and monastic orders, see Alejandro M. Fernandez, "The Spanish Governor and Captain-General in the Philippines," M.A. thesis, Cornell University, 1955. In the Spanish system of government separation of powers was largely unknown. Because of the lack of precise differentiation of governmental functions, the *Audiencia* was the high court but at the same time shared with the governor-general certain executive and political functions. Created in 1583 to serve "the interest of good government," it was abolished in 1589 and reestablished in 1595. It was not until 1861 that the *Audiencia* was divested of its administrative and consultative functions; thereafter its function was confined to the administration of justice and became truly a supreme court.

[19] James LeRoy, *The Americans in the Philippines,* Vol. I, p. 53.

[20] Cf. John Foreman, *The Philippine Islands,* 3rd ed. (New York: Charles Scribner's Sons, 1906), pp. 207-208.

Estimated transportation expenses of missionaries ..   10,000.00
Anticipated total outlay for State support of Church,
    Missions, monasteries, convents, etc., including the
    above items 724,634.50

In the budget for 1888, the *"sanctorum* or Church tax of 18-3/4 cents (i.e., 1-1/2 reales) on each *Cedula personal* (personal tax), say on 2,760,613 *Cedulas* in 1888, less 4 per cent of collection . . . [was] ₱496,910.00." [21] Since there were Filipinos who did not or could not pay these personal taxes, a decree of Governor-General Terrero, dated November 23, 1885, ordered said men to furnish free labor "for Church architectural works, provided it was made clear that the cost of such labor could not be covered by the surplus funds of the *Sanctorum.*" [22]

3. *Duties of the Parish Priest.* In actual practice the parish priest exercised a most important social and political function in the Philippines during the Spanish regime. According to the *Schurman Report,* the parish priest assisted in choosing the members of the municipal tribunal (a unit of local government), saw to it that these officials were properly elected, and then signed the certificate of election. He also helped choose and nominate the *cabeza de barangay.* He assisted the tribunal with regard to taxation, construction of public works, its financial accounts and expenditures. He even decided the time and the date of the meetings of the tribunal. He also rendered his opinion on the accounts prepared by the tribunal before these are sent to the provincial council. And more than this, he was even a member of the provincial council. He was also the chief of the local census bureau, and all baptisms, marriages and deaths were required to be recorded in his files.[23] No testimony on the civil functions of the parish priest can be more eloquent than that given by Father Juan Villegas, head of the Franciscan Friars in the Philippines. During an investigation made by the Philippine

---

[21] *Ibid.,* p. 207.

[22] *Ibid.,* p. 208.

[23] For duties of the parish priest, cf. *Report of the Philippine Commission,* Vol. I, p. 57; *Senate Document No. 112,* 56th Congress, 2nd session, pp. 24-27; *Census of the Philippine Islands for 1903* (Washington: United States Bureau of the Census, 1905), Vol. I, pp. 369-370.

Commission on the status of the religious orders in the Philippines in 1900, Villegas volunteered the following information:

> The following may be mentioned as among the principal duties or power exercised by the parish priest: He was inspector of primary schools; president of health board and board of charities; president of the board of urban taxation (this was established lately); inspector of taxation; previously he was the actual president, but lately honorary president of the board of public works.
>
> He certified to the correctness of the cedulas—seeing that they conformed to the entries in the parish books. They did not have civil registration here, and so they had to depend upon the books of the parish priest. These books were sent in for the purpose of this cedula taxation, but were not received by the authorities unless vised by the priest.
>
> He was the president of the board of statistics, because he was the only person who had any education . . . . He was the president of the census-taking of the town.
>
> Under the Spanish law every man had to be furnished with a certificate of character. If a man was imprisoned and he was from another town, they would send to that other town for his antecedents, and the court would examine whether they were good or bad. They would not be received, however, unless the parish priest had his vise on them. The priest also certified as to the civil status of persons.
>
> Every year they drew lots for those who were to serve in the army, every fifth man drawn being taken. The parish priest would certify as to that man's condition . . . . By law he had to be present when there were elections for municipal offices . . . . He was censor of the municipal budget before they were sent to the provincial governor . . . . He was also counselor for the municipal council when that body met. They would notify him that they were supervisors of the election of the police force . . . . He was examiner of the scholars attending the first and second grades in the public schools. He was censor of the plays, comedies and dramas in the language of the country, deciding whether they were against the public peace or the public morals . . . . He was president of the prison board, and inspector (in turn) of the food provided for the prisoners . . . . He was a member of the provincial board . . . . Before the provincial board came all matters relating to public works and other cognate matters. All estimates for public buildings in the municipalities were submitted to this board . . . . He was also a member of the board for partitioning crown lands . . . . In some cases the parish priests in the capitals of the provinces would act as auditors.[24]

---

[24] *Senate Document No. 190,* 56th Congress, 2nd session, pp. 64-66. According to the Philippine Commission, Father Villegas spoke with authority,

Some of the duties of the parish priest came about by law, while others were acquired by actual practice. In 1898 there were 746 regular parishes, 105 mission parishes, and 116 missions, or 967 in all. Of these all but 150 were administered by the monastic orders. The total Catholic population at this time being 6,559,998, only about one-seventh of these were entrusted to the secular clergy, the majority of whom were Filipinos.[25] In 1892, the spiritual charges of the various religious communities were as follows:[26]

Augustinians	....	2,082,131
Recollects	....	1,175,156
Franciscans	....	1,010,753
Dominicans	....	699,851

In 1895

Jesuits	....	213,065

and in 1896, the

Secular clergy	....	967,294

From control of the parishes to control of the municipalities was not a difficult step; and since the friars controlled most of

having been in the Philippines for twenty-five years, out of which twenty were spent in the northern provinces, as curate.

[25] *Senate Document No. 112,* 56th Congress, 2nd session, p. 23. In 1870, according to LeRoy, there were 792 parishes, excluding the 10 mission parishes of the Jesuits. The friars at this time controlled 611 of these, while the Filipino priests had only 181 of them. Whereas the parishes under friar control averaged 6,000 persons each, that controlled by Filipinos averaged 4,500. In the 196 parishes under Augustinian control, the average of each went as high as 10,000 souls. When in 1898, the number of Filipino priests and coadjutors increased to 600, the number of parishes under their control .did not increase. Cf. *The Americans in the Philippines,* Vol. I, pp. 60-61.

[26] These figures are found in Charleson Shane, "A Sketch of Catholicity in the Philippines," *The Catholic World,* Vol. LXVIII (August, 1898), p. 696; and Le Roy, *The Americans in the Philippines,* Vol. I, p. 61.

In a report furnished by the Jesuit fathers, the membership of the religious orders, before the Revolution, numbered as follows: 644 Augustinians, 528 Dominicans, 522 Recollects, 475 Franciscans, 164 Jesuits, 36 Capuchins, and 14 Benedictines. *Report of the Philippine Commission,* Vol. IV, p. 108.

Senate Document No. 112, 56th Congress, 2nd session, p. 23, gives a much reduced figure for 1896. It states there were 1,124 Spanish priests in the Philippines in 1896, and that in 1896-1898, 40 of them were killed, while 403 were imprisoned by Philippine Revolutionary forces. By 1900, only 472 of the total remained—the rest having died or gone to Spain, China or South America.

the parishes, they also controlled most of the municipalities. Out of "the 850 municipalities into which the Archipelago was divided, 670 were in the power of the monks, leaving 180 municipalities under the administration of the Jesuits and clericals of other orders." [27]

The friar-curate's tenure of office was permanent; and once he had his parish, he continued in office until death or superannuation. This was also true of the prelates of the Church. On the other hand, the civil and military authorities in the Islands did not usually hold office for more than four years, and in many cases they stayed for a shorter period. Civil and military authorities came and went, but the friar stayed.[28]

The above discussion throws light on the claims of the friars and their apologists to the effect that the whole Spanish government of the Philippines rested on their shoulders. On this point the provincial of the Augustinian Order, José Lobo, went so far as to claim boldly that the friars were "the pedestal or foundation of the sovereignty of Spain in these islands," and when removed, "the whole structure would topple over." [29] Retana, while still an avid apologist for the friars, wrote that the State had in each friar an active sentinel, ever-watchful of the integrity of Spanish territory. He further added that the official intervention of the friar in official matters was a right based on the days of the Spanish Conquest; and in addition he was, as a rule, the only peninsular in the town, being "all patriotism and love for the natives." [30] Actually, the government in times of emergency had to rely on the friar in order to secure and tighten its authority on the Filipino masses. In some provinces the governor-general had only two or three officials representing him, and they may have been ignorant of the language spoken in the area and also

---

[27] T. H. Pardo de Tavera, "History of the Philippines," *Census of the Philippines for 1903*, Vol. I, p. 346.

[28] From 1835 to 1897 the Philippines had almost 50 governors-general, each averaging one year and three months; while from 1581 to 1898, there were only 25 archbishops of Manila. Cf. LeRoy, *The Americans in the Philippines*, Vol. I, p. 52; and J. Taylor, *Philippine Insurgent Records*, Vol. I, 14 FZ.

[29] *Senate Document No. 190*, 56th Congress, 2nd session, p. 73.

[30] W. Retana, *Frailes y Clerigos* (Madrid, 1890), p. 33. In 1765, a viceroy of Mexico told Charles III: "In each friar who steps on Filipino soil, Your Majesty has both a captain-general and an army." *Ibid.*, p. 27.

unable to take care of all the routine work of administration. As a sympathizer of the friars said

> . . . government would be impossible were if not for the twenty or thirty friars living in their respective parishes who educate the natives, guide, discipline and control them.[31]

It was precisely this attitude held by such apologists and sympathizers that irritated and exasperated Filipino intellectuals. In their view, the friars intentionally did not want to educate them fully; and that they even tried to draw all political powers into their own hands, refusing to allow power to be shared with the people so as to maintain their position and power.

Actually, the friars comprised a powerful political class; and when they combined with the bishops, they presented a well-organized political force which was difficult for any civil official to combat with impunity. In the Revolution of 1896, when the friars were dissatisfied with what they considered Governor-General Blanco's apathy in fighting the revolutionists, they were able by means of a telegram to Madrid, to have him relieved of his duties within 48 hours. The ordinary Filipino who crossed their path could always be easily imprisoned or exiled as either a mason or *"filibustero."*

It is to be expected that when a class acquires a great amount of power it will not easily relinquish it. Therefore, it is easily understood why the friars should fight any attempt to secularize the parishes, to grant to the people greater participation in local government, or educate them to a higher level; for if these were done their function would rather either become superfluous or begin to be questioned. It is no wonder then that they fought the Propaganda Movement with such fury; and during the Revolution itself, many of them joined the ranks of the Spanish Army. The

---

[31] Stephen Bonsal, "The Work of the Friars," *North American Review*, DLI (October, 1902), 458. Bonsal quotes various governors-general who affirmed the usefulness of the friars in governing the country. *Ibid.*, pp. 458-459. This "dependence" of governors-general on friars led many Filipinos to believe that the Spanish government was utilized to serve the interests of the monastic orders. As M. H. del Pilar put it in 1890: "Es ya un proverbio en Filipinas que el Gobernador General es el sacristán general de los conventos monásticos." Quoted from Teodoro M. Kalaw's *La Masonería Filipina*, p. 33.

Propaganda Movement and the Revolution threatened their very existence in the Philippines.

Taylor correctly pointed out that the trend of legislation after the middle of the nineteenth century was away from the continued ecclesiastical control of the Philippines. But he carefully noted that this in no way implied that in practical matters ecclesiastical authority and influence had diminished. He continued:

> To a contemporary observer who judged merely by what was taking place about him and not by the general tenor of events, the influence of the ecclesiastics may even have seemed to be increasing. When evidence appeared in the Philippines of that feeling of the nineteenth century, which makes for the subordination of the theological to the secular spirit in national affairs, they were met by a fierce spirit of repression on the part of the religious orders. The Spanish spirit does not admit of conciliation by concession. The Spanish clergy seeing themselves attacked, defended themselves, and the government, although its representatives frequently disagreed with them, was still dependent upon them, as the parish priests were more in touch with the people than with any other officials and were the only ones who lived with them and knew their language. And the mass of testimony shows that a man who becomes involved with the priests becomes involved with the civil authorities.[32]

4. *Filipino Attitude Towards the Political Power of the Friars.* The claim of the friars that they were the sole and indispensable supporters of Spanish sovereignty in the Philippines was not allowed to go unquestioned by either the Filipino propagandists or the leaders of the Revolution. It was maintained that their claim was basically false or that the need the government had for them was not inevitable. In one of his official communications to Major-General Otis, Aguinaldo wrote:

> The same priests (sacerdotes religiosos) tried . . . to cheat the Spanish Government, making it believe that they were the only upholders of Spanish sovereignty in the Philippines, and although the Spanish authorities recognized the fraud, they did not want to admit anything, as they were influenced by the gold of the religious corporations.[33]

---

[32] *Philippine Insurgent Records,* Vol. I, 20 FZ.
[33] *Senate Document No. 208,* 56th Congress, 1st session, part 1, p. 43. This communication was penned by Mabini.

This statement of Aguinaldo, written in 1898, is but a restatement of what M. H. del Pilar and the other propagandists were saying in the early days of the movement for reforms. The propagandists claimed that, instead of safeguarding Spanish sovereignty in the Philippines, the friars were, because of their class interest and their abuse of the people, actually endangering it. It was also pointed that the friars separated the people from the Government because their interests were opposed to those of both the people and the Government. And more than this: according to M. H. del Pilar, writing in 1889, the friars in order to preserve their position, power and wealth, saw to it that some form of enmity should always exist between the people and the government.

> Such is the method of dominance developed by the friars: before the people, they accuse the government of every kind of despotism; before the government, they accuse the people of being rebels and filibusters. And so, by alarming one another, and maintaining this antagonism, they are able to put themselves in the position of interceders—a position which they now possess and which enables them to deal with the antagonistic forces, in the manner they so desire.[34]

---

[34] *Frailocracia Filipina* (Barcelona: Imp. de F. Fossas, 1889), p. 9. Del Pilar's observations were expressed almost identically by Felipe Calderón, before the Taft Commission on October 17, 1900. What Calderón stated was that the friars "were the expression of the most exaggerated despotism, not of the Government of Spain, but of their own despotism, which they exercised, using the name of the Kingdom of Spain, because their system was to deceive both Spain and the people. That was the line they had laid down, and unfortunately, they are still following it . . . . They would say to the people, 'If it were not for me the government would annihilate you.' And then they would say to the government, 'If it were not for me the people would overthrow you.' And even at the present time there is not the slightest doubt that they have said to the American authorities that all of the Filipino people were a lot of anarchists and insurgents who were conspiring to overthrow constituted authority, while to the people of the Philippines, they say the American Government will place a chain around the waist of each of them; I do not make this assertion as an emanation of myself. I have seen it in writing. In the confessional they say to them, 'How can you be in favor of the Americans when they are absolutely the enemies of our religion?' And they say that constantly to the secular clergy [Filipino clergy], adding that woe betides the poor Filipinos who deliver themselves over unconditionally to the American Government, and I have heard them from the very lips of Monsieur Chapelle [papal delegate to the Philippines in 1900]." *Senate Document No. 190,* 56th Congress, 2nd session, p. 141. This was the testimony of a man who wanted the Catholic religion to be the State religion of the Philippines.

M. H. del Pilar believed that the preservation of the wealth of the friars was based on this continually encouraged antagonism between the people and the government.[35] He also maintained the friars had so much political power, that the "national integrity" had begun to fall into their hands—a situation counter to the interests of both the King and the Filipino people.[36] Graciano López-Jaena pinpoints the conflict of interests between the friars and the people in the political sphere, when he complains that the local officials (i.e., the *cabezas de barangay, gobernadorcillos,* and other municipal officials) were not at all local authorities, except on paper.[37] This essentially means that any attempt on the part of the Filipino people to appeal for a greater share in local government would be likely met with opposition on the part of the friars, who would be reluctant to relinquish it.

The contention that the interests of the friars were opposed to those of the King and government revolved around the charge that the friars had become so strong politically as to disobey the Government with impunity and to utilize it to further their own ends. According to the lengthy *Memorial* of Isabelo de los Reyes, some specific charges on this point are as follows:

> That the friars flout . . . the laws and decrees of the Government and of the Church, disregarding everything with impunity . . . .
> That they are opposed to the progress of the country, even impeding Spanish immigration because they believe the Spaniards would fiscalize and curtail their abuses . . . .[38]

---

[35] "La base del enriquecimiento monacal es la desunión entre el pueblo y el gobierno." M. H. del Pilar, *La Soberanía Monacal* (Barcelona: Imp. de F. Fossas, 1888), p. 9.

[36] *Ibid.,* p. 17.

[37] *Discursos y Artículos Varios,* p. 88. Also cf. *ibid.,* pp. 78-96.

[38] "Memorial of I. de los Reyes," quoted from Teodoro M. Kalaw, *The Philippine Revolution,* pp. 55-56. This memorial created a great sensation and number of discussions in both Spain and the Philippines, gaining for De los Reyes some notoriety. After this, the Spanish Minister of Foreign Relations gave him a modest job in the Publicity Board Department in Spain. Cf. *ibid.,* pp. 54-55. The specific charges number fifteen and are also found in the original of Retana's *Vida y Escritos del Dr. José Rizal,* pp. 94-95. Retana says that the complaints are somewhat exaggerated, and this is probably so, but a lot of truth is also found in them. It is writings like this, plus the belief on the part of Spaniards that the friars were a source of the troubles in the Philippines, that may have prompted the friars to present their "Friar Memorial of April 21, 1898." This long document, directed to the Spanish Minister of Colonies, was in effect

W. Retana, in defending the role of the friar in state matters, unwittingly revealed their interference in governmental affairs—

> The Friar desires that kind of progress which is *reasonably proper* for the Philippines; it is for this reason that when he sees that a Minister implants reforms which may cause some form of disorder in that country, he laments the errors of the Minister. Yet, he dares to combat them, in private, but not in public, because first of all, he knows more of the Philippines than that very Minister, and secondly, because the Friar is *permanent* in the Philippines, while the Minister is a mere *passing bird* in the Department of State.[39]

It was not only interference on the part of the friars in governmental affairs that irked Filipinos; even more intolerable to them was the friars' attitude in thinking themselves the only ones who knew what was good for the Filipinos.

One of the most serious charges hurled by Filipinos against the friars was that they utilized both the Government and the Church as tools to increase their power and preserve their hold on the masses. This is one of the arguments of the *Noli Me Tangere* and Rafael Palma, a Filipino scholar, in his interpretation of this political novel, wrote that what the novel exposed was that

> the regular clergy utilized the Catholic religion as an instrument of domination and prostituted it with many external ceremonies in order to give it the appearance of a cult, but which actually served as a source of wealth. The civil guards do not protect peaceful citizens nor those of the humble classes, but only the priests and Spaniards; they commit excesses and abuses, with the result that for every bandit they capture, many of those born not to be so become bandits . . . . As yet, there is no filibusterism in the Philippines, but with these excesses and abuses of both the friars and the government, there will be one.[40]

Retana, after he became a fervent admirer of Rizal, interpreted this novel (*Noli Me Tangere*) to mean, in part, that the friars

an apology for the friars' stay in the Philippines. It claimed that the Filipino masses loved them, and so did many of the educated ones. It also vehemently warned that they would oppose secularization and episcopal intervention in their affairs. Apparently, either the lessons of 1896 were forgotten by them, or they were living in terms of wishes.

[39] W. Retana, *Frailes y Clerigos*, p. 72.

[40] *Biografía de Rizal*, p. 83.

utilized the Church as an instrument of domination so that "instead of having a system of disinterestedness and lofty sentiments, they converted it into a system of abominable deceit." [41]

5. *Filipino Attitude Towards the Control of Education by the Friars.* Another contention of the Filipino propagandists was that separation of the Government from the people was also the result of control by the friars of the education of the masses of the people. M. H. del Pilar went to the extent of claiming, in general, that the friars discouraged the learning of the Spanish language in order to better secure their hold on the masses; for, if and when the majority of the Filipinos learned this language then it would be easier for the governors and the governed to reach an understanding.[42] The fact the Government did not exert great efforts in this direction or failed to secularize all education was interpreted by Filipinos as approval of the control of education by the friars. Mabini wrote, as was widely believed by Filipinos generally,

> . . . the Spanish government in conjunction with the friars attempted to isolate the Filipinos, both intellectually and physically, from the outside world, in order that they would not receive any impression other than that which was convenient to allow them to have.[43]

The *Noli* also tried to demonstrate that the friars attempted to keep the Filipinos perpetually ignorant, and therefore any attempt on their part to educate themselves led either to ridicule or

[41] W. Retana, *Vida y Escritos del Dr. José Rizal,* p. 127. With reference to the time of the publication of the *Noli,* Retana gives the information that when the book was circulated in the Philippines, "it was noticed that contributions to the parochial box reduced, and in the towns that were relatively more politically advanced than others like Taal, Lipa, Malolos, etc., very few paid baptisms were accompanied by organ-playing and bell-ringing, neither were there many masses officiated by three priests and subchanters, nor celebrations in honor of such and such a saint or saintess. . . . Rizal was able with a simple book to hurt the friars in that which they most esteemed, that is, the pocket book. At the same time. he was able to convince many of his countrymen that in order to merit heaven, it was not necessary to enrich the friar, nor to follow blindly everything the friar preached to them; the friar was simply an exploiter of the simplicity and meekness of the faithful; and, what was more important, the respect for the priest need not be converted into dishonorable servility." *Ibid.,* p. 308.
[42] *La Soberanía Monacal,* pp. 11-13.
[43] *La Revolución Filipino,* Vol. II, p. 281.

persecution. Their own country came to be conceived by Filipinos as not for them; and any idea of progress looked upon as to be harbored only by foreigners. This meant that any man who could manage to educate himself along liberal lines was a man incompatible with the interests of the friars; as such it was not possible for him to live peacefully in his own country. On these points, De los Reyes stated "that . . . friar provisors and fiscals persecute the cultured Filipinos and even those who hardly speak Spanish." [44]

In truth, many friars believed the Filipinos would never be able to attain the educational and cultural level of the Spaniard. The testimony of Nozaleda, the Archbishop of Manila, to the Philippine Commission, was to the effect the Filipinos had "no proper individuality," had "an absolute want of character," had "just sufficient of the logical faculty to be rational beings" and "they have not sufficient mental capacity to digest any abstract question." The Archbishop also said the Filipinos "could hardly be called an artistic race except in a very limited degree"; that "soon after they leave an educated atmosphere, they lose all they have learned"; and "their affection for their children is more that of the animal than human," etc.[45]

Historically considered, the evidence proves the friars were actually attempting to keep the Filipinos in medieval isolation. How the friars believed this isolation could still be maintained with the coming of newspapers, books, telegraphic communications, and men of liberal ideas, is difficult to understand.[46] According to Taylor,

---

[44] I. de los Reyes, "Memorial," *op. cit.*. p. 56. The ridicule of those speaking Spanish could not have been prominent in the metropolitan area of Manila, where there was a concentration of many foreigners and educated Filipinos, and where a good command of the language was to some extent imperative for commercial and academic reasons. In all probability the ridicule was localized in the provinces, where as a rule the parish priest held sway, and where most sermons and religious instruction were done in the local dialects. However, the Crown always favored the teaching of Spanish.

[45] Cf. *Senate Document No. 190.* 56th Congress, 2nd session, pp. 96-112. Were it not for the fact that Nozaleda knew that he was speaking for the official records, one would suspect that he was jesting.

[46] Austin Craig wrote: "Though they are in the Orient. the Filipinos are not of it. Rizal once said, upon hearing of plans for a Philippine exhibit at a European World's Fair, that the people of Europe would have a chance to see themselves as they were in the Middle Ages. With allowance for the changes due to climate and for the character of the country, this statement can hardly be called exaggerated. The Filipinos

The Philippines was the last and greatest of the Spanish Catholic missions, the Benjamin of the Spanish Church, and were to be held uncorrupted. It was a dream which lasted for three hundred years in the secular calm behind the ramparts of Manila.[47]

The friars, understandably, viewed themselves as absolutely needed for the enlightenment of the people; and any Filipino who combatted them was consequently ungrateful. When in 1898, Halstead interviewed Archbishop Nozaleda, the latter said the Catholic teachers raised the Filipinos from savagery to Christianity; and since these teachers educated the very men who were leading the Revolution, Filipino rebels were "false, unjust and ungrateful." [48] Upon the above principle, Rizal was considered "ungrateful" when he wrote his political novels. In the official censure of the *Noli* on December 29, 1887, the friar Salvador Font pronounced that

> . . . the Filipinos are the happiest race which has lived under the beneficent shadow of the paternal Laws of the Indies—that monument which heroic and peerless Spain has raised amidst modern civilization to protect and assimilate infantile peoples whom God has entrusted to her, not to enslave and degrade them, as other nations have done, but to instruct and enlighten them, and to make to shine upon them the dawn of Christian liberty and the resplendent sun of a new life, of social culture and modern civilization.[49]

The claims on the part of the friars—that their guiding hands were vitally needed, that without them a return to savagery was inevitable, and that the Filipinos were innately inferior to Spaniards as evidenced by their present state of indolence, gambling habits, etc.—did not escape attack. Rizal actually blamed the

in the last half of the nineteenth century were not Orientals but Medieval Europeans—to the credit of the early Castilians but to the discredit of the later Spaniards." *Lineage, Life and Labors of José Rizal* (Manila: Philippine Education Company, 1913), p. 7.

[47] J. Taylor, *Philippine Insurgent Records,* Vol. I, 11 FZ. One is led to suspect that the frustrations of friars in Europe due to the rise of the national states and the Reformation's cleavage of the Christian community, led them to desire to preserve a theocratic Utopia, along medieval lines, in the Philippines.

[48] *Op. cit.,* p. 87. The Archbishop of Manila also added that European anarchistic education influenced Filipinos who went to Europe to be educated, and since the Church did not believe in "murderous anarchy" the revolutionists were against the Church.

[49] "Official Censure of Noli Me Tangere," Manila, December 29, 1887; in *Rizal's Political Writings,* ed. Austin Craig (Manila: Oriental Commercial Company, 1933), pp. 304-305.

bad educational system of the Filipinos and even their so-called "moral degradation" on the example of the friars. In the *Noli,* in the words of Isagani in a conversation with Padre Fernandez, he wrote:

> What we are, you have made us. A people tyrannized over is forced to be hypocritical; a people denied the truth must resort to lies; and he who makes himself a tyrant breeds slaves . .... . If after three centuries and a half the artist has been able to produce only a caricature, stupid indeed he must be.[50]

Here Rizal reveals a principle that permeates all of his works—that those who rule have certain obligations to their subjects; and if there is something amiss with the social order, to a great extent the ruler is held accountable. In believing the friar served as a factor in the degradation of the moral fiber of the Filipino people, Rizal was a proponent of the idea that all education should be secularized, and that the Government should encourage primary education, to the complete exclusion of friar interference.[51] This idea of Rizal is found more clearly stated in one of the ideals expressed by the *Hongkong Junta:*

> We desire a system of public instruction less clerical in its nature and in which greater attention is paid to the natural and positive sciences . . . an instruction which will be free in all its branches and obligatory in its lowest grades. We desire to apply to this object all the property, whose products are today set aside to defray the expenses of the same, placing a Board of Public Instruction in charge of such property, and not leaving it for an instance longer in the charge of the religious institutions as the latter only teach superstition and prejudice . . . .[52]

The Revolutionary government and the Philippine Republic, in accordance with the above ideal, actually established an educational system completely divorced from religious interference.

6. *The Secularization Problem.* The claim of the Spanish friars that they are of vital importance for the preservation and spread of Christianity in the Philippines was also contested by the pro-

---

[50] *The Reign of Greed,* p. 266.
[51] Stated in a conversation with Carnicero. Cf. "De Ricardo Carnicero al Gral. Despujol," Letter No. 565, August 30, 1892, *Epistolario Rizalino,* Vol. IV, p. 29.
[52] "First Manifesto of the Hongkong Junta," *op. cit.,* p. 210.

pagandists and the Filipino clergy. The early Spanish missionaries were recognized for their disinterestedness, their inspired character, and for the incalculable debt owed to them for the effective and beneficial spread of Christianity in the country. But the latter-day friars were believed to possess so much power as to be completely different from the earlier missionary friars. The Filipinos, quite naturally, claimed that a Filipino clergy would be competent and adequate to handle parochial duties and also, largely, the Church administration in the country. When the friars discouraged, nay, even opposed the rapid development of Filipino clergy, it was believed this was a plan on their part to prevent the loss of their prestige and power. Whatever may have been the motives and rationalizations of the friars in their opposition to the development of a Filipino clergy, it is quite clear that the secularization of the parishes would benefit only the Filipino priests; therefore, it is not surprising that the first leaders for general reforms— and these included the increase of chances for Filipino priests to hold parishes in their own country—should be Filipino priests like Burgos, Gómez, and Zamora. It must also be considered that the Filipino priests were those who had all the chances for a relatively better education. Therefore they would represent an enlightened class that would be more sensitive to all forms of inequalities and injustice.

Assuming that the power of the friars was inversely proportional to the increase in the power of the Filipino clergy, it is not hard to understand why they argued before the Spanish Throne that the Filipino clergy was inefficient and ignorant. There was, to some extent, ignorance and inefficiency among Filipino priests, as has been attested by writers like T. de Comyn and Jagor; but Filipino writers claimed this situation came about during the beginning and middle of the nineteenth century because of a concerted plan to keep the Filipino priests ignorant, so that they could not qualify for the positions held by the Spanish friars. If it is at all valid, as Rizal argued, that many Filipinos were ill-educated due to the educational system perpetuated by the friars, then, as many propagandists claimed, some Filipino priests were ill-prepared for their duties. They were the victims of both the inefficiency and the bad example of their instructors. And more than this, it was also thought the friars would not be able to control the best and richest parishes, if it were demonstrated that there were secular priests better prepared to handle them.[53] The *Memorial* of De los Reyes, which expresses some truth for all its rhetoric, lists the following complaints:

> That the native clergymen are oppressed by being sent to prison or suspended arbitrarily, by being transferred from one province to another . . . .
>
> That friar bishops, in order to favor the Spanish priests, order changes in assignments to parishes to the prejudice of the native priests . . . .
>
> That the parishes are not apportioned after a test and in accordance with equity, as ordered by the Council of Trent, so that the most deserving may hold them, but that, in order to discredit the native priests, the most inefficient among them . . . are made acting parochial priests . . . .[54]

The clash of interests between those of the friars and those of the Filipino clergy, the sympathy and the support of the Filipino population for their cause, together with the belief that the Spanish government supported the cause of the friars, are instances of the principle stated by M. H. del Pilar that the friars had served to separate the people from the Government. Del Pilar maintained that the sympathy and identification of the Filipino people with their clergy had become a national issue and, further, that the Government had alienated itself from the people by supporting a class whose interests were directly in opposition to the people; therefore, since government must consider the wishes of the people and have their confidence, the friars acted as a force opposed to the interests of the Government. For the Filipino reformers, whether clerical or laymen, the secularization problem was definitely one of nationalism. On this point, LeRoy states:

> The fight against the friars was a fight in behalf of the Filipino clergy, and in that way formed another aspect of the revolution in behalf of a new and a *national* life.[55]

This was a point never understood fully by the Spaniards. They could not quite grasp the nationalistic element involved in the secularization problem. It was only when events of the Revolution were viewed retrospectively, so as to tie together the separatist

---

[53] Cf. "Evidence of Florentino Torres (October 31, 1900)," *Senate Document No. 190, 56th Congress, 2nd session*, p. 181.

[54] *Op. cit.*, p. 55.

[55] *Philippine Life in Town and Country*, p. 160.

movement and nationalism, that enemies of the Filipino clergy blamed them as the incipient instigators of the Revolution. Although it is true that Filipino priests joined the ranks of the Revolution later on, during the Propaganda days they were not separatists. If ever they were authors of the Revolution, it was only in the sense that Rizal was also an author; that is, they made the people more aware and alert to social issues and the existence of injustice and inequalities with the aim of correcting them.

On this point, Governor-General Primo de Rivera sheds light on the conditions that led Filipino priests to desire social emancipation. Regarding the events of 1896 he reflected:

> . . . . the statement can be made without possibility of error that the native priests have been the real propagators of ideas of separation, receiving orders from the centers of the conspiracy or their inspiration from their doctrines, and when it came to the time of their execution, some of them were sufficiently brave as to follow the rebels . . . .
> Hence the native priest, having the Christian spirit, educated in the seminary, enlightened by the friar ordinarily living with him, is probably the most hostile and most dangerous of those who confront us. And this is as it should be. When you instruct a man and give him a superior education; when you ordain him, train him in the gospels . . . that man can be no man's servant. He will look as equal on the men who exercise analogous functions, and he will hold himself the superior, if he knows more . . . . When he is given a parish, it must be a very poor one, since the religious orders keep those which produce anything. This explains the outcry for the expulsion of the friars . . . . Upon the decision taken upon the question of the friar depends the preservation or loss of this country.[56]

---

[56] From the "Memoria Dirigida al Senado, por el Capitán General D. Fernando Primo de Rivera, acerca de su gestión en Filipinas." J. Taylor, *Philippine Insurgent Records*, Vol. I, 60 FZ, Exhibit 6.

The "secularization controversy" had its roots in the "visitation controversy." This was a continuous conflict between the Archbishop of Manila and the friar curates. When the archbishop tried to exercise episcopal visitation on them, the friar curates resisted him on the pretext that they were not seculars. Since they were regulars, they claimed to be subject to the discipline of their respective provincials. Especially, the controversy was a struggle for the ecclesiastical control of the country. It was to the interest of the archbishop to have a greater secular clergy. This was achieved by the ordination of Filipino priests. In a conflict between the Filipino clergy and the friars, the archbishop usually sided with the Filipino priests, who as seculars were his subordinates. In the light of the above digression, the "visitation controvery," which was in effect a struggle for power among Spaniards, made it unwittingly provide for a more fertile soil for Filipino nationalism.

7. *Social Grievances Against the Friars.*

Beginning with myself, my mother is the daughter of a Franciscan friar. I do not dishonor myself by saying this, because my family begins with myself.[57]—Felipe Calderón.

Besides the complaints that the friars charged excessive rates for baptisms, weddings, funerals, etc. (to the complete disregard of the schedule of fees promulgated by Archbishop Santa Justa y Rufina), Filipino revolutionists and propagandists charged the friars with leading immoral lives. The novels of Rizal are permeated with this charge. The "Manifesto" in the first number of the *Kalayaan* asserted that the friars have alienated themselves from the teachings of the Sermon on the Mount.[58] The *Memorial* of Isabelo de los Reyes complained of the friar curates that

. . . instead of being examples of Christian conduct to their flock in the town over which they rule, they are the embodiment of scandal because of their vices and incontinence, sacrificing to their carnal appetites the peace of happy homes.

It further added that the friars

. . . would not bury the poor free of charge, as is their duty, and that they charged excessive rates for the performance of religious rites, enforcing excommunication to punish the erring and intimidating the poor to force them [to] give to the Church what little they possess in payment for the funeral services over their relatives.[59]

The above views on the friars was not a monopoly of Filipinos. They were also shared by foreigners who lived in the Philippines. To take a particular case, it was General Charles Whittier who testified before the United States Peace Commission in Paris with the following:

The rapacity, stealing, and immoralities of the priests [friars] are beyond question, and the bitterness of the natives against them has been caused and aggravated by years of iniquity. To demand a wife or daughter from a native has been a common occurrence. Failing to obtain acquiescence, the husband's or father's goods have been seized, he

---

[57] *Senate Document No. 190,* 56th Congress, 2nd session, p. 139.
[58] Cf. Retana's *Archivo,* Volume III, pp. 140-141, for this first number. Judging from the "Manifesto," the *Katipunan* was decidedly anti-friar.
[59] *Op. cit.,* pp. 55-56.

deported into jail, under an order easily obtained from the government in Manila. The priests' influence was paramount—they are rich, and fathers (not only of the Church), despised and hated by the people.[60]

The testimony presented before the Schurman and Taft Commissions with regard to friar immorality is so extensive that one can scarcely escape believing that they have a basis in fact. In an investigation on the friar orders and lands carried by the Taft Commission in 1900 wherein the provincials of different orders and the Manila Archbishop and other bishops cooperated, it appears that the friar-witnesses, although admitting isolated cases of immoralities, denied its universal character. But according to the Commission, the evidence collected from the different testimonies showed that the pattern of immorality was universal. However, the Commission concluded, the immoralities charged on the friars were not *the* chief ground of hostility towards them on the part of Filipinos, for "it did not shock the common people or arouse their indignation to see their curate establish illicit relations with a woman and have children by her." [61]

It may be admitted with the Taft Commission that immorality was not *the* chief ground of hostility toward the friars, but it was certainly one of the reasons stated by Filipinos as to why friars should have been expelled from the country. But what is most important to consider (and this Taft was probably not aware of) is that the main teachings of the propagandists were in part designed to open the eyes of the people in order to abhor and not tolerate friar immoralities. One of the aims of the *Noli Me Tangere* was to demonstrate the demoralizing effects of a system where immoralities were either ignored or tolerated. This novel tried to instill a sense of dignity among Filipinos—a dignity incompatible with the maintenance of the *status quo* of this mentioned pattern in the social order. That Rizal's novels succeeded in their attempts, at least partially, is not to be doubted. The evidence is that a new attitude towards friars came about with the net

[60] *Senate Document No. 62,* part ii, 55th Congress, 3rd session, p. 499.
[61] The conclusions of the Commission were based on a series of investigations where at least eleven priests were interviewed. These included the Manila Archbishop, two bishops, four provincials, one Jesuit, etc. About twenty-five Filipinos and a few Americans were also interviewed. Some of the opinions expressed represented that of a group. The results of the interviews are found in *Senate Document No. 190,* 56th Congress, 2nd session.

result that the friars attempted to repress his novels vigorously. The testimonies before the Commission in 1900 given by Filipinos of various social strata all point out that friar immoralities had become intolerable—at least among the witnesses. It may have been the case that immoralities were tolerated or at least considered as a normal part of the pattern of the Filipino parish up to the last quarter of the nineteenth century; but the disapproval of it that became more manifest during the few years preceding the Revolution cannot be explained more adequately except by the assumption that the work of the propagandists was bearing fruit. It was truly an age of doubts, questionings, and evaluation that preceded the Revolution.

8. *Filipino Belief that the Spanish Government Had Supported the Cause of the Friars.* From the time of the Propaganda Movement to the Revolution, and then up to the establishment of American sovereignty in the Philippines, the friars were singled out as either *the* cause, or part of the cause, of all the ills in the Philippines. The propagandists continually warned Spain that, if the problem of the friars was not solved immediately, to remedy affairs at some future time would be too late. As early as May 31, 1889, Rizal wrote an article in which he said:

> The people fight the friars, and if the government aligns itself with them unconditionally, it makes itself an enemy of the people and admits that it is an enemy of their progress. If this is the case then the government will itself open a new and disgraceful era.[62]

M. H. del Pilar advised that Spanish officialdom look at the lessons of history.

> Serious reflection is necessary on the sovereignty of the friars in the Philippines, which should not properly be theirs. History and Philosophy offer great and severe lessons on this point, and a great harm will be done to society and its institutions, if at these moments, these lessons are forgotten.[63]

Mariano Ponce, in a letter to the German scientist F. Blumentritt, repeated what his other propaganda colleagues had warned.

[62] Quoted from R. Palma, *Biografía de Rizal*, p. 147.
[63] *La Soberanía Monacal*, p. 50.

We have repeated to the governing powers . . . that, as long as a theocracy dominates the Philippines, there will be no peace in the hearts, no tranquility in the homes, and no security for the individual. We have also said that the tears, sighs and continuous fears, the constant lack of confidence in the government officials (who have become converted into instruments of the friars) may appear in the streets one day in a form of violent and desperate protest.[64]

The great error of Spain or of its government, was to make common cause with the friars. These are consummately incompatible with the life of the Filipinos, and cannot be hated more than they already are.[65]

When the second phase of the Revolution began, Aguinaldo declared in a presidential message that one of the causes of the Revolution was the Spanish government's identification with the cause of the "religious corporations whose interests have always been opposed to that of the Filipino people." [66] In a letter to Major-General Otis, he wrote

. . . it is a widely known and notorious fact, recognized by all the foreigners who have studied Philippine affairs, that the primary causes of the Filipino Revolution were the ecclesiastical corporations, which, taking advantage of the corrupt Spanish government, have robbed the country, preventing progress and liberty.[67]

According to historian Leandro H. Fernandez, even the most conservative elements of the Revolution demanded the expulsion of the friars. When the Filipino-American War broke out and the likelihood of American victory was becoming evident, Felipe Calderón told the Schurman Commission on June 5, 1899:

The friar is the principal question here, and I say to you, Mr. Schurman, that I am a Catholic and have defended the Catholic faith in the Congress of Malolos, and I am certain that the friars must be expelled if we are to have peace in the country.[68]

---

[64] "Carta a Blumentritt" (May 11, 1897), *Cartas Sobre la Revolución, 1897-1900* (Manila: Bureau of Printing, 1932), pp. 11-12.

[65] *Ibid.,* "Carta a Blumentritt" (October 21, 1897), p. 56.

[66] A. Mabini, "Message of the President of the Philippine Revolution," *La Revolución Filipina,* Vol. I, p. 184. This message was penned by Mabini.

[67] *Senate Document No. 208,* part i, 56th Congress, 1st session, pp. 43-44. This letter was also penned by Mabini.

[68] *Report of the Philippine Commission,* Vol. II, p. 146. There were some Filipino leaders who had more radical ideas about the manner in which to deal with the friars. In a letter to Aguinaldo, Felipe Agoncillo suggested that friars be killed if necessary, and that an order be made secretly to kill those who were captured. Cf. J. Taylor, *Philippine Insurgent Records,* Vol. III, Exhibit 147. This attitude was not typical.

The friars were, rightly or wrongly, identified in the minds of Filipinos with all the elements of misgovernment. According to the Taft Commission

> . . . every abuse of the many which finally led to the two revolutions of 1898 was charged by the people to the friars. Whether they were in fact to blame is perhaps aside from our purpose, but it cannot admit of contradiction that the autocratic power which each friar curate exercised over the people and civil officials of his parish gave them a most plausible ground for belief that nothing of injustice, of cruelty, of oppression, of narrowing restraint of liberty, was imposed on them for which the friar was not entirely responsible. His sacerdotal functions were not in their eyes the most important ones, except as they enabled him to clinch and make more his civil and political control. The revolutions against Spain's sovereignty began as movements against the friars.[69]

After an exhaustive series of questionings of dozens of witnesses, including bishops, provincials and friars, the Philippine Commission (Taft), with reference to the general Filipino attitude toward the clergy, presented the following conclusion:

> . . . the statement of the bishops and the friars that the mass of the people in the islands, except only a few of the leading men of each town and the native clergy, are friendly to them, cannot be accepted as accurate. All the evidence derived from every source, but the friars themselves, shows clearly that the feeling of hatred for the friars is well-nigh universal and permeates all classes.[70]

If the observations and conclusions of the Taft Commission are correct, it appears the revolutionists fought Spain in order to get rid of the friars. This is not equivalent to the friars' contention that the propagandists and revolutionists fought them in order to get rid of Spanish sovereignty. The following is LeRoy's view:

> . . . so intimately have the religious orders been connected with the history of the Philippines, so largely have they dominated the writing of this history, and so thoroughly did they identify themselves with the reactionary campaign against the expansion of Filipino freedom, social and political, in recent years, that one must pause to protest exemption from religious bias when he but relates the facts with rigid impartiality.[71]

---

[69] *Philippine Information Series,* Vol. I, No. 1, May 1, 1901, p. 19.
[70] *Senate Document No. 112,* 56th Congress, 2nd session, p. 30.
[71] *Philippine Life in Town and Country,* pp. 8-9.

The declarations of the acknowledged leaders of the Filipinos and the official pronouncements of the governments established by the revolutionists, all indicate the Filipinos considered the friars their national enemies. During the days of the Propaganda Movement, the friars claimed the propagandists wanted them expelled or reduced to insignificance in the affairs of the Philippines, since without them Spanish sovereignty would cease. This implied, to the friars, that the Filipinos were masking their real desire for separation from Spain with the pretense of blaming the friars for the ills of their country. José Lobo, provincial of the Augustinian Order, told the Philippine Commission on August 2, 1900, that:

Rizal, Bloomentil [Blumentritt], Gregorio del Pilar [M. H. del Pilar?] . . . began a movement against the friars, knowing very well that if they are removed the pedestal or foundation of sovereignty of Spain in these islands, at that moment the whole structure would topple over . . . .[72]

Lobo's criticism of the members of the Propaganda movement was not based on facts, although it might be applied partially to the actual revolutionists. The propagandists, especially Rizal, maintained it was not at all necessary for the friars to stay in order for the Philippines to be better assimilated as a part or province of Spain; a better social life was possible without them; and whatever function they had of service to the country could have been handled by Filipino laymen and clericals. This means their parochial functions could be taken over by Filipino priests, their educational functions could be taken over by the government, and their civil and social services could be undertaken by a system of local government in which the direct participation of the people would be greater. It was only when it became fixed in the mind of the revolutionists that the Spanish government identified itself with the cause of the friars that it became essential to do away with both the Spanish government and the Spanish friars. Since the friars up to the early days of the Revolution had political power and were doing their best to maintain Spanish sovereignty to the extent of joining the ranks of the Spanish army, it became necessary on the part of the revolutionists to capture a great number of them. When their positions were taken over by

[72] *Senate Document No. 190*, 56th Congress, 2nd session, p. 73.

Filipinos, both secular and clerical (these giving their allegiance to the Revolutionary government), Spanish administration in the provinces collapsed.

9. *The Status of the Friars during the Revolution.* In view of the conclusions of the Taft Commission regarding the virtually universal attitude toward the friars, it is no wonder, then, that one of the principal reforms demanded by the revolutionists during the negotiations at Biak-na-Bató was the "expulsion of the religious orders, or at least regulations prohibiting them from living together in cloisters." [73] The ideal of the first *Manifesto of the Hongkong Junta,* of having as priests and ecclesiastical authorities in the Philippines only Filipinos, left no room for friars in the social life of the Filipinos. Mabini's proposed "Constitutional Program of the Philippine Republic" has in Title I, section 14:

> . . . there shall never be permitted in the territory of the Republic the establishment of the Religious Orders governed by a General of the Order under the immediate authority of the Roman Pontiff. The Congregations and confraternities which are under the full jurisdiction of the Ordinary are solely excepted.[74]

Aguinaldo's Message to Congress dated January 1, 1899, proposed the following amendments to the Malolos Constitution:

> All members of the regular Spanish clergy will be expelled from the Territory of the Republic even if they occupy positions of high ecclesiastical rank.
> All persons who lead the monastic life will also be expelled even though they may not have received holy orders.[75]

Following these, in the Presidential Decree of January 23, 1899, it was ordered that:

> All regular Spanish clergy, even those who are ecclesiastical dignitaries, and also the persons who, although they are not in holy orders, are yet connected permanently with said clergy, will be expelled from the Philippine Territory.[76]

---

[73] "Draft of Agreement of Biak-na-bató," *The Philippine Social Science Review,* Vol. III, No. 1 (August, 1930), 84.

[74] *The Philippine Social Science Review,* IV (October, 1932), 317.

[75] Quoted from J. Taylor, *Philippine Insurgent Records,* Vol. III, Exhibit 352.

[76] J. Taylor, *Report on Organization,* Exhibit G, p. 44.

Due to war conditions and the eventual defeat of the Philippine Republic by American forces, orders for the expulsion of the friars never went into full effect. However, after the Revolution a few hundred friars chose to go back to Spain or to other foreign missionary territories.

10. *The Economic Problem.*

> . . . men forget more easily the death of their fathers than the loss of their patrimony.[77]

The Schurman Commission, in 1900, anticipated that a return of the friars to their parishes would alienate Filipinos sympathetic to the American cause, since they were as bitterly hostile to the friars as were the revolutionists who were in the field fighting the Americans. The Commission noted that this hostility and resentment towards the friars on the part of the Filipinos would be shifted to the Americans, if they were believed to be guardians of the interests of the friars.[78] Governor Taft testified before a U.S. Senate Committee on February 7, 1902, that this report of hostility towards the friars, found "through all the Filipino people," had been confirmed by later events. He also pointed out that this hostility was twofold, for "it is against them as political enemies, and also in certain provinces it is against them as landowners, and in those provinces the two feelings coincide and become exceedingly bitter." [79] In this statement is found one of the clues as to why the bulk of Filipino tenants and peasants easily joined the ranks of the army of the Philippine Republic. The belief that the United States was to reinstate the friars to their former parishes and to allow them to exercise their former control over large agricultural tracts of land in certain provinces induced in a great part of the population a willingness to protect the new-born Republic. It is thus important to know what economic elements were at stake.

The Taft Report for 1900 estimated that the friars owned 403,713 acres of agricultural property, while the 4th Report of the Philippine Commission estimated it at 420,000 acres. Since

---

[77] Niccolo Machiavelli, *The Prince* (N.Y.: Modern Library, 1950), p. 62.
[78] Cf. *Senate Document No. 112*, 56th Congress, 2nd session, pp. 31-32.
[79] *Senate Document No. 334*, part i, 57th Congress, 2nd session, p. 178.

the Franciscans were by their own rules not allowed to own agricultural properties, this amount represented the holdings of the other three friar-orders. The value of the total land holdings was estimated by the 4th Report to amount to about ₱12,086,431.11, a calculation made by the surveyor Villegas, and judged at that time to be accurate by the Commission.[80]

At this point it is important to distinguish "Catholic Church property" from "monastic property" or "friar lands." The former refers specifically to church buildings and rectories (*conventos*), which in 1903 numbered 1,573, with a total value of ₱41,645,297. The latter refers to agricultural holdings owned by the monastic orders, and is the main topic of the present discussion.[81]

Out of the total landholding of the friars, nearly three-fourths were concentrated in the area around Manila; that is, they were concentrated in the Tagalog provinces. A report of the United States Philippine Commission, dated November 30, 1900 gave the following figures:[82]

Cavite	....	121,747	acres
Laguna	....	62,172	"
Manila	province	50,145	"
Bulacan	....	39,441	"
Morong	....	4,940	"
	Total	278,445	"

---

[80] For figures, cf. "The Taft Report of 1900," *Senate Document No. 112*, 56th Congress, 2nd session, p. 28; "4th Report of the Philippine Commission," *House Document No. 2*, part i, 58th Congress, 2nd session, Vol. VI, 1903-1904, pp. 38-41; *Census of the Philippines for 1903*, Vol. I, p. 346, footnote 1.

At the turn of the century it was difficult to determine accurately how much land were owned by the friars, and the Schurman Commission experienced this difficulty. (*Report of the Philippine Commission*, Vol. IV, p. 91.) In an exchange of letters between Major-General Otis and Archbishop Chapelle from February to April, 1900, it appears clearly that the friars, a few years before the Revolution, began slowly to transfer estates to "profane syndicate purchasers." (*Senate Document No. 129*, 56th Congress, 2nd session, pp. 7-11.) In *Senate Document No. 331*, part i, 57th Congress, 1st session, pp. 175-180, Taft revealed that the "titles" of friar lands were transferred to certain companies or trusts but that the friars retained the majority of the stocks pertinent to the lands.

In all probability, the friars saw the handwriting on the wall, and took pains to secure their properties.

[81] Cf. *Senate Document No. 331*, part i, 57th Congress, 1st session, p. 186, for Taft's distinction of these two types of properties. For figures on Church properties, cf. *Census of the Philippines for 1903*, Vol. IV, p. 412.

[82] Cf. *Senate Document No. 112*. 56th Congress, 2nd session, p. 27.

This total of friar lands probably represented about 48 per cent of the total agricultural land of the five Tagalog provinces listed above. In the province of Cavite, the lands of the friars amounted to about 82 per cent of the total agricultural area.[83] The opinion was general that the neighborhood of the city of Manila included the best cultivated lands. In an investigation of friar lands by the American Senate, Governor Taft was asked whether these lands were among the best in the Philippines. The answer was in the affirmative. Taft also added:

> The friars in Cavite have spent a good deal of money in improving lands . . . . In Cavite alone there is the largest number of acres of friar lands, about 125,000 acres. There the insurrection has always started. It was largely due to the agrarian question and the feeling against the friars.[84]

The economic origins of the hostility towards the friars and the economic aspect of the Revolution, in certain provinces at least, are thus evident. It is not a mere coincidence that the violence of the Revolution was concentrated in the area of Cavite. Felipe Calderón, keenly alert on all the events around him, told American authorities: "Nearly the whole of the province of Cavite is in the hands of the friars; that is the reason that the revolution is con-

[83] The *Census of the Philippine Islands for 1903* (Volume IV, p. 199) stated that the total agricultural area of the above provinces was 233,052 hectares (575,871.5 acres). It also gave the figure of 40,881 hectares (101,016.95 acres) for the province of Cavite. General Mariano Trias, a revolutionary leader who later became governor of Cavite province, in an annual report to the civil governor of the Philippines on January 14, 1902, stated that in the province of Cavite, nearly all of the productive lands were in the hands of the friars. (Cf. *Senate Document No. 331*, part iii, 57th Congress, 1st session, p. 2405.) The above figures are estimates.

The general statements of American correspondents and army officials to the effect the friars owned ½ to ¾ of the total area under cultivation in the Philippines are an exaggeration. Major-General Greene shows this inaccuracy when he stated that the friars owned "the greater part of the land." (See his memorandum in *Senate Document No. 62*, part ii, 56th Congress, 3rd session, p. 374.) In 1900 the Taft Commission estimated that out of 73 million acres of land in the Philippines, 5 million were in private ownership (exact figure—4,940,000). (Cf. *Senate Document No. 112*, 56th Congress, 2nd session, pp. 6 and 33.) Since at this time Taft testified that the friars owned about 403,713 acres of agricultural property it is clear that the friars did not own more than 8% of the total agricultural area of the Philippines. Other estimates assert that at this time the friars owned about ⅛ of the lands owned by individuals. Cf. the editorial of *The Independent*, LIII, March 21, 1901.

[84] *Senate Document No. 331*, part i, 57th Congress, 1st session, pp. 180-181.

centrated there." [85] Governor-General Primo de Rivera, as quoted by LeRoy, stated a similarly relevant point:

> . . . the Tagalog outbreak [in 1896] was due to the fact that there had been more abuses by the friars, and they had greater possessions of land, in the territory of the Tagalogs.[86]

In answer to the question why the Jesuits were not hated or treated in the same manner as the other friars, Miguel Saderra Mata, representing the Jesuit superior in Manila, testified clearly:

> In the first place, we have no haciendas; and another reason is that nothing has been said against our habits up to the present time; and further, the fact of our teaching.[87]

Actually, in the history of the Philippines, the major agrarian troubles were closely associated with monastic properties. In the first two centuries of Spanish rule in the Philippines, titles to land were generally unknown and thus landed properties were undefined. According to John Foreman, all land nominally belonged to the State during these two centuries, with the state granting no titles. However, "squatters" took up the lands desired, without limits—and it was around this time that the friars began to take possession of rich arable lands. Foreman continued:

> About the year 1885 the question was brought forward of granting Government titles to all who could establish claims to land. Indeed, for about a year there was a certain enthusiasm displayed both by the applicants and the officials in the matter of "Titulos Reales." But the large majority of land-holders—among whom the monastic element conspicuously figured—could only show their title by actual possession. It might have been sufficient, but the fact is that the clergy favored neither the granting of "Titulos Reales" nor the establishment of the projected Real Estate Registration Offices . . . . Agrarian disputes had been the cause of so many armed [up]rising against [the friars] in particular, during the nineteenth century, that they opposed an investigation of the land question, which would have revived old animosities, without giving satisfaction to either native or friar, seeing that both parties were intransigent.[88]

---

85 *Senate Document No. 190,* 56th Congress, 2nd session, p. 135.
86 *The Americans in the Philippines,* Vol. I, p. 146.
87 *Senate Document No. 190,* 56th Congress, 2nd session, p. 95.
88 *Op. cit.,* p. 4. With regard to the legislation referring to the application for "Titulos Reales," J. Taylor writes: "The religious corporations were

The most notorious case of conflict between tenants and their friar landlords was the Calamba Affair, where the family of José Rizal played a prominent part. In December, 1887, Governor-General Terrero ordered the investigation of friar estates in order to ameliorate agrar an problems. Because of their feeling this was a chance to state their grievances, a petition, penned by Rizal and signed by about 70 tenants and leading citizens, was presented to the government.[89] This incidentally was the first major pronouncement presented publicly by tenants in their fight against the friars. In 1890, while the trial of the suit against the friars was going on before the proper judicial authorities, Governor-General Weyler surrounded the town of Calamba with troops and artillery, drove the tenants out of the town, burned their homes, confiscated their animals, and exiled the most prominent people of

---

apparently in favor of this legislation, but when it was enacted they proceeded to protect their interests. As they were the largest landholders in the richest agricultural provinces the sum of the animosity which they excited was greater than that produced against any other proprietor." *Philippine Insurgent Records,* Vol. I, 24 FZ.

[89] This refers to the "Informe al Administrador de Hacienda publica de la Laguna acerca de la Hacienda de los P.P. Domínicos en Calamba," which is found in M. H. del Pilar's *La Soberania Monacal,* Appendix.

As early as 1697, the Spanish King ordered Auditor (*oidor*) de la Sierra to investigate the legality of the holdings of the friars; but these refused to furnish any data to the auditor, claiming that they were exempt from such formalities; and "as subsequently they were unable to prove the legality of their titles they were declared to be 'occupants in bad faith' and an embargo was laid on the lands held by them. When Archbishop Camacho arrived in the islands the friars appealed to him for protection, and this prelate ordered the auditor to stop his proceedings or he would excommunicate him. Taking advantage of this crisis as they also did on other occasions, the friars threatened to abandon the islands, and the governor, in order to avoid a conflict, which had taken on alarming proportions, got the new *visitador* who had succeeded Sierra to accept the titles to the land held by the friars as valid . . . ." *Census of the Philippine Islands for 1903,* Vol. I, p. 342 (by Pardo de Tavera in section entitled, "History of the Philippines"). Later on in 1751, an investigation of Dominican and Augustinian haciendas was carried out due to the usual agrarian troubles, and since the friars were not able to show legal titles, Auditor Calderón ordered that their estates revert to the State. Needless to say, the fulfillment of the order never took place. On this point, cf. R. Palma, *Biografía de Rizal,* p. 4.

It is interesting to note that when the lands of the friars were involved, the Church, in the person of the Archbishop, would combine with the friars against any other third party, for the protection and maintenance of the estates. For all practical purposes, "church property" and "monastic property" were jealously treated alike by the Church.

the area. Among them was the family of Rizal.[90] John Foreman, who was familiar with this incident, wrote:

> In September, 1890, a lawsuit was still pending between the Dominican Corporation and a number of native residents in Calamba (Laguna) who disputed the Dominicans' claim in that vicinity as long as the Corporation was unable to exhibit its title. For this implied monastic indiscriminate acquisition of real estate several of the best native families (some of them personally known to me) were banished to the Island of Mindanao.[91]

The petition penned by Rizal revealed that the whole town of Calamba was actually a part of a Dominican hacienda and presented specific causes for grievance. Among these were the following: when tenants improved the land by the erection of buildings and storages, they had to pay extra *canon;* that payment for parcels of land that yielded three or four *cavans* were treated as if they yielded nine to twelve *cavans;* that the percentage for the products to be delivered to the Hacienda was increased; and also, that the increase of the *canon* was not in any manner beneficial to the material development of the town as this was not used for the social activities of the town.

The alleged economic abuses of the friars played a prominent part in De los Reyes' *Memorial* to Governor-General Primo de Rivera:[92]

> That the friars from year to year increased the rate of the land rent, despite the serious commercial and agricultural crises through which

---

[90] For details of the Calamba affair, cf. Pardo de Tavera, *op. cit.,* p. 382; "Letter of Narcisa Rizal to José Rizal," Letter No. 443 (March 10, 1891), pp. 167-168, and "Letter of Felipe Buencamino to José Rizal," Letter No. 438 (February 7, 1891), *Epistolario Rizalino,* Vol. III, pp. 148-157. It is believed that at least 300 families were affected by Weyler's action. According to Manuel Artigas y Cuerva: "La cuestion de Kalamba fué sin que de ello quepa la menor duda, el principio del fin de la *debacle* española en sus dominios de la Oceanía, porque ella hizo que las ideas tanto tiempo comprimidas, pugnaran por salir, y acumuladas las cien mil causas que aprisionaran á los habitantes de estas Islas en las mas terrible red de esclavitud, llenaron la atmósfera esparciendo por do quiera las ideas de vindicación, ante el chasquido del látigo extranjero, de aquellos que veían al pueblo como *homo homini lupus* olvidándose que el más sagrado de la patria, se amasa con sangre proporcionada por las venas del mismo pueblo." *Andrés Bonifacio y el Katipunan; Reseña Histórica Bio-Bibliográfica* (Manila, 1911), p. 10.

[91] *Op. cit.,* p. 4, footnote 2.

[92] *Op. cit.,* p. 55.

the country had been passing for a decade . . . . That, besides the land rent, the friars exacted . . . a surtax on trees planted by the tenants on the lands they had leased, instead of being gratified for this favor which constituted improvement of such lands. That the friars, instead of using the legal measure when receiving the tax in kind, computed the rice in sacks of 30 to 33 gantas instead of 25, which is the legal content of a *cavan,* or sack, of rice.[93]

Putting aside these alleged abuses, there was a widespread belief that the friar lands were, in general, acquired through fraud or deceit. In general, the friars based their rights on the long period of time over which they had possession of the lands. This applied especially to the lands around the Manila area, some of which had been held for more than a century, and probably none, less than one generation.[94] A typical Filipino argument objecting to such a claim was:

. . . that legal provisions in regard to prescriptions require a condition *sine qua non* of the possessor of the thing, in order to be the legitimate owner of the same, the period of time which the law prescribes having been accomplished, that he should have a transferable title of possession, and as the friar administrator cannot prove . . . the legitimate means by which the lands came into his hands which he had converted into large estates, it is clear that the prescription, for that reason, is not based on law.[95]

---

[93] This assertion is a bit exaggerated. If true at all, it can only refer to very isolated cases. Calderón's criticism of the friars on this point is more moderate. On October 17, 1900, he told American authorities that the planting of fruit trees increased the *canon* of the land and that the friars used a measure that contained more than the legal measure, that is, their *cavans* contained 26 "liters (dry measure)" [gantas], instead of the legal 25. Cf. *Senate Document No. 190,* 56th Congress, 2nd session, p. 137. The friar's *cavan* was called the "devil's cavan."

[94] Some of the lands acquired by the friars were by government grants, among which the most extensive were in the then sparsely populated provinces of Cagayan (49,400 acres) and Mindoro (58,455 acres). But it is significant that the agrarian troubles did not start there, and that they were normally found in those areas which the friars claimed by prescription and where the population pressure was relatively higher. For figures of state grants, cf. *Senate Document No. 112,* 56th Congress, 2nd session, p. 27.
As a rule the estates of the friars were rented on shares in small holdings. Leases were given for three years and any renewal had to have the approval of the Order or Corporation. In general, tenancy continued in the same family for generations. Cf. *Senate Document No. 112,* 56th Congress, 2nd session, p. 28.

[95] From the article, "Causes of the Dislike of the Filipinos for the Friars" (February, 1900), J. Taylor, *Philippine Insurgent Records,* Vol. I, 63 FZ to 68 FZ, Exhibit 8. The author is unknown but probably a Filipino priest, according to Taylor.

Mariano Trias, in an official report to Governor Taft, mentioned that the people claimed friar lands were "usurped from the legal owners through religious deceit, usury, fanaticism, craft and other illegitimate or violent methods." And he argued that if a proper investigation were made, the friars would undoubtedly be dispossessed.[96] Manuel Xerez y Burgos described to the Schurman Commission four means by which the friars got their lands: by threats which obliged people to sell them their lands at reduced prices; by illegal and devious encroachments into other lands; from rich people about to die; and by inheritances from devout people. This last means was quite illegal, according to Xerez, as the law provided that no man could donate more than a small part of his property to the Church; but he added, where were the sons who would dare sue the friars? [97] The *Memorial* of De los Reyes stated that "the friars would confiscate lands which the Filipinos had inherited from their forefathers, all that is needed to this being the inclusion of such lands in the drawings or maps of the friars . . . ." It further added,

. . . the friars mercilessly prevented those who dared to resort to legal means, even going to such lengths as to have the Government deport such tenants and protestants, thus causing the ruin of many families.[98]

In a letter from Aguinaldo to Major-General Otis on November 3, 1898, Otis was told for his own information:

The religious corporations of the Philippines have acquired large agricultural colonies by means of fraud. In older times the Filipinos prompted by their religion, gave away a part of the products of their lands to the old priests (Sacerdotes religiosos) for their support. But in the course of time that which was prompted by spiritual motives they made obligatory . . . .[99]

11. *The Revolution and the Disposition of Friar Lands.* According to the Schurman Commission, the following is a clear statement as to what the Filipino revolutionists desired:

[96] *Senate Document No. 331,* part iii, 57th Congress, 1st session, p. 2405.
[97] *Report of the Philippine Commission,* Vol. II, p. 413. Xerez y Burgos was a nephew of the executed Filipino priest, Burgos.
[98] *Op. cit.,* p. 55.
[99] *Senate Document No. 208,* part i, 56th Congress, 1st session, p. 43. This letter was penned by Mabini.

Restitution of all lands appropriated by the friars to the townships, or to the original owners, or in default of finding such owners, the State is to put them up to public auction in small lots of value within the reach of all and payable within four years, the same as the present state lands.[100]

The *First Manifesto of the Hongkong Junta* declared:

We desire the absolute and unconditional respect of personal property, and as a consequence of the same legal recognition of the exclusive right of possession of the tenant of the so-called farms of the religious orders, of the land which he cultivates and has improved by his labor, land which the religious orders have usurped and stolen . . . . We desire that the possession of these tenants be respected without their being under the necessity of paying any fee [*canon*], rent or tax whatever of an oppressive or unjust character, thus terminating the illegal and anti-social retention of the land by the monastic orders . . . . .[101]

Mabini, in the *Ordenanzas de la Revolución,* a guide written for the successful management and termination of the Revolution, inserted the rule:

Rule 21—All usurpations of properties made by the Spanish government and the religious corporations will not be recognized by the Revolution, this, being a movement representing the aspirations of the Filipino people, true owners of the above properties.[102]

In his message to Congress dated January 1, 1899, one of Aguinaldo's proposed amendments reassured the people that "all real property which has been held by the religious communities in the Philippines is restored to the State." [103]

In spite of the section in the Malolos Constitution which, though temporarily suspended, provided for separation of Church and State, the Philippine Republic also inserted specific legal recognition of policies already officially carried out by the former Dictatorial and Revolutionary governments.

Additional Article: From the 24th of May last, on which date the Dictatorial government was organized in Cavite, all the buildings, pro-

---

[100] *Report of the Philippine Commission,* Vol. I, p. 84.
[101] *Op. cit.,* p. 208.
[102] *La Revolución Filipina,* Vol. I, p. 112.
[103] J. Taylor, *Philippine Insurgent Records,* Vol. III, Exhibit 352.

perties, and other belongings possessed by the religious corporations in these islands will be understood as restored to the Filipino government.[104]

It is important to note in the Additional Article of the Official Constitution of the Philippine Republic that only the properties of the monastic orders are declared restored (not confiscated) to the State. These include not only cultivated lands but also other types of properties; yet these do not include "Church properties." Those churches in territory held by the Republic were placed in the hands of the Filipino priests. On this point, the Republic did satisfy one of the aspirations of the Filipino clergy.

In spite of the war that ensued between the Republic and the United States troops in the Philippines, the Filipino government passed a law on February 19, 1899, to regulate administration of the lands recovered from the friars. The law provided:

> Article 11. The property of religious corporations restored to the state in accordance with the additional article of the constitution will be administered by men of means who will be designated by the secretary of Treasury, local chiefs (presidentes) preferred, who will furnish such security, in cash or by bond, as the secretary of the Treasury may deem necessary.
> Article 12. Those who administer the property of the religious corporations will receive in payment for their services a percentage of the annual rent received from the property . . . . .[105]

John Taylor, in another of his attempts to discredit the Revolution and its leaders, especially Aguinaldo, maintained that "the demand for the secularization of the property of the orders come from men who would profit by it." [106] And he added that these men are not necessarily identical with the small tenant-farmers. What Taylor meant to imply is clear: the control of the former friar lands was designed by Aguinaldo and other government officials to enrich themselves personally and to perpetuate their power. This imputation of Taylor is, however, refuted by the facts. Yet it must be admitted the former properties of the monastic orders did provide a new source of income for the Re-

[104] Quoted from Maximo Kalaw, *The Development of Philippine Politics (1872-1920)*, p. 445.
[105] J. Taylor, *Report on Organization*, Exhibit L, pp. 72-73.
[106] *Philippine Insurgent Records,* Vol. I, 24 FZ.

public. The *canon* formerly paid to the Order was now paid to the Filipino government. This situation was to be expected, considering that the infant Republic was badly in need of a new source of income to forestall the expected efforts of the United States to forcibly impose its sovereignty on the Filipinos. But it is of greatest importance to note that there was no intention of keeping the land from individual owners, who may have had a legal claim to it. A report from the Secretary of the Treasury to the President of the Republic, dealing with sources of income for the new government is quite revealing, for it stated in part:

> As a new source of income, however, the property of the religious cor porations enters into the bill by virtue of the sole additional article of the constitution, and are considered restored to the State; this, however, will not be a bar to future adjudications concerning the claim of private individuals. An intelligent and honest administration of these estates, or, in default of this, their lease, will undoubtedly yield (to the treasury) an income of no slight importance.[107]

In the view of the men guiding the process of the Revolution, the friar lands were to revert either to the State or to individual owners having a legal claim to them. Mabini's rule in the *Ordenanzas* that these lands should revert to the people may be interpreted to mean: either the land reverted to individual owners; or it reverted to a Filipino government, which would administer it for the welfare of the people. In any case, the land would be in the hands of Filipinos and not Spaniards. How many Filipinos would willingly fight for a system in which a change of ownership would mean government ownership is another problem. The evidence is that they did not entirely oppose the idea of this system, although it may be safely assumed there was some expectancy on the part of the tenant-farmer that he would ultimately inherit the land tilled by him and his family.

In any case, regardless of whether the Filipino government was to control all of the friar lands, the fact that there was fear the Americans would reinstall the friars in their former possessions gained the Republic additional recruits in its struggle with the

---

[107] "Letter written by the Secretary of Treasury to Aguinaldo," Malolos, February 12, 1899, in J. Taylor, *Report on Organization*, Exhibit L, pp. 70-71.

United States. A testimony by a Filipino before the Schurman Commission on May 14, 1899, was:

> One of the reasons that resistance to America was decided on in the Philippines was the fact that the friars' property was seen to be respected, and they remained here. You know in the treaty of peace it was provided that the property of the Church should be respected.[108]

Another testimony before the same Commission laid renewed emphasis on the danger of having the friars regain their property with American help.

> It is impossible to retain here the religious corporations as they existed before, for they caused a great problem—one state within another state . . . . If the friars remain here in the country their property must all be thoroughly scrutinized—their right to the property. If the property is returned to the friars an agrarian war will result; that is, such a war as we have now, a war of the agricultural classes against the property owners.[109]

In spite of the testimonies of many Filipino intellectuals as to the economic aspect of the Revolution and essential part played by the friars in it, American authorities did not immediately give assurances to the Filipino people that the problem was one to be solved by them. On the contrary, on account of their lack of full realization of the impact of the problem, not only did they

---

[108] *Report of the Philippine Commission,* Vol. II, p. 93 (Testimony of Señor Melliza).

The "treaty of peace" here referred to is the Treaty of Paris (December 10, 1898), and Article VIII of the treaty stated that all public domains belonging to the Crown of Spain such as buildings, forts, public highways, etc., are relinquished by Spain but this relinquishment ". . . cannot in any respect impair the property or rights which by law belong to the peaceful possession of property of all kinds, of provinces, municipalities, public or private establishments, ecclesiastical or civil bodies, or any other associations having legal capacity to acquire and possess property in the aforementioned territories renounced or ceded, or of private individuals, of whatever nationality such individual may be." *Senate Document No. 62,* part i, 56th Congress, 3rd session, p. 7.

Article VIII of the Treaty of Paris, the apparent friendship between Major-General Otis and Archbishop Chapelle, and the general impression that the U.S. Government was protecting the friars, led Filipinos to conclude the friars were going to be reinstated to their former privileged position. Reassurances that the American tradition demanded a strict separation of Church and State did not help much, because of the fresh memories of bitter experiences.

[109] *Report of the Philippine Commission,* Vol. II, p. 99 (Testimony of Señor Rosario [Arcadio?]).

appear to disregard Filipino aspirations, but they were led to hope optimistically that resistance to American sovereignty would be terminated in the space of a few months.[110]

The discussion of the economic aspect of the Revolution may be concluded by mentioning the testimony of Florentino Torres, who became an attorney-general in the U.S. Military Regime in the Philippines. Torres, who was one of the leading Filipinos to cooperate in the United States administration of the Philippines, stated:

> The socialistic character of the revolution of 1896, maintained up to date against the American sovereignty, is a patent and positive fact, for although the rebellion was promoted morally through the propaganda of the middle class of certain towns in the center of Luzon . . . it found decided support . . . among the plebeians or the laboring people that worked and labored in the fields and towns, and this socialistic character is due in part to the existence and manner of being of many haciendas belonging to the religious communities of these islands, for reasons which require special study; hence it was that the first acts of the revolutionists upon the outbreak of the rebellion to the north as well as to the south of the center of Luzon was to take possession of the haciendas and properties of the friars. . . .[111]

---

110 It was the Taft administration that sought to do something to lessen the agrarian troubles, although not entirely eliminate them. After a long series of negotiations, where the Vatican was involved, it was finally agreed on December 22, 1903, to have the government pay the friars the amount of $7,239,784.66 for 23 estates (165,000 hectares or 407,715 acres). ". . . the contract stipulated that the sum was to be reduced if surveys should reveal that the estates were actually smaller than they had been assumed to be. When the negotiations between the government and the friars were finally concluded on October 20, 1905, the purchase price was set at $6,934,433.36, a sum that was raised through the sale of Philippine government bonds authorized by the United States Congress. This transfer brought the greater part of the friar lands with their tenants, estimated at more than sixty thousand persons, under direct control of the government. The friars, however, were not willing, in 1903, to sell all of their land; moreover, the Church itself also possessed a number of estates; so that, in spite of great efforts on the part of the American administrators, the question was not completely solved." *Philippine Land Tenure Reform: Analysis and Recommendations* (Special Technical and Economic Mission, Mutual Security Agency, United States of America, Manila, 1952), Appendix C, pp. 3-4.

111 *Senate Document No. 190,* 56th Congress, 2nd session, p. 191. The term "socialist" most probably is used in a sense that is intended to lay emphasis on the mass character of the agrarian rising in Central Luzon. If Torres implied by "socialism" the public control of all agricultural property taken from the friars, then he was not fully aware of Government intentions to restore lands to those who could legally claim them.

In brief, the friars in the Philippines had gone a long way from those days when they were mere missionaries, dedicated to the spiritual welfare of the Filipino people. So much trust was placed in their hands and so much respect given to their office that power ultimately fell into their hands. The result in the nineteenth century was that they had become a powerful class with political, economic, and social interests. To this extent they could be viewed as "a State within a State." This class was looked upon as one whose existence was so inimical to the interests of the people seeking educational and social emancipation, that its existence was a danger to both Church and State.

Yet, so closely were the friars related to the political and religious development of the country, so much (it was believed) were they then protected and their interests defended by the Spanish Church and the Vatican, and so much was the Church in the Philippines administered by Spanish priests (among whom, including many archbishops, were friars) that the attitude toward the Church became a function of the attitude toward the friars.

The revolutionary leaders had to consider, too, the aspirations of the Filipino clergy. These aspirations were not confined to the control of the parishes in the country. They also included the desire to control some if not all of the highest ecclesiastical offices of the Church in the Philippines. The problem now is to find out what ideas the revolutionary leaders had with regard to the problem of Church and State and how they set about dealing with this issue in the official constitution of their Republic. This, as will be seen later, leads to a discussion of the conception and plans for the formation of a Filipino National Church.

CHAPTER SEVEN

The Problem of
Church and State

1. THE MALOLOS CONGRESS. In the Revolution, no decision with regard to the future relations of Church and State is more clear than that found in the *Constitution of the Philippine Republic* as adopted by the Congress assembled at Malolos. And no section of the Constitution was more energetically debated than the one dealing with future relations between Church and State. Whereas the section was supposed to have been discussed on October 28, 1898, the delegates, anticipating the time that would be utilized in the discussion, agreed among themselves to defer the discussion. In this manner the approval of the other sections of the proposed constitution was left unhindered by a controversial issue. According to Felipe Calderón, the author of the Constitution, the problem of religion was one of the most debated problems in Congress, and when the time to vote came, many of the delegates who on other sessions may have been absent, appeared to vote on the matter.[1]

The original section (Section III) as proposed by Calderón made the Roman Catholic religion the official religion of the State, allowing non-Catholics, however, the freedom to practice their own religion. This section provided:

> Article 5. The nation shall protect the cult and the ministers of the Roman Catholic Apostolic religion, which is the religion of the State, and shall not utilize its revenues for the support of any other cult.
> Article 6. Any other cult may be exercised privately, provided that it is not against morality and good customs, and does not endanger the security of the State.

---

[1] *Mis Memorias sobre la Revolución Filipina* (Manila: Imprenta de "El Renacimiento," 1907), p. 243.

Article 7. The acquisition and discharge of all duties and official functions of the Republic, as well as the exercise of all civil and political rights, are independent of the religion of the Filipino citizens.[2]

The two assemblymen who were the most notable opponents of this section were Tomás G. del Rosario and Arcadio del Rosario.[3] The amendment proposed by T. del Rosario was the following:

Section III. The State recognizes the equality of all religious worships and the separation of the Church and the State.[4]

There was no better defense of the original Section III than that given by its author. His arguments in Congress, and those that later crept into his memoirs, in retrospect, are as follows: First of all, considering that the Filipinos belonged to different linguistic groups and were divided into regional groupings, it was necessary to have some cohesive force or tie that would bind all of them together. Considering that the Filipinos had a Christian tradition and also that the majority of them were Catholics, this cohesive force should be the Catholic Church and religion. Therefore, the separation of Church and State might hurt the sensitivities of the Filipinos. Secondly, to demand the separation of Church and State was to disregard the struggle and sacrifices of the Filipino clergy, who had been the first to ask for reforms and among the first to shed their blood in the movement for reforms. Besides, since separation of Church and State implied either the abandonment of the Christian tradition or the de-Christianization of the Philippines, then the labors of the Filipino priests Pelaez, Burgos, Zamora, Gómez and others would have been in vain. In all, the second argument suggested that the unity of Church and State in the Philippines was to be an explicit recognition of the work and aspirations of the Filipino clergy. The third argument was a practical one. It warned that in the event of a separation of Church and State, nothing could be done if the Vatican decided not only to nominate foreign ecclesiastical authori-

[2] *Ibid.,* p. 241.
[3] Both T. del Rosario and A. del Rosario were Masons with a strong anti-friar attitude. The former was a member of the committee that drafted the Malolos Constitution. The latter was one of the members of the *Liga Filipina.*
[4] Quoted from F. Calderón, *op. cit.,* p. 71 (Appendix I).

ties for the Philippines but even to take away the power of the Filipino clergy. On the other hand, if Church and State were united, then a concordat might be negotiated with the Vatican to arrange these matters. A concordat might also finally solve the problems of the final disposition of the properties of the religious orders. On this point Calderón presented a dilemma: either there was a unity of Church and State and, therefore, the properties of the religious orders remained in Filipino hands to be used for the Church in the Philippines; or Church and State would be separated and the religious corporations will be indemnified. In this situation money would leave the Philippines.[5]

It may be wondered why Calderón viewed the above alternatives as not only exclusive but also exhaustive. Actually what he had in mind was that the mere fact the tenants had for generations paid *canon* for their occupancy of the land implied that the friars had to be dealt with as owners of the land. That the friars' acquisition of the land was "vicious in its origin" mattered less than their long occupancy. What was not anticipated was a third alternative, the one adopted by the Filipino government. This was embodied in the Additional Article in the Constitution which declared all friar lands and properties restored to the State.

Manuel Gómez a member of Congress who shared Calderón's views, presented some theoretical and theological considerations. In brief, he said religion was necessary because it was based on man's rationality and that it was found as a demand in all societies, since the idea of a Supreme Being was found in the consciences of all men. Now, since the Catholic religion was the most perfect religion and had the best moral code, and since it was the one professed by the Filipinos, it should therefore be the religion of the State. Gómez also reflected that if Church and State were united, then men would be governed by two forces, one "internal force," that is, by religion, the other, the "external force" of governmental coercion—the first, Church rule,

---

[5] For Calderón's arguments, cf. his *Memorias,* pp. 242-243, 83-93 (Appendix); Arsenio Manuel, *A Portrait of Felipe G. Calderón: Father of the Malolos Constitution* (Bookman Inc., Manila, 1954), p. 21; Teodoro M. Kalaw, "The Memoirs of Felipe G. Calderón," *Philippine Review,* IV (June-July, 1919), 475-476.

is conciliatory and humane, while the latter, governmental coercion, is harsh and tyrannical.[6] Presumably, the first force tended to moderate the second.

Calderón and Gómez were typical Filipino conservatives, weaned and educated by the Mother Church. Whereas the latter rationalized his preconceptions in terms of philosophical speculations, the former sincerely believed that the separation of Church and State, although an admirable ideal, was inapplicable to Filipino society on account of its historical past; that is, the Filipino people had their social life so intertwined with the Church that without the Church a powerful cohesive force in their social life would disappear. In this, the fears of Calderón were not well founded. In the first place, as Tomás del Rosario pointed out, the mere fact that it was not religious ideals that united the people in the Revolution showed that there were other factors unifying the Filipinos. Besides this, a separation of Church and State did not necessarily imply the abandonment of Christian morality and other Christian elements that had become part and parcel of the cultural pattern of the majority of the Filipinos.

Tomás del Rosario was the most vehement of the delegates who favored the principle of separation of Church and State. Besides pointing to a growing unity among the Filipinos not due to religion, and which therefore must be rooted in secular values common to all the people, Del Rosario presented various other arguments. In his first talk, which lasted five hours, he promised to deal with the problem "without love or hate and with the strictest impartiality." He accepted the legal competence of the framers of the Constitution but stated that he was surprised when he read Section III, which made him feel as if he were back in the Middle Ages. For such a section showed a disregard of all the lessons of modern history and the advances of philosophy. Even admitting that Christianity was the best of all religions, it had nevertheless "become altered by the passions of men, to the extent that it had bred intolerance and religious wars, especially when the Papacy had a hand in [its] affairs." He also warned of the dangers that might come about, when both civil and religious

6 For the arguments of Gómez, cf. F. Calderón, op. cit., pp. 77-78 (Appendix); Arsenio Manuel, op. cit., p. 19.

powers were concentrated in the same hands. He added numerous historical examples to substantiate his point. Del Rosario then went to a more practical point. He mentioned that not all of the inhabitants of the Philippines were Catholics, and that some were Moslems. Amidst this mixture of faiths "imposition of a religion may provoke civil war, and the mere granting of a privilege to one religion may lead to serious conflicts, demanding that serious reflection be given to the problem." Besides this, he continued, it was no use having a state religion which was not the real Catholic religion, for what was taught in the Philippines by Spanish friars was a perversion of Christianity. It was also important to consider, he added, that the "feudal theocracy" in the Islands had been one of the sources of discontent and therefore had contributed to the Revolution. In one of his interpolations, T. del Rosario declared:

> I maintain the theory that the State must not protect any particular religion and that no religion should depend on the State. There should be a complete separation between the two, for, on the contrary, it will have to admit of a State within a State, a principle which is now rejected by modern civilization.[7]

Calderón, probably in order to allay the fears of those congressmen who accepted the last-mentioned principle, reassured them that, because of their tested patriotism, the Filipino clergy would not attempt to usurp governmental powers. To this Arcadio del Rosario answered that there was little fear of the Filipino clergy but rather of the Pope as the possible author of the interference.[8]

Arcadio del Rosario also contributed arguments in favor of the amendment, of which he was a co-author with Tomás del Rosario. Among his arguments were the following:

> The ministers of a religion protected by the State begin their ministry in the role of martyrs and with self-denials, but end up as tyrants and executioners.

---

[7] F. Calderón, *op. cit.,* p. 81 (Appendix). Also cf. pp. 72-75 (Appendix); A. Manuel, *op. cit.,* p. 18. The interpretations of the arguments presented above are mostly based on the notes and reports of a member of Congress, Don Pablo Ocampo, who sometimes quoted verbatim or condensed what he heard. Most of the parliamentary debates were reported in the revolutionary papers of the day.

[8] F. Calderón, *op. cit.,* p. 95 (Appendix).

A state religion does not necessarily constitute a more efficient brake on passions, and statistics show the contrary.

In the United States, where there has been religious freedom for more than a hundred years, the Catholic Church is most flourishing . . . while the decline of Spain is principally due to the denial of religious liberty and the existence of a powerful clergy.

To protect a religion is to grant a privilege, and all privileges are like money loaned at a usurious rate which sooner or later will ruin the State.

In this country today there is real tolerance, and it would be a crime to one's conscience to insist that a system be given another chance after it has been tested for 350 years and has given nothing but sterile results.[9]

The arguments in favor of the amendment shifted from objections to the Church as such, to objections to its ministers. As Calderón remarked, "it is a grave mistake to confuse the ministers of the Catholic religion with the religion itself." [10] Yet, his defense of the merits of the Catholic Church and his assertion that having the Catholic religion as a state religion did not imply a lack of tolerance for other religions, did not at all touch one of the basic contentions of Arcadio del Rosario. The latter argued that the unity of Church and State in the Philippines, in all the years of Spanish occupation, did not further the progress of the Philippines and had on the contrary hindered it. The discussions in the Malolos Congress clearly show that the Filipino delegates were torn between loyalty to their religion and the bad experiences of the past with that religion, especially when Church and State were united. The first argument of Arcadio del Rosario implied that although there was a distinction between the Church and its ministers, there was no guarantee that the ministers would not attempt to use both Church and State for the furtherance of their own interests.

In any case, when the amendment came to the vote, the results were twice a tie. Chairman Pablo Tecson broke the second tie by voting for the amendment. The results were 26-25, and the decision of Congress was to adhere to the principle of separation of Church and State. Thus instead of the three articles of the

[9] *Ibid.,* pp. 79-81 (Appendix).
[10] *Ibid.,* p. 110.

original Section III, the amendment proposed by Tomás del Rosario was adopted.

It was to be expected that the Filipino clergy was disappointed with the outcome of the voting. During the sessions of Congress, many Filipino priests interested in the outcome of the discussions were seen occupying seats reserved for guests. Actually, one priest, Gregorio Aglipay, was a member of the Congress at Malolos, and he tried to have the amendment suspended.[11] According to Calderón:

> The action of those who desired the separation of Church and State brought about a great disappointment to the Filipino clergy, and since then I have noticed in them a certain withdrawal from public affairs; but when their spirit revived, they agreed to publish a newspaper called *El Católico Filipino* to protect the interests of the Filipino clergy . . . and I edited the newspaper.[12]

It is to be expected, and quite understandably, that with the loss of the power of the friars, the Filipino clergy had no intention of rejecting the possibility of a theocratic Filipino government. They expected to have a share in the government for which they had sacrificed so much. In January, 1899, a petition by the Filipino clergy was addressed to Aguinaldo, asking him to use his influence in establishing the freedom of one religion only, that of the Catholic Church. A typical rationalization for the unity of Church and State is found in the *Memorial* of Padre Garces to Congress.

> Neither society nor good government can exist without morality, order and authority, that is, without law, and therefore without religion; for this is the basis of all three, as it is the life of the nation and the organ of the government. Civil society is conceived . . . as a moral person, and as such is obliged to have a religion . . . . To permit the liberty of all religions, is to concede liberty to both error and impiety.[13]

The problem of Church and State assumed such importance that it had to some extent separated the supporters of the government into two camps:

---

[11] José Lopez del Castillo y Kabangis, *Malolos y sus pronombres: Estudio Crítico Histórico* (Manila, 1950), pp. 189-190 and 207-208.

[12] *Op. cit.,* p. 244.

[13] "Memorial del Padre Garces al Congreso," F. Calderón, *op. cit.,* pp. 116-117 (Appendix).

> Mabini himself, who was a fierce sectarian and a mason with grave commitments, did not dare accept the form in which it was presented by Congress . . . .[14]

Mabini, in his "Proposed Amendments" to the final form of the constitution passed by Congress, attempted to suspend Title III, Article 5 to such time as the meeting of a future constitutional assembly. This amendment was accepted by Congress as part of the official constitution and it ran as follows:

> Temporary Provisions: Article 100. The execution of the 5th article of title 3 is hereby suspended until the meeting of the constituent assembly. In the meantime, the municipalities of those places which may require the spiritual offices of a Filipino priest shall provide for his maintenance.[15]

It would appear strange that Mabini, who personally adhered to the theory of the separation of Church and State, was the one to propound the suspension of this provision of the Constitution. Actually, Mabini did not entirely abandon his principle and he saw to it that the suspension was temporary. He was already anticipating the outbreak of hostilities with the American Army and he knew that the government (and at this time he was the chief adviser of Aguinaldo) could not afford to have a segment of the population alienated from the government. He was fully aware of the prestige of the Filipino clergy and the sympathy of part of the population for the clergy. On the more positive side, he believed that he could count on the support of the clergy, in case of war, if they were not indifferent or alienated. This action was one of political expediency. During the week that Congress was discussing the problem of Church and State, Mabini wrote to Aguinaldo:

> There is now going on in Congress a heated discussion on the religious question. If you favor one faction, then the other will separate itself from the government . . . . It is imperative that you commission a Secretary to inform Congress that, unless the times become

---

14 F. Calderón, *op. cit.,* p. 244.
15 Quoted from M. Kalaw, *The Development of Philippine Politics,* p. 444.

normal, such problems should not be discussed . . . . This is just a warning of what may happen in the future.[16]

In the same letter, Mabini added a postscript, which in some ways showed his preferences on the factions involved: "If you accept the unity of Church and State, those men from whom one could expect more services in critical times, will break with you."

Mabini, who for various reasons did not personally favor the promulgation of a constitution by the Malolos Congress, used Title III, Article 5, as one of the reasons why the Constitution should not have been passed at all. In an official memorandum to the council of state (*consejo de estado*), he stated that it was not wise to accept the constitution because "To establish openly the separation of Church and State during these difficult times . . . may give cause for the withdrawal of the supporters of religion." [17]

It is thus clear that in spite of Mabini's recommendation for the suspension of the clause on religion, he did not as a matter of principle believe in the unity of Church and State for the Philippines. In his proposed constitution for the Philippine Republic, the first two paragraphs of Article 12 provided that

> The Republic as a collective entity does not profess any determined religion, leaving to individual consciences full liberty of selecting that one which may appear most worthy and reasonable.
>
> Thus no one will be molested within the Philippine territory because of his religious opinions or on account of the exercise of his respective worship, except when it violates public morals.[18]

It is significant that in the Malolos Constitution and in Mabini's proposed constitution, the provision for the separation of Church and State was joined with a provision for the religious liberty of any sect. This might have been due to a tacit recognition on the part of some of the revolutionary fathers that the two provisions were inextricably bound together. They suspected that in a political society where there existed a state religion, it would not have been easy to practice any other religion. Mabini and the

---

[16] Quoted from J. L del Castillo y Kabangis, *op. cit.*, p. 186. This letter is also found in J. Taylor, *Philippine Insurgent Records*, Vol. III, Exhibit 349.
[17] *La Revolución Filipina*, Vol. I, p. 231.
[18] "The Constitutional Program of Mabini," *op. cit.*, pp. 316-317.

members of the Malolos Congress who desired separation of Church and State, had their suspicions based on justifiable grounds. During the Spanish regime they lived in a society where foreign non-Catholic missionaries were not allowed. Calderón, however, believed that the existence of a state religion was not incompatible with the free practice of other religions. His original three articles of Title III provided not only for the unity of Church and State but also for the free practice of any other religion. But an argument of Arcadio del Rosario subtly implied that there was no guarantee that the ministers of the State religion would not attempt to control the State. And this situation would have undoubtedly been detrimental to other religions. Padre Garces' presumption that to allow the liberty of other religions "is to concede liberty to both error and impiety" was a preview of what the future might hold if men like him were to be the high ecclesiastical authorities of the Church, and at the same time have political power.

Actually, the tradition of the separation of Church and State in the Philippines was found as early as the Propaganda days. An article written on September 15, 1892, by M. H. del Pilar, partially inspired by an injustice done to Rizal due to a decree deporting him to Dapitan, presented arguments pointing out the absurdity of punishing a man politically for some religious reason. He denied that to combat the friars and the Church was an act of disloyalty to Spain. And he inquired as to the sense in which the Church was the "irrevocable bond of the national integrity" of the Philippines, when Filipinos were not entirely Catholic by any means, and, in addition there existed no civil law forcing a man to be a Catholic.[19] Whatever be the validity of Del Pilar's arguments, it is important to note that his article was essentially an appeal for the separation of Church and State. That such an appeal was a bold and radical one can be appreciated only when the Philippine situation is understood as a system of intertwined relations between Church and State. The appeals of other propagandists may not have been as explicit as Del Pilar's; but their desire to secularize education and to have the government control the lower levels, their objections to the excessive interference of ecclesiastical officials in governmental affairs and their desire

19 "Contraproducente," *La Solidaridad,* Vol. I, No. 86 (September 15, 1892).

for religious freedom (a situation absolutely incompatible with the Spanish Church in the Philippines), resulted in a conjoining of ideals possible only of systems in which Church and State were separated.

Many of the undesirable events of the past were blamed on the unity of Church and State: the maladministration of the Spanish government, the power of the Church and the friars, the view that the government had become a tool in the hands of either the Church or the religious orders, and the personal power and interference of the friars in the social life of the people. This view of the past led many Filipino leaders to believe that a complete separation of Church and State might ameliorate political and social conditions. Calderón contended that in "pure reason" the separation was possible, but this was not the case in the Philippines where the social structure of the Filipinos was already constructed and determined along lines such that unity of Church and State was a constant and fixed pattern. But what Calderón failed to consider was that in the eyes of farsighted statesmen, like Mabini and Arcadio del Rosario, a system productive of bad or empty results should give way to another system. This involved, naturally, a radical reorientation of attitudes towards traditional institutions; but Filipino statesmen were looking towards the future, in the belief that time and the development of expectations among the people along lines traced by their leaders would eventually secure for Filipinos a system leading to progress and more liberty.

2. *Relations between the Filipino Government and the Filipino Clergy.* But the weight of historical background in the Philippines was such that in the transition from Spanish rule to the Philippine Republic, the Filipino government found it necessary to the very last days of its existence to recruit support from the parish priests. This the government had to do, as heir of the Spanish system in which the priest had political and social functions, in order that it might secure greater consent and support of a great part of the masses. In some cases, actual interference with the affairs of the clergy was necessary, to the extent of legislating for the disposal of parish funds.

The fact was that the Filipino clergy enjoyed a great deal of prestige. And they had partially acquired the social influence of the former friars, either because of habit on the part of the populace or because of a deep sympathy with their cause—a cause for which, it was widely believed, Filipino priests had given their blood. The memory of the martyred priests Burgos, Zamora and Gómez was still fresh in the minds of the people. This fact was clearly recognized by government officials. It is interesting to note that in a letter of July 26, 1898, written by Leandro Ibarra, Secretary of Interior at the time, to Aguinaldo, the former advised:

> One of the measures which our Revolutionary Government can and must utilize . . . is the disposition of the Filipino secular clergy to extend to us all the aid possible in the work of our independence, an aid which undoubtedly has a certain efficacy on account of the prestige which said clergy enjoys among the populace [20]

This recommendation was approved by Aguinaldo, and in his decree of July 26, 1898, it was ordered:

> The heads of the provinces are to call upon the patriotism of all Filipino clergy in charge of parishes in towns which have submitted to the revolutionary government, urging them to impress upon their parishioners, both from the pulpit and the confessional, that in order that our independence should be secured it is necessary to give absolute adhesion to the revolutionary government and its worthy president, Don Emilio Aguinaldo. The secretary of the interior is to inform them that they can collect the tithes and allowances prescribed in the regulations of Archbishop Santa Justa y Rufina.[21]

The government took pains to avoid friction with the Filipino clergy, and the Decree of September 1, 1898, ordered ". . . civil authorities to use the utmost care to avoid conflicts with the clergy (native clergy—T)." [22]

The reaction of the Filipino clergy was always taken into consideration in certain pieces of legislation, as if it were a gauge

---

[20] J. Taylor, *Philippine Insurgent Records*, Vol. III, Exhibit 126.

[21] J. Taylor, *Report on Organization*, Exhibit G, pp. 37-38.

[22] *Ibid.* Military authorities were not allowed to interfere with the religious duties of priests, and in a letter of the Secretary of Interior to a military chief of Nueva Ecija who wanted parochial services to be given to the poor *gratis*, it was informed that for the President of the Revolutionary government to interfere in such particular affairs would be to do an arbitrary act. Cf. Taylor, *Philippine Insurgent Records*, Vol. III.

indicating whether the populace would consent. To take a particular example: when the Filipino government wanted to make civil marriages compulsory and canonical marriages optional, Calderón cautioned Aguinaldo's friends and advisers on the project. He suggested that it might do "violence to the consciences of the Filipinos, nearly all of whom were Catholics," and at the same time might give the impression that the revolutionary movement was anti-Catholic.[23] Actually, this implied a consideration of the attitude of the Filipino clergy, who would not be expected to favor legislation inimical either to their religious beliefs or to their personal interests. In any case, when the above legislation took effect, the Revolutionary government still had so much need of the civil services of the parish priests that they were ordered not to prevent the recording of civil marriages in the parochial registers.[24]

Filipino revolutionary leaders had to bear in mind two things: not to alienate the Filipino clergy by recognizing their part in the struggle for emancipation and, at the same time, to see to it that the Filipino clergy did not perpetuate those abuses that were so common among the friars. It was the second consideration that led Aguinaldo to declare in his Manifesto of October 17, 1899:

> The clergy should not meddle in civil or military matters, in order that they may be justly respected in their high offices. They will live at the foot of the altar, respected and esteemed by all, and in conformity with the regulations of Archbishop Santa Justa y Rufina.[25]

To prevent the Filipino clergy from becoming economically powerful and from following the footsteps of the friars, another

[23] T. M. Kalaw, "Memoirs of F. Calderón," *Philippine Review*, IV (June-July, 1919), 468.

[24] Cf. J. Taylor, *Philippine Insurgent Records*, 97 LY. Also cf. Taylor, *Report on Organization*, Exhibit G, p. 38, on the Presidential decree of August 22, 1898 making civil marriage compulsory.

[25] J. Taylor, *Philippine Insurgent Records*, Vol. IV, Exhibit 700. Archbishop Santa Justa y Rufina was the prelate who regulated the amount of fees to be charged for religious services in the 18th century. One of the charges of the revolutionists against the friars was that they completely disregarded this schedule of fees and charged amounts much higher than it.

It was such experiences in the past that may have prompted the Presidential decree of October 20, 1898, to prohibit priests from selling wax candles. Cf. J. Taylor, *Report on Organization*, Exhibit G, p. 41, for this decree.

proposed amendment in Aguinaldo's message to Congress dated January 1, 1899, stated

> Any religious association which in the future may be established in the territory of the Republic is prohibited from possessing real property exceeding 50,000 pesos in value.[26]

In general it may be maintained that the Filipino government did not interfere with the fees charged for religious services except when there were abuses and other forms of illegal exaction. The standard schedule of fees was that set by Archbishop Santa Justa y Rufina.

In order that the Revolutionary government could secure better its authority over its territory, it was also imperative that the spiritual allegiance of Filipino priests should not be paid to Bernardino Nozaleda, the Archbishop of Manila, who was not only a Spaniard but also a friar.[27] But it so happened that whenever the Archbishop had an excuse to do so, he did attempt to exercise some canonical jurisdiction over Revolutionary territory, such as nominating Filipino priests to take care of certain parishes. It was not easy for the Filipino government to dispossess these priests of their newly acquired parishes, for not only were the priests Filipinos but their religious services were needed by the parishes. And so, in order to face this problem, a Presidential decree of Aguinaldo on October 20, 1898, ordered "Priests nominated by the Archbishop of Manila will not be recognized unless approved by this government." [28]

It appears that some of the Filipino clergy were correct in their patriotism and in their support of the Revolutionary government. For, according to Taylor, around October, 1898, certain priests informed Aguinaldo that they had received appointments from Nozaleda to administer certain parishes; and these priests requested him to confirm their appointments. Upon receipt of their appointments the President issued signed confirmations, which in turn were countersigned by the Secretary of the Interior.[29]

---

[26] J. Taylor, *Philippine Insurgent Records,* Vol. III, Exhibit 352.

[27] It is to be recalled that the Revolutionary government never had direct jurisdiction over the city of Manila, as this city was under the control of the United States Military Government.

[28] J. Taylor, *Report on Organization,* Exhibit G, p. 41.

[29] J. Taylor, *Philippine .Insurgent Records,* Vol. II, 96 LY.

But it seems that the Archbishop was interested, too, in taking his share of the parish funds. On this the Filipino government had one and only one decision. The Presidential decree of June 24, 1899, stipulated that

> . . . in order to avoid parish funds in the future being delivered to Archbishop Nozaleda . . . by parish priests, as has been done, and as this is a highly unpatriotic act, Father Gregorio Aglipay is appointed a commissioner of the government to make a careful inspection of the parish funds of every town in Luzon.[30]

The official attitude towards Nozaleda was partially dictated by reasons of administrative and financial security. But there must also have been some anxiety that the Archbishop might utilize his ecclesiastical office and canonical discipline to influence some Filipino priests to act against the interests of the Revolutionary government. This archbishop was one of the fiercest antagonists of the Revolution and obviously hated by many Filipino leaders.

It so happened that when the Republic was at war with the United States and hard pressed for funds, a Presidential decree on August 10, 1899, stated:

> In order that parish funds and cash belonging to churches be removed from danger of loss by the hazards of war, they will all be invested in the national loan.[31]

Actually, before this decree the parish priests were only requested to invest in the national loan; and the evidence is that the majority complied with this request. The province of Pangasinan was a rare case when it refused to invest, except by direct orders of Gregorio Aglipay. It was in June, 1899, when Aglipay was appointed commissioner to take charge of parochial funds and invest them in the national loan.[32] It clearly appears that the Filipino government had made great demands on the Filipino clergy. And one cannot but wonder at and admire the sacrifices made by the

---

[30] J. Taylor, *Report on Organization*, Exhibit G, p. 49. Gregorio Aglipay was the Chaplain-General of the Filipino Armed Forces.

[31] *Ibid.* This decree was addressed to the provincial governors of 25 provinces, and as such is interesting because it shows the extent of the jurisdiction of the Republic in August, 1899.

[32] J. Taylor, *Philippine Insurgent Records*, Vol. II, 100 HS—1 KK.

clergy and the manner in which they threw their lot in with that government to which they were already tied by bonds of sanguinity.

Yet the Filipino government and many secular revolutionary leaders went so far as to exert great efforts to see to it that some of the major aspirations of the Filipino clergy were realized. It had become a matter of conscience‚ to some of the leaders to extend this recognition. For they realized that, initially, one of the ideals of the Revolution was to grant those rights which their countrymen-priests had so long demanded. And they knew if these were not granted the Filipino clergy, then the Revolution was bound to fail, simply because of the abandonment of some principles viewed as essentially moral in character. The secularization or the Filipinization of the parishes was almost a reality; and in this respect, the Revolution did satisfy part of the aspirations of the Filipino clergy. But this was not enough in the opinion of some of the political leaders, especially Mabini. To them, as long as the highest ecclesiastical officers in the Philippines were foreigners, especially Spaniards, the newly acquired gains of the Filipino priests were imperilled. This reason, plus others which will be discussed later on, led to the demand for a Church in the Philippines administered completely by Filipino ecclesiastical officials. These demands paved the way for the conception of a national Church.

3. *The Idea of a National Church.* One of the earliest references to the idea that all ecclesiastical authorities in the Philippines should be Filipinos is found in the *First Manifesto of the Hongkong Junta* in April, 1898:

> We desire that Christianity, which is the basis of present civilization, and the solid foundation of its religious institutions, be without coercion or imposition, and that the native clergy of the country be those to direct and teach the people from every step of the ecclesiastical hierarchy.
>
> By right of one's political fatherland and native soil . . . . whosoever among you wants to be a clergyman, dignitary, provisor, bishop, archbishop and cardinal, must as an indispensable condition have been born on your proper soil.[33]

This resolution was made by laymen, and in fact the initial impetus toward the formation of a national Church was made by

---

[33] F. Calderón, *Memorias,* pp. 33 and 40, respectively.

laymen, principally Mabini. The Filipino clergy in 1896 and throughout the days of the Revolutionary government in 1898, did not appear to have initiated this move. There is evidence many of them rendered canonical obedience to the Archbishop of Manila, although they were working for the consolidation of the Revolution. In a letter written to Galicano Apacible, one of the propagandists who later became a member of the Hongkong Junta, on October 28, 1898, Mabini complained:

> It is true that our priests still recognize the authority of Nozaleda. I try convincing them to entreat the Pope to nominate Filipino bishops for the Philippines. I do not know whether I can convince them, because they are very stubborn.[34]

Mabini, who at this time was Aguinaldo's chief adviser, was definitely in a position to use governmental authority to support the Filipino clergy as long as they desired to follow the bold lines of Mabini's thinking. At this time, the clergy did not heed Mabini's advice or "instructions," to use the word of Del Castillo y Kabangis, a Filipino writer and lawyer. Whatever might have been the motives of the Filipino priests at this time, the kindest description of their motives is that they did not follow the advice of Mabini because of "their innate humility and submission to the chair of St. Peter." [35]

It appears, then, that the primary force and soul of the movement for the establishment of a national Church was Mabini. In his view, a national Church was one where the highest ecclesiastical authority in the Philippines would be a Filipino, although subject to the Pope in Rome. This would, at one stroke if Mabini is to be believed, solve permanently the secularization problem and at the same time eliminate foreign influence (Spanish influence in particular) from the affairs of the Church in the Philippines. To one quite familiar with the interrelations of Church and State in the Philippines during Spanish times, Mabini's suspicions of foreign prelates is quite understandable.

Just how governmental authority and pressure might be used to aid the cause of the Filipino clergy, provided they asked for

---

[34] Quoted from J. L. del Castillo y Kabangis, *op. cit.,* p. 94.
[35] This is the opinion of Del Castillo y Kabangis. Cf. *ibid.*

it, may be gleaned from two of the official letters (penned by Mabini) sent by Aguinaldo to Major-General Otis, on November 3 and 18, 1898. These letters were part of a series of correspondence begun when Otis requested Aguinaldo to release some Spanish clerics and civil officials who were prisoners in the hands of the Revolutionary army. In the first letter, Aguinaldo wrote:

> When the Filipino priests, unjustly spurned by the Vatican, have obtained the right to appointment to the duties of bishops and parochial priests, then there will be no danger to the public tranquility in setting at liberty the ecclesiastics. The Spanish Government and the Pope have proven themselves ignorant of law or justice when one deals with their interests. For that reason the Filipinos wish to hold the civil officials in order to obtain the liberty of the prisoners and deported Filipinos, and the priests in order to obtain from the Vatican the recognition of the Philippine clergy.[36]

Mabini's arguments for the establishment of a national Church rested, usually, on two points: The first was that ". . . an independent nation has the right that one of its sons should be the chief ecclesiastical superior within its own territory." [37] The second was that it was time for the Filipino priests to manage their own affairs and to organize themselves, especially since the Archbishop of Manila, being in territory held by the Americans, could not validly exercise his jurisdiction on revolutionary territory.[38] Other reasons were both patriotic and rhetorical like the following:

> The Filipino clergy cannot recognize as its chief the bloody enemy of the Filipino people [Nozaleda], without antagonizing them. The

---

[36] *Senate Document No. 208,* part i, 56th Congress, 1st session, p. 44. It is amusing to note that Otis, in his reply to Aguinaldo, said in part: "The expressed intention of holding these Spanish priests as prisoners of war in order to force the Vatican of Rome into certain acknowledgments with appropriate action I can not conceive to be well founded in law, custom, or precedent, and am convinced that such a position is untenable." *Ibid.,* p. 46. In all probability, Otis did not fully understand the problems of the Philippine Revolution. It may be suspected, too, that Otis, having a different social, religious and cultural background, must have been entirely amazed by what was going on between the revolutionists and friars.

[37] "Al Pueblo y Clero Filipino" (August 19, 1899), *La Revolución Filipina,* Vol. II, p. 40. This manifesto was dictated by Mabini, to be signed by Aglipay.

[38] Cf. A. Mabini, "Organización del Clero Filipino" (October, 1899), *ibid,* pp. 114-118.

Filipino clergy must not be an enemy of the people, and should recover those rights that have been willed to them by the blood of
Burgos, Gómez, Zamora, and other Filipino priests . . . .[39]

The Filipino government actually recognized a Filipino as the
highest ecclesiastical official in the Philippines. He was Gregorio
Aglipay, a preeminently patriotic man. His title was "Vicario General Castrence de la Republica o Clero Filipino."[40] Aglipay, during the days of the Revolutionary government, was already looked
up to as the leader of the Filipino clergy. And during the Malolos
Congress, he was the only priest who served as delegate. His support of the Revolutionary government was inestimable. On October
22, 1898, he issued a circular addressed to the Filipino clergy
asking them to give their full support to the Revolutionary government.

Since the revolution has triumphed and the independence of our country has been solemnly proclaimed by a duly established government,
patriotism demands that we should recognize it since we now clearly
see that its intention concerning the Catholic religion professed by
the Filipino people is to preserve it in all its purity; and we should
not only recognize it but we should cooperate with all our strength
and in accordance with the obligations of our mission in the efficient
attainment of its noble purpose, never for a moment doubting that
they are and have been to liberate our country from a foreign domination . . . .[41]

In addition to the appeal to the patriotism of the Filipino clergy,
Aglipay also implied that to side with the Revolutionary government was considered by the government to be incompatible with
loyalty to the Manila archbishop. He also suggested that full support for the government might give them greater hand in fashion-
ing the future of the Church. The result would serve both the
interests of the Church and their own.

. . . . we ought to consider the advantages and the benefits which
will accrue to religion and to our personal interests if we place ourselves on the side of the revolutionary government, because if we

---

[39] A. Mabini, "Al Pueblo y Clero Filipino," op. cit., p. 42.
[40] According to Isabelo de los Reyes, it was Mabini who was the author
of the designation of Aglipay as "Jefe Supremo del Clero Filipino" and
with the above official title. Cf. I. de los Reyes, Catedra (Sermonario)
de la Iglesia Filipina Independiente [Manila:] Edición Oficial, 1932, p. 55.
[41] J. Taylor, Philippine Insurgent Records, Vol. II, 98 LY—1 AJ.

continue recognizing the supremacy of the Spanish prelate, or even if we remain in an expectant and neutral attitude without definitely and clearly defining our position this might lead to the separation of Church and State in our country and other conflicts consequent upon it will assuredly not fail to gravely prejudice the interests of the clergy and above all the service of religion . . . .[42]

It is hardly necessary to assert that Aglipay had the full backing of the Filipino government, for Aglipay's views were identical with Mabini's, who was once the most powerful man in Aguinaldo's government. In September, 1899, the Secretary of Interior of the Republic wrote that the cause of Aglipay and the cause of the government were so closely linked that

. . . any attempt against his legitimate authority, authority which has been recognized by our government, means an attempt against our independence, which the secretary of interior is charged with maintaining and strengthening.[42]

Armed with government encouragement, Aglipay in October, 1899, wrote a circular addressed to the Filipino clergy asking them to establish and organize a national Church. And then this organization was to elect a commission to deal with the Vatican, stating the needs of the Filipino Church.

The Filipino clergy has the undeniable right of meeting as soon as possible to elect an ecclesiastical chapter (cabildo), which, as representatives of the clergy, will establish a provisional government for the Filipino Church in harmony with its needs and the relations of mutual support which should exist between it and the Filipino government, and appoint a commission charged with informing the Holy See of the real needs of the diocese and of proposing the names of those most fit for appointment as bishop or as bishops.[44]

To ease the consciences of those priests who were to attend the meeting and at the same time to suggest that much could be lost if the Filipino clergy would not organize, the circular-letter of Aglipay on August 19, 1899, stated:

. . . canon law, like all human laws, is adopted for normal cases; in abnormal or unforeseen cases, it is left to the prudent judgment of

---

[42] *Ibid.*
[43] J. Taylor, *Philippine Insurgent Records,* Vol. II, 94 LY.
[44] "Organización del Clero Filipino," *op. cit.,* p. 119.

those charged with the preservation of society, to choose the most facile and expedient means in order to save it when it is threatened; for if society is allowed to live, then the rule of law can be reestablished later on, but if it is allowed to die—everything is finished.[45]

On October 23, 1899, members of the Filipino clergy met at Panique, Tarlac. A decision to "filipinize" the church was made and a commission was formed to get Papal approval for their activities.[46] Thus, to all intents and purposes, a Filipino National Church was formed. But the war with the United States and the defeat of the Republic disrupted all plans for future activities.[47]

[45] A. Mabini, "Al Pueblo y Clero Filipino," *op. cit.,* p. 43. This letter was penned by Mabini.

[46] Cf. Juan A. Rivera, "The Aglipayan Movement," *Philippine Social Science Review,* IX (December, 1937), 303.

[47] The Filipino Church, which was established formally on October 23, 1899, should be carefully distinguished from the "Philippine Independent Church," which came into existence in 1902 and was commonly known as the "Aglipayan Church." It was on October 1, 1902, that Aglipay accepted the designation of "Obispo Maximo" of this new Church and presided over a council which framed its new constitution. The major difference between these two churches was that while the former wanted to establish firm and direct relations with Rome, the latter broke away from Rome completely. One of the prime movers, if not *the* prime mover of the Independent Church, was Isabelo de los Reyes, a layman; and it appears that Aglipay accepted the position of "Obispo Maximo" on account of pressures from some priests and a part of the Filipino population, who signified adherence to the new Church.

Yet there are logical and historical relations between the two Churches, for the Independent Church may be conceived of as either a radical transformation of the first or a mere substitute for it. Calderón, in his *Memoirs,* maintained that the rise and spread of the movement of the Philippine Independent Church was due initially to the refusal of Archbishop Chapelle, the Apostolic delegate, to reconsider the complaints and denunciations made against the friars, his actual espousal of their cause, and his rash acts in replacing certain Filipino parish priests with others; in all, to his refusal to satisfy the aspirations of the Filipino clergy. This was also the contention of Aglipay. In a published article he stated that it was necessary to separate from Rome, since it took the side of the friars; besides this, he added that if Filipinos were capable of holding high offices like those of the Supreme Court in the Philippines as well as posts of provincial governors, then he saw no reason why they should not also be capable of governing their own Church. (Cf. "Independent Catholic Church in the Philippines," *The Independent,* Vol. LV, No. 2865, October 29, 1903.)

The nationalistic element of this Church is clearly evident in its canonization of Rizal and the three priests, Burgos, Gómez, and Zamora, on September 24, 1903. The Church has also incorporated in its doctrines some of the patriotic doctrines of Rizal Bonifacio, Mabini, *et al.* (Cf. I. de los Reyes, *Catedra,* p. 68.)

Juan A. Rivera (*op. cit.,* Vol. X, No. 1, February, 1938, p. 27) correctly stated that: "The Aglipayan Church is one of those developments

The discussions in the Malolos Congress emphasized the separation of Church and State in the Philippines as an ideal found among many Filipino political leaders and thinkers. It should be pointed out that some of the proponents of the principle of separation were Masons who were closely aware of or in contact with the liberal movement in Spain. As such, they had definite ideas on the problem or possibly even some commitments. This is what Calderón might have meant when he said that Mabini was a Mason with *"compromisos graves."* Yet the major reason was fear that the predominance of the Church would duplicate a historical pattern of the past, the memory of which was so bitter. Incidentally, it is interesting to note that Calderón's rationale for the unity of Church and State was to the effect that, in such a situation, it would be easier to control the clergy. In all probability, Calderón was looking forward to the day when the clergy would be entirely Filipino, and their patriotism would be manifest in great loyalty to the Filipino government. They would then be, in all likelihood, easier to control. One is led to suspect that Calderón was also fearful of a possible increase in the power of the clergy if no governmental checks were to be applied to them. Could it be possible, then, that some Filipino revolutionary leaders were thinking of the same end, but with contradictory techniques?

If the above views are substantially correct, the formation of a Filipino Church was therefore a tool to further the aims of the Revolution. Revolutionary leaders wanted its support and, also, the institution of a system whereby abuses attributed to the friars and other church officials, who in many cases fought civil authorities, would be totally eliminated. This naturally assumed that a new clergy, so conceived, would not perpetuate such abuses. In any case, it was probably hoped that if the Church were entirely in the hands of Filipinos, it would be much easier for the Filipino government to discover a *modus vivendi* with it. Or, at least, it was hoped that Filipino bishops would be patriots. Since the Revolution fought the friars vehemently, the revolutionary leaders tried to avoid being judged anti-religious by demonstrating that they

which crystallized out of our past struggle for recognition as a people. As the struggle for reforms finally culminated in the agitation for political emancipation, so the demand for the recognition of the Filipino priesthood—a part of the general demands for reforms—finally resulted in the organization of an independent Filipino Church."

had no intention of taking away the Faith from the people; and this could best be done by supporting a national Church. The formation of a national Church may also be viewed as a preventive measure against control by foreign religious corporations. According to De los Reyes

> [Mabini] desired political independence; but he also considered that without religious independence. the country would be at the mercy of powerful foreign religious corporations.[48]

Yet, without overlooking the newly developed national pride that might have entered into the picture, the formation of a Filipino National Church may also be conceived as due to a tacit recognition that the Filipino clergy had to be rewarded for its important part in both the movement for reforms and the Revolution. Considering the nationalistic element of the Philippine Revolution and the manner in which the emancipation of the Filipino clergy played a conspicuous part in the reforms sought by the propagandists and the revolutionists of 1896, it would have been quite surprising if there were no attempt made to form a national Church.

[48] *Catedra,* p. 55.

CHAPTER EIGHT

A Legislature
or a Dictatorship

THE REVOLUTIONARY CONGRESS was inaugurated in Malolos, Bulacan, on September 15, 1898. After ratifying the independence of the Philippines, previously proclaimed by Aguinaldo on June 12, 1898, Congress decided immediately to draft a constitution for a future republican system of government. On this point a controversy ensued in Congress. Mabini, who at this time was Aguinaldo's chief adviser, maintained that Congress had no power to draft a constitution since it was originally convoked as a consultative body and not as a constituting assembly. Calderón, who had the support of the majority of Congress, claimed that Congress had the power to draft and promulgate a constitution. Regardless of the merits of Mabini's arguments, the fact was that Congress, once convened, was not satisfied in remaining a mere consultative body. In any case, Aguinaldo as President of the Revolutionary government, was led to recognize that Congress had the power of promulgating the fundamental laws of the land. Congress formed a committee to study various proposed constitutional drafts. The draft made by Calderón was accepted by the committee and Congress discussed each and every article of it from October 25, 1898, to November 29, 1898. Except for one change that referred to Church and State, the draft of Calderón was approved by Congress.

When Mabini and his supporters were convinced that nothing could deter Congress from promulgating a constitution, they devised certain amendments to the draft approved by Congress. These amendments, penned by Mabini, were presented to Congress on January 1, 1899 by one of the government Secretaries in the form of a message by Aguinaldo. The committee that presented Calderón's draft, in answer to these proposed amendments, presented a reply (*dictamen*). This was in defense of Calderón's constitution. Congress rejected Mabini's amendments almost *in toto*. However, to prevent a serious split in Congress, and in view of the fear of an outbreak of hostilities with American troops which made it necessary for all factions to join, a series of "temporary provisions" were added to the Constitution. These provisions represented a compromise between the two factions. The Constitution was officially announced on January 21, 1899 and the Republic with Aguinaldo as President was inaugurated two days later.

The discussions in the Revolutionary congress thus revealed two distinct approaches to the problem of the structure of the Philippine government. It was initially on the question as to whether or not a constitution could and should be adopted by Congress that two groups sprang into existence: the "constitutionalists" (Calderón and his supporters) and the "absolutists" (Mabini and his supporters). But once Congress decided on a constitution, the problem discussed by these two groups became that of whether the provisions of the Constitution were adequate to secure the gains of the Revolution. Since the accepted constitution provided for a strong legislature as against a weak executive, the merits or demerits of a strong legislature during revolutionary days became the bone of contention.

1. *Calderón's Support of a Constitution and of a Strong Legislative Power.* The promulgation of a republican charter was defended by Calderón on the grounds that a "modern and progressive" constitution was needed to achieve recognition of the independence of the Philippines by other nations. As later discussions will demonstrate, there were other more fundamental reasons—based on the social system and political traditions of the Filipinos.

A salient feature in the Malolos Constitution was the provision for a very powerful legislature. This legislature reduced the President of the Republic to a mere symbol or figurehead directly responsible to Congress. It also held a great power over the judiciary. In the words of Calderón, on the subject of the general characteristics of the Constitution:

> In fact, the legislative power, although I proclaimed at the beginning the separation of the three powers, had been vested with such ample powers in the proposed constitution that it controlled the exe-

cutive and judicial powers in all their acts, and in order to make this control a constant one . . . I had established a so-called permanent committee, that is, a committee composed of members of the congress which, during the recess of congress, assumed all the powers of the same, with full authority to adopt emergency measures. In one word, it may be affirmed that the congress of the republic was the omnipotent power of the entire nation.[1]

The omnipotence of the legislative power was partially secured by provisions in the Constitution (Title VI, Articles 54-55) providing for a Permanent Commission (*comisión permanente*). This consisted of seven members elected by Congress. Their functions included the convocation of Congress for extraordinary sessions, and serving as a Court of Justice in order to try the President of the Republic and other high officials believed to have committed high treason (Title V, Article 44). In practice, the Permanent Commission was intended to watch the actions of high government officials, such as the President of the Republic, the Chief Justice of the Supreme Court, and the cabinet or council of government (*consejo de gobierno*).

The cabinet was supposed to be directly responsible to Congress (Title IX, Article 75). Also, Congress elected the President of the Republic and had the power to impeach him. Similarly it appointed the Chief Justice of the Supreme Court and the Procurator-General and had the power to try them in cases of high crimes. The convocations, suspensions, and dissolutions of Congress could not be carried out by the President of the Republic, except in concurrence with Congress or the Permanent Commission. With such a system, the President of the Republic was deemed irresponsible. All of his official acts had to be countersigned by a secretary of the cabinet, to whose authority or province such an act properly belonged.

One of the major reasons why Calderón favored a strong legislature was that it was designed to serve as a counter force to the

---

[1] Quoted from T. M. Kalaw's "Memoirs of F. Calderón," *Philippine Review,* IV (June-July, 1919), 474. The idea of a permanent commission appears to have been copied from the constitutions of some South American republics and possibly Spain. The idea is found in the Constitution of Spain (1812 and 1856), Mexico (1857, as amended), Guatemala (1879), Chile (1833, as amended), Peru (1860) and Costa Rica (1871, as amended). Cf. "The Revolutionary Government," *Philippine Review,* I (April, 1916), 27.

growing strength of the military element in the Philippines. Calderón was convinced that the bulk of the military forces, including most of the officers, were ignorant; and as he himself recalled, many persons who belonged to the humbler strata of society were initiated into the Katipunan by Bonifacio. In his *Memorias,* he wrote:

> Being fully convinced . . . that in case of obtaining our independence, we were for a long time going to have a really oligarchic republic in which the military element, which was ignorant in almost its entirety, would predominate, I preferred to see that oligarchy neutralized by the oligarchy of intelligence, seeing that the congress would be composed of the most intelligent elements of the nation. This is the principal reason why I vested the congress with such ample powers . . . . In one word where oligarchies were concerned, I preferred the oligarchy of the intelligence of many to an ignorant oligarchy.[2]

The above digression of Calderón regarding the control of the executive by an "intellectual oligarchy" becomes more significant when related to the person of Aguinaldo, who was the supreme military chief of the revolutionary forces and the recognized leader of the government. It must be noted that Aguinaldo could not strictly be said to belong to the *ilustrado* group. It would be more exact to say that he sprang from the masses. Calderón, who exemplified the typical aversion of the *ilustrado* to the military, did not want to see the military predominate in the affairs of the country. Nor did he want a strong chief executive, in the person of a military man who was not an *ilustrado,* to exist in the Philippines. This was due to the fact that Aguinaldo, who was the supreme military chief and had the loyalty of the masses, would have to remain the chief executive of the Philippines for an indefinite time. Were the chief executive in the Philippines not a military man but rather an *ilustrado,* the desire for a strong legislative as against a weak executive might not have existed.

Mabini also feared that the military might get out of hand. It was for this very reason that he wanted to vest greater powers in Aguinaldo, on the assumption that Aguinaldo, being the supreme military chief, would be in a better position to curb the abuses

[2] *Ibid.*

of his subordinates and followers. But it must be observed that possibly in the back of Mabini's mind was the assumption that there would always be an *ilustrado* like himself guiding and advising Aguinaldo. Thus, with regards to the fear of the military, both Calderón and Mabini utilized different techniques to achieve similar ends.

It is quite understandable why an *ilustrado* like Calderón would fear or feel averse to allowing the masses or their leaders to have a powerful hand in the control of the government. And in desiring to have a country led by an "intellectual oligarchy," he may be judged as merely following the tradition of Rizal: that only the *ilustrados* knew what was good and beneficial for the people; that reforms to be beneficial had to come "from above," for those "from below" were "irregular and uncertain."

It is interesting to note with regard to the "primacy of the intelligence" that the Malolos Constitution (Title V, Article 40), provided that in case of the death or resignation of the President of the Republic, the Chief Justice of the Supreme Court would temporarily assume the presidency until the election of a new one by Congress. Now, this demonstrates the high premium on the intelligence and education of a person, for it was and is still assumed in the Philippines, that the position of Chief Justice is usually intended to be held by a man of great learning—not only with respect to knowledge of legal matters, but of other disciplines as well.

Calderón's notion of an "intellectual oligarchy" was closely bound up with his reasons for the choice of a unicameral system of legislature. In the first place, knowing that the number of educated persons in the Philippines was relatively small, he said that having two Houses in the legislature would not be possible as there were not enough men in the country competent to fill both Houses. Another reason given was that there were no conflicting interests in the country to justify the existence of more than one House.[3] With regard to this second reason (assuming the con-

---

[3] Cf. Calderón, *op. cit.,* pp. 240-241. J. L. del Castillo, in order to illustrate Calderón's dislike for the military class, quoted the following story to the effect that during a recess from one of the sessions of Congress at Malolos, Calderón, noting a revolutionary general strutting about with certain presumptuous airs, said to his companions: "Es a éste y a otros como éste a quienes hay que atarles por la cintura, para evitar que mas tarde quieran

tention that the desire for independence did actually unite various classes in the Philippines, and that a common purpose might have pushed conflicting opinions to the background), it is probable that Calderón did not consider that in time of peace there would be no guarantee even among the *ilustrados,* with their different economic backgrounds, that conflicts would not arise. One of the few things upon which they probably would have agreed was that only they should control the governmental processes of the country. Not only was a conflict among the *ilustrados* possible, but considering that many of them belonged to the *cacique* class, a conflict with the peasants would be inevitable. The history of the Philippines after the Revolution has demonstrated that most of those best prepared to hold governmental offices in the country were *caciques.* Now, since the interests of this class were not only different from but actually opposed to those of a great part of the population, it is obvious why agrarian disturbances loomed large in the second quarter of twentieth century Philippine history.

2. *Mabini's Opposition to the Constitution and His Defense of a Strong Chief Executive.* On a technical ground, Mabini questioned the claim of Congress to promulgate a constitution or any law, since it was originally convoked as a consultative body and not as a constituting assembly.[4] The Revolutionary Congress was created, according to Mabini, to secure a greater popular support for Aguinaldo and to advise and help him in the prosecution of the Revolution. In addition, the formation of a revolutionary Congress served primarily as a visible sanction for Aguinaldo's leadership. With regard to the description of the Revolutionary Congress as merely a consultative body, Mabini had a case to stand on

cabalgar sobre las espaldas del pueblo." *Op. cit.,* p. 27. It is important to note, however, that some *ilustrados* were able to attain high positions in the army. General Antonio Luna was one of them. It may be suggested that the assassination of General Luna was a symptom of a basic rift between two groups that wanted to control the army. The rivalry between Luna and Aguinaldo portrayed the struggle between the *ilustrados* and mass leaders for the control of the army. Mabini's regret on the death of Luna, his contention that Luna was more capable of presenting stiffer resistance to the American offensive, and his charge that Aguinaldo was to some extent to be blamed for the death of Luna, all add up to the conclusion that Mabini had the same ideas as Calderón as to the nature and control of the army. In the above conflict we see a divisive element that plagued the Revolution.

4 Cf. *La Revolución Filipina,* Vol. II, p. 310.

for he was the very author of the Decree of June 23, 1898, which defined the functions of the Revolutionary Congress.[5]

The primary reason Mabini had in opposing the promulgation of a constitution by the Revolutionary Congress was that he realized the proposed constitution was aimed to make Congress supreme in all matters of government—reducing the functions of Aguinaldo to those of a mere figurehead. Not only did he believe that the country was unprepared for the proposed constitution, but that he also clearly anticipated an outbreak of hostilities with American troops—an event that demanded "the concentration of the three divisions of power in the same hands." His *Memorandum* to the council of government on December 13, 1898 cautioned against the adoption of the proposed constitution:

> Nor would it be advisable that said constitution should govern in what relates to the organization and operation of the three powers. The ship of State is threatened by great dangers and terrible tempests, and this circumstance, in my opinion, renders it advisable that the three powers be to a certain extent combined for the present in a single hand, so that she may be guided with the force necessary in order to avoid all reefs.[6]

When Mabini realized that Congress would sooner or later promulgate a constitution, he did his best to convince Aguinaldo that he should use his powers as President of the Revolutionary Government to amend it—this by virtue of Article XXIV of the Decree of June 23, 1898, which provided that the President could explain to Congress why certain acts of Congress should not be carried out, and even veto them. In a letter written to Aguinaldo in January, 1899, Mabini tried to explain the consequences to be expected from the adoption of the proposed constitution. The letter said in part:

> . . . you have to repose full confidence in your Secretaries and sign anything they may propose to you. Otherwise, they will tender their resignation, since Congress will censure them, because they, and not you, are responsible, and therefore you must give way to their opinion.[7]

---

[5] Cf. M. Kalaw, *The Development of Philippine Politics,* p. 426. Article XV and Article XVI provided for these advisory functions.

[6] "For the Council of Government: Points and Considerations," Taylor's *Philippine Insurgent Records,* Vol. III, Exhibit 320.

[7] J. Taylor, *Philippine Insurgent Records,* Vol. III, Exhibit 350.

It might have been that Mabini feared delays might accompany the passing of laws by an unwieldy assembly—when precisely what was needed in time of war was the fast and efficient promulgation and execution of laws. But of even greater importance to Mabini, over and above mere efficiency in war, was the strengthening of the chief executive. This applied more specifically to Aguinaldo, in order that abuses of the civilian by the military might be avoided or curbed. In spite of a firm belief that a democracy should be based on a municipal foundation (a foundation that determined provincial government), Mabini was led by reasons of expediency to try to increase the powers of the central government over these areas. But in attempting to strip the provincial councils of whatever legislative or consultative functions they might have had, he still advised the council of government that some amount of power should be allowed to the provincial councils in order that "the abuses to which the armed force gives rise should in some manner be contained." [8]

When war with the United States troops started and there was evidence of abuses of the civilian population by Filipino soldiers, Mabini must have felt that his plea for a stronger "politico-military" president was based on justifiable suspicions. It may have even strengthened his demand for a virtually dictatorial leadership. In a letter to Aguinaldo on February 28, 1899, he, who at this time was the head of the first Cabinet of the Republic, wrote with regard to military abuses in some towns:

> Under these circumstances a military dictatorship is very necessary, not in order to subjugate the town people, but in order to repress the abuses of the army, which can only be done by the chief.[9]

Since Aguinaldo was the supreme military chief, a major reason Mabini wanted to increase Aguinaldo's power by freeing his actions from the fetters of congressional discussions is clear: it was essential to have a strong leader who would curb abuses among his own subordinates. Assuming that Aguinaldo, as supreme chief of the Revolutionary army, would be able to control the army and prevent possible abuses, the problem was actually raised as to what would prevent the supreme chief from abusing his own powers.

---

[8] J. Taylor, *Philippine Insurgent Records*, Vol. III, Exhibit 320.
[9] *Ibid.*, Vol. IV, Exhibit 615.

In answer to this question, Mabini maintained that a dictator need not be likened to a horse without reins, for

> . . . the reins are public opinion which is manifested in the press, in the public assemblies, and in the literary works of critics—all censuring such a power if it decreed an unjust law.[10]

Now, this "public opinion," which Mabini believed could serve as a moderating influence on the actions of a dictator, has to be understood in terms of the social system of the Philippines during the time Mabini wrote. If there was any criticism of either the chief executive or the government of the Philippines, such criticism would in all probability originate from the *ilustrados* and not from the masses. These masses had been so imbued with a cult of leadership as to avoid questioning the actions of Aguinaldo. Thus what was meant by "critical public opinion" could not have been extended beyond the confines of a relatively very small group in the Philippines. In any case, regardless of criticism, Aguinaldo's popularity and control of the bulk of the army would not have been reduced considerably. Relative to this point, it is noteworthy that one of the other reasons Mabini mustered to prevent the promulgation of the constitution was that its 5th Article (Title III), providing for the separation of Church and State, would alienate some of the supporters of the Revolutionary government.[11] He further maintained that the elaborate constitutional guarantees in favor of individual liberties as provided for in the Bill of Rights in the proposed constitution could not be fully maintained in practice, since the country was still under the "predominance of the military element." [12]

It is important to emphasize that Mabini was arguing for a strong politico-military dictatorship only as a temporary expediency. To have called him an "absolutist" as opposed to a "constitutionalist," as some have done, must be qualified. Actually, he was a firm believer of constitutional government, as evidenced by the

[10] "Al Señor Zersarian" (October 5, 1899), *La Revolución Filipina*, Vol. II, p. 88. It will be recalled that when Mabini wrote his reflections on the Philippine Revolution, he said that one of the reasons the Revolution failed was that its Director (Aguinaldo) did not guide his actions in the manner expected of a person in authority.
[11] Cf. "For the Council of Government: Points and Considerations." Quoted from Taylor's *Philippine Insurgent Records*, Vol. III. Exhibit 320.
[12] *Ibid.*

framing of his *Provisional Constitution for the Philippine Republic*. But it is doubtful that he welcomed the proclamation of the Republic on January 23, 1899, for he believed that the recognition of the independence of the Philippines by various foreign nations was a prerequisite—a condition that was never fulfilled. His service as head of the first Cabinet of the Philippine Republic up to May, 1899 could be interpreted as his response to the need for his services by Aguinaldo and others, as well as an act of patriotism.

Mabini, who insisted that the work of the Revolution was not fully terminated even with the defeat of the Spanish forces in the Philippines, and who maintained during the war with the United States that the conflict was still of a revolutionary character, believed that no constitution of a "static" or permanent character should be adopted during the process of revolution—for the process of the revolution was fraught with unpredictable changes. In an article written after he left political office, he wrote:

> No revolutionary people should adopt a perfect constitution, but should confine themselves to a declaration of the principles upon which they intend to complete their work. The form to be adopted must be variable, in order to accommodate it to the conditions of the times, and place. The revolution does not constitute; it prepares. It prepares the people for a more perfect constitution upon the advent of peace, and this should be carefully observed, because the best system applied at the wrong times gives very bad results. The science of government does not consist in knowing how to select the best and most perfect, but what is most useful and timely. Thus, as two individuals exactly alike cannot be found, so are there no two revolutions which are identical: hence the necessity of initiative. A revolution that knows only how to copy and has no initiative, does not deserve the name of such.[13]

In the same article, he distinguished two aspects or parts of a constitution: one was the statement of certain fundamental principles that referred to individual rights and the moral aims of a

[13] From the article "Algo Para El Congreso," written on July 19, 1899 and published in the newspaper *La Independencia* on July 24, 1899. The above translation was taken from Taylor's *Philippine Insurgent Records*, Vol. IV, Exhibit 683.
. This article so upset Pedro Paterno, who headed the Cabinet succeeding the one headed by Mabini, that the government of the Republic was led to resort to some form of censorship of the press.

revolution; the other referred to the administrative technique that was to serve in the securing and the maintenance of the first.

> This Constitution is a purely provisional and transitory one and in such case we can still distinguish therein what is fundamental and what is accessory, what is material and what is contingent. The declaration of individual rights, of independence and of republican principles belong to the former and cannot be repealed, without our national honor being injured and all our past work lost. But the remainder, all that relates to the form of revolutionary Government entrusted with the duty of cementing that declaration, can and must be repealed, as this Government must accommodate itself to conditions.[14]

The above exposition implies that a Bill of Rights, as incorporated in a constitution, is in a certain manner independent of the constitution in the sense it is a mere statement of the recognition of certain immutable principles. These, to Mabini, would have meant principles of natural law. However, governmental techniques which aim at maintaining these principles must change in accordance with the conditions and needs of time and circumstances. According to Mabini, the exigencies of the times demanded a military dictatorship, simply to protect these principles. Mabini's article concluded:

> Could it not happen that the salvation of our ideals might depend upon a dictatorial Government? And if this should occur as a result of the contingencies of the struggles, would it be wise not to adopt such a form on account of its unconstitutionality? Drown the Constitutions and save the principles—we could and should then say.[15]

3. *The Proposed Amendments of Mabini.* When the Constitution was approved on November 29, 1898 by Congress, it was sent to Aguinaldo for his approval. However, Mabini urged Aguinaldo not to sign the document. But since Aguinaldo had already recognized that Congress had the power to promulgate a constitution, Mabini devised twelve proposed amendments that aimed principally to increase the power of the future President of the Republic—more specifically Aguinaldo. These proposed amendments are found in Aguinaldo's *Message* to Congress dated January 1, 1899. Aguinaldo was empowered to present such

[14] *Ibid.*
[15] *Ibid.*

proposals by virtue of Article XXIV, of the Decree of June 23, 1898.

The first amendment stated that the President of the Republic could, with the council of government and while the independence of the Philippines was not yet recognized by other nations, assume legislative powers when Congress was not in session. Both could also convoke Congress under critical circumstances. The seventh amendment empowered the President of the Republic to exercise a second veto on any act of Congress if either the internal or external security of the country was endangered. This veto was to be solely his responsibility. The eighth provided that when Congress assumed a hostile attitude towards the council of government and the circumstances of the nation were grave, the President of the Republic could dissolve Congress without the consent of the latter. The second and sixth amendments were intended to curtail the powers of the Permanent Commission— more specifically its legislative function—in favor of the council of government. The sixth amendment limited the Permanent Commission to the protection of the Constitution while Congress was not in session; to call Congress as a Court of Justice; and to carry out functions assigned to it by Congress. The third provided for the temporary suspension of the separation of Church and State, as provided for in Title III, Article 5, of the proposed constitution. However, the last amendment (Number 12) emphasized that all the above previous amendments were of a "provisional and transitory character." [16]

4. *The "Dictamen" of Calderón.* The Committee that drafted the proposed constitution, under the leadership of Calderón, reacted violently against the proposed amendments of Mabini as expressed in the *Message* of Aguinaldo. The specific objections of the Committee were formulated in the celebrated *Dictamen,* the author of which was Calderón. It is probable that this document reinforced congressional decisions to reject most of the amendments of Mabini. The lengthy document asserted that the proposed amendments were objectionable on two general grounds: the first was the suspicion that the strengthening of the Executive in the person of the President of the Republic resulted in a

---

[16] Cf. Taylor, *Philippine Insurgent Records,* Vol. III, Exhibit 352. The Spanish original may be found in Del Castillo y Kabangis, *op. cit.,* pp. 34-42.

corresponding weakening of the legislative power. This in turn could lead to the creation of "a despotism which, at a given moment, could absorb the whole country and convert an individual into both an autocrat and tyrant of the Islands." Further, "if an individual or dynasty could aggrandize a people, such an aggrandizement can only be temporary, and would exist only during the life of that individual . . . ." [17] Relevant to this point, the Committee objected to granting the President power of a second veto, for such power

> . . . was so extensive and omnipotent, that the labors of Congress would result into sterility; and neither would public opinion, nor the aspirations of the people, nor any other force, be able to prevail against the will of whosoever can employ the veto power.[18]

The Committee reacted quite negatively to Mabini's fourth amendment, which enabled the government to arrest any member of Congress believed to have acted against the security of the State. Symptomatic of a deep fear of the army and distrust of a possible military dictator was the action of the Committee in trying to reduce this proposed amendment to its logical conclusion: at the most unexpected moment there was nothing to prevent the whole of Congress from being declared a group of conspirators against the State—a situation that would surely engender tyranny.[19]

The second reason for opposing the amendments was based on more theoretical grounds. With regards to the veto power that Mabini desired to give the President, the Committee asserted that the granting of such a power violated the

> . . . indisputable principle and fundamental basis of constitutionalism, which is the division and absolute separation of the attributes of the powers of society; a principle that states that it is never the case that anyone of these powers could invade the sphere of action of the other . . . .[20]

It appears that to Calderón and the Committee, the theory of the division of the three powers of government was not con-

---

[17] Calderón, op. cit., Appendix, p. 107.
[18] Ibid., p. 108.
[19] Ibid., p. 110.
[20] Ibid.

ceived as a system of checks and balances. The division of power would rather be a system for the specialization of definite functions. The desire to have an omnipotent legislature demonstrates that the notion of "balance" was not at all important; and whatever "checking" was to be found amounted to nothing more than seeing to it on the part of the legislative that both the executive and the judiciary did not exceed the functions assigned to them. To Calderón, the division of powers was based on the different origins of these powers. To him, Congress, whose members were to be elected by the people, was the "true representative of the people" and its power was directly based on popular sanction. On the other hand, the government (or cabinet, in this sense), since it was appointed by the Chief Executive who in turn was elected by Congress, did not have as much a direct popular sanction as Congress. Thus, in any conflict between the government and Congress, the former should give way to another government. As Calderón put it:

> On the assumption that Congress is the true representative of the people, if it is in conflict with the government, it would then follow that the government is the one that does not have either the prestige or vote of the popular sanction. It is in cases like this, where grave political crises occur in constitutional governments, that the government must give its place to another.[21]

In connection with this particular discussion of the theory of the separation of powers in government, it is interesting to note briefly Mabini's general theory. On this count, Mabini's theory is similar to that of Calderón, and demonstrates further that his desire for a strong executive was a matter of temporary expediency. Mabini believed strongly in the predominance of the legislative power of government—but apparently only for peacetime practice. This theory of Mabini acquires greater significance in view of the fact that it was written on September 20, 1899, after the downfall of his cabinet. His general ideas on the separation of powers are as follows:

[21] *Ibid.,* Appendix, p. 111. Calderón wrote that in drafting the Malolos Constitution he based his studies on the French constitution at that time and on some South American constitutions, principally Costa Rica; he further asserted that there were similarities between the social system of South American countries and that of the Philippines.

> Society should have à soul: authority. This authority needs an intellect to guide and direct it: the legislative power. It also needs a will that is active and will make it work: the executive. It needs, too, a conscience that judges and punishes what is bad: the judicial power. These powers should be independent of one another, in the sense that one should never encroach upon the functions of the other; but the last two should be subordinated to the first, in the same manner that both will and conscience are subordinate to the intellect.[22]

These views clearly paralleled those of Calderón, in that they suggested the supremacy of the legislative to the other two powers. Mabini also implied that the division of powers was based partially on their origin and electoral responsibility. Like Calderón, he believed that both the executive and the judiciary were directly responsible to the legislative, which, in turn, was directly responsible to the people.

> The executive and the judiciary cannot depart from the laws passed by the legislative, in the same manner that it is said that a citizen cannot infringe upon the laws. Whereas the executive and the judiciary are judged by the legislative, this has no other judge but public opinion, or better said, the people. The guarantee for the proper functioning of the legislative is its truly representative character (*pluralidad de sus miembros*), and the public character of its sessions.[23]

Mabini characteristically concluded:

> The power to legislate is the highest manifestation of authority, just as the intellect is the noblest faculty of the soul. But this subordination is not one of hierarchy but of both order and harmony. If from the three faculties of the soul (intellect, will, and conscience) virtue is born, from the harmony of the three powers of government, good government emerges. Virtue produces the happiness of the individual; similarly, good government produces the greatness of society and the well-being of its members.[24]

Going back to the amendments of Mabini, it was the strength of the opposition by Mabini and his group that led Congress to add certain "Temporary Articles" to the proposed Constitution. Also, the threat of war with the United States made it imperative

---

[22] "La Trinidad Política," *La Revolución Filipina,* Vol. II, p. 69. The above and following arguments of Mabini are significant in regard to his opinion that society may be viewed as having a collective mind. Cf. *ibid.*

[23] *Ibid.*

[24] *Ibid.*

for all factions to settle their differences. From this view, the "Temporary Articles" may be seen as a compromise between the group led by Calderón and that of Mabini.

"Temporary Articles" 99 and 101 of the approved Constitution did in effect strengthen the executive power. Article 99 provided in part that during the struggle for independence the government could issue decrees on questions or difficulties not provided for by law. The decrees were then to be communicated to either the Permanent Commission or Congress. Article 101 provided that

> . . . the laws returned by the President of the Republic to Congress can not be replaced until the legislature of the following year, the President and his council of government being responsible for the suspension.[25]

"Temporary Article" 100 provided for the temporary suspension of the 5th Article of Title III of the originally proposed constitution. This is the article which provided for the separation of Church and State. "Temporary Article" 100 was in consonance with Mabini's third proposed amendment.

5. *General Support of a Strong Government.* Both Mabini and Calderón believed in a strong government. Yet this belief did not contradict their desire to have a "limited" government, a concept involving the recognition of an area in man's personality to be protected by government. Filipinos, in general, looked forward to government to make the good life possible for them. Even during the Spanish regime, in spite of the fact that the foreign character of the government was dimly recognized, people looked to government for guidance in the improvement of their social and economic life. When an opportunity for a Filipino government materialized during the days of the Revolution, it was to be expected that a great part of the population would desire and believe that their government would be able to give them many of those liberties and material aids they had never before possessed. In brief, a Filipino government was conceived as a positive tool to give the people something they never had during the Spanish regime.

But in any case, historically speaking, Filipinos were used to a strong government. This was probably due, principally, to both

[25] M. Kalaw, *The Development of Philippine Politics*, p. 444.

the nature of the highly centralized form of Spanish government in the Philippines and also to the existence of a normally strong Governor-General directly representing the Spanish King.[26] The proclamation of Aguinaldo's dictatorship and the Decree of June 23, 1898, establishing the Revolutionary government with Aguinaldo as President, were therefore consistent with this past. During the regime of the Revolutionary government, direct intervention in local and provincial elections was provided for by law—however, with the reservation that this intervention was only for a "transitory period." Even in the Malolos Constitution, which represented a shift in the control of governmental powers from the sole monopoly of military leaders of the Revolution to its sharing with the *ilustrados,* the Central government was empowered to intervene in provincial and municipal governments. Article 82 of the 11th Title provided, among others, for the

> Intervention of the government, and in the proper case of the national assembly in order to prevent the provincial and municipal corporations from exceeding their powers, to the prejudice of general and individual interests.
>
> Determination of their powers in the matter of taxes, in order that the provincial and municipal taxation may never be antagonistic to the system of taxation of State.[27]

With regard to the intervention of the Central government of the Philippine Republic in provincial and municipal affairs and with the above Article no doubt in mind, the Schurman Commission wrote:

> The idea of "intervention" which is foreign to American practice, is fundamental to the whole political life and thought of the Filipinos. Acquired from long experience with Spanish methods of government, the idea has taken such a firm hold in the mind of the Filipinos that they find government of any kind inconceivable without it.[28]

The observation of the Commission may be accepted as valid in so far as they assert that the idea of "intervention" may

---

[26] One of the main conclusions of Alejandro Fernandez in his researches on the office of the Spanish Governor-General was that it served as a basis for the tradition of a strong executive in actual practice in the Philippines; even after the Revolution. Cf. Fernandez, *op. cit.* (Conclusion).

[27] M. Kalaw, *The Development of Philippine Politics,* p. 442.

[28] *Report of the Philippine Commission,* Vol. I, pp. 91-92.

have been greatly influenced by the Spanish system of government, and that the Spanish system was the only form of government which the Filipinos were intimately acquainted with. But it should be added that the idea itself was just an instance of the desire for a strong government—a government which needed great powers to give the people benefits they never had before.

The Schurman Commission further pointed out that Filipinos never dreamt of the "American plan" of giving the chief executive large powers and then holding him directly accountable for them This, the Commission added, was because they made the chief executive irresponsible and his Secretaries responsible directly to the legislature. In general, it was further asserted, the Filipino system of government was a system of general distrust, of divided power, and of indirect responsibility. Also:

> This complex system, which violates so many of the vital principles laid down by Hamilton and Madison in *The Federalist*, is undoubtedly an attempt along these Spanish lines with which alone the Filipinos were familiar, to circumvent knavish and oppressive rulers whom a long experience had accustomed them to regard as an inevitable part of government.[29]

The Commission's assertion that there was a general fear and distrust of a strong chief executive among the Filipinos must, so far as valid, be confined solely to the ideas expressed in the Malolos Constitution. Actually, the proclamation of he dictatorship and the decree establishing a revolutionary government, which in effect gave the Revolutionary President dictatorial powers, were quite in consonance with the general trend of Filipino habits and expectations at that time. Thus, the Malolos scheme of government may be viewed as a temporary reaction to the idea of a strong chief executive, less because a strong executive as such was feared, but because the *ilustrados* feared a strong executive in the person of Aguinaldo, who did not come from their ranks If Aguinaldo had come from their ranks, it is probable that the system of government created at Malolos might have followed another course. Malolos witnessed a contest between a leadership of the masses and a leadership of the *ilustrados*. However, during the war with the United States, the Filipino government in prac-

[29] *Ibid.,* p. 93.

tice reverted to the kind of system conceived in the Decree of June 23, 1898. That is, Aguinaldo was still the strong chief executive.[30] However, all throughout Aguinaldo's leadership and even after his capture, he always received from all the respect and deference due to the position he acquired in Filipino society. The *ilustrados* were among the first to offer him the symbolic courtesy befitting his office.

Regardless of the problem as to whether the executive or the legislative was to predominate, it was agreed by both Mabini and Calderón that the Central government had to be a strong one. They also agreed that personal despotism had to be eliminated. Mabini believed that a dictator need not be a despot. Calderón believed that the absence of a dictator automatically eliminated this possibility; but, ironically, he did not consider that tyranny could also be exercised by an "intellectual oligarchy." In spite of what might be said against Calderón, he deserves credit for his desire to create a governmental system that would acquire the character of durability and adequacy—for war or for peace.

The Revolution unmistakably showed a trend towards strong centralized government. The desire to have a national Church that could be to some extent controlled by the government showed this. Further evidence of this trend was the dissolution by Aguinaldo of the *Katipunan* on July 15, 1898 on the pretext that the country had been converted into a huge *Katipunan* and that therefore its nature as a secret society was no longer necessary.[31] Aguinaldo also declared any form of secret society to be illegal. It may be suggested that the dissolution of the *Katipunan,* which was a society signifying a mass movement, also previewed the coming to power of the *ilustrados* who were to share in the control of the governmental functions of the Philippine government.

6. *The Bill of Rights of the Malolos Constitution.* The Bill of Rights of the Malolos Constitution is the most elaborate document which expresses some of the deepest aspirations of the Filipino

---

[30] Cf. Taylor, *Report on Organization,* p. 15.
[31] When war with the United States commenced, various local *"katipunan"* groups came into existence to stiffen resistance against the United States Army.

people. It was a testimony to the principle held by their leaders that a function of government was to maintain freedom in a society where law prevailed. It also reveals why a revolution was launched. The Bill of Rights comprised nearly thirty per cent of the text of the Constitution.

Articles 7, 8, and 9 stated that no person could be subject to arbitrary arrest and detention and that certain judicial procedures for both arrest and detention were required. Article 14 provided that no Filipino could be prosecuted or sentenced except by a competent judge or tribunal and in accordance with law. Article 15 stated that any person detained or imprisoned without judicial procedures should be discharged on either his petition or that of any other Filipino.

Article 10 provided for the right of domicile. It stated that no person may enter the domicile of either a Filipino or foreigner without his consent except in cases of emergencies like flood, earthquake, fire, etc. Article 13 provided among other things that in case of forcible entry the aggrieved party had the "right to demand the responsibilities which ensue." [32] Article 11 provided that no person may be compelled to change his residence except by virtue of law. Article 25 allowed any person the freedom to change his residence provided that he was in the full enjoyment of his civil rights. Part of Article 30 specifically prohibited the government to banish any Filipino away from the country. This article, more than any other one, demonstrates that the lawmakers at Malolos were conditioned by the experiences of the past.

Article 12 provided for the freedom of correspondence, while Article 13 stated among other things that any detention or search of correspondence had to be done in accordance to law and had to be "justified."

Articles 16 and 17 provided that no person could be deprived of his property except by virtue of a judicial sentence. The property that is temporarily or permanently taken is to be used for reasons of "necessity and common welfare" and the person deprived of his property is to be indemnified.

[32] In this section all quotations from the Malolos Constitution are taken from: "The Political Constitution of the Philippine Republic." Found in Maximo Kalaw's *The Development of Philippine Politics, 1872-1920*, Appendix. D.

Article 18 provided that no taxes shall be imposed upon the people unless decided upon by Congress or other legally authorized "popular corporations."

Article 19 stated that no Filipino "who may be in the full enjoyment of his political and civil rights shall be hindered in the free exercise of the same." Article 20 provided that no Filipino could be deprived of the freedom of speech, communication and association. Neither could an individual or a group be denied the right to petition to the "public powers and to the authorities." The freedom of religious worship was found in Article 5 of the Third Title.

A most interesting provision was that of Article 28. This stated that the enumeration of rights did not "imply the prohibition of any other not expressly delegated." This article suggests that the framers of the Constitution believed in the existence of natural rights, and therefore natural law that create these. It could have expressed a fear that there existed other rights not expressedly stated in positive law.

Article 30 stated that Articles 7, 8, 9, 10, 11, and 20 (except the particular provision of the right of petition) could be suspended provided three conditions were satisfied. These were that the suspension had to be done in accordance with law; had to be temporary; and had to be based on a reason involving the security of the state. It is important to note that in no case could the right to petition by either an individual or a group be suspended by the government. This reflected an attitude of hope among Filipinos that as a paternalistic system, government was a positive agent to redress grievances.[33]

7. *Actual Exercise of Rights during the Revolution.* A judgment of the merits of the Bill of Rights of the Malolos Constitution, in so far as its actual applicability was concerned, is quite difficult. The reason is that within a month after it went into effect, war broke out between American and Filipino troops. It may be asserted that the Republic was disrupted the moment the

[33] According to Justice Malcolm of the Supreme Court of the Philippines, some elements of the Malolos Constitution found their way into the Philippine Constitution of 1935. These were the provisions regarding the right of domicile, freedom of correspondence and communications, and the right to form associations. Cf. Arsenio Manuel, *A Portrait of Felipe G. Calderón: Father of the Malolos Constitution* (Manila, Bookman Inc., 1954), p. 26.

Filipino Army was disbanded into different guerrilla groups, under their respective commanders in November, 1899. Since the Constitution went into effect in January, 1899, the Republic did not survive for more than ten months. These months witnessed a republic that was losing territory day by day and a capital that was changing from site to site.

The Bill of Rights of the Malolos Constitution actually made explicit some of the "rights" already exercised during the days of the Revolutionary government. Among these was the frequent practice of petitioning the government to redress grievances. It was quite usual for leading citizens of a town to write petitions to Aguinaldo, as president of the government, complaining about certain irregularities in the elections of officials and the interference of military officers in the elections.[34] Other complaints signed by a number of inhabitants requested the abolition of taxes on vehicles and draft animals.[35] Complaints against the abuses of civil authorities were also found.[36] That these complaints could exist and the petitioners not suffer imprisonment or exile (unlike the Spanish regime) demonstrates that the government did not intend to perpetuate the ways of the Spanish government. The situation permits the inference that Filipinos felt that the government was their own and would listen to their grievances.

The press during the Revolution was relatively free. Not only did the government establish an official organ on July 4, 1898, but it also encouraged the people to contribute articles to it with the intention of raising the level of the political education of the Filipino people. The government also encouraged the publication of privately owned newspapers. However, in at least one case, Aguinaldo actually asked the editor of La Independencia, a revolutionary paper, not to print articles that were prejudicial to the government. This happened on July 31, 1899, after some government officials did not like some of the views of Mabini in his article, "Something for Congress." [37]

---

34 File 1200 of the "Philippine Insurgent Records Compilation" belonging to the U.S. War Department in the National Archives in Washington, D.C., contains many original copies of these kinds of complaints by Filipino citizens.

35 J. Taylor, Philippine Insurgent Records, Vol. II, 95 HS.

36 Cf. ibid., Vol. III, Exhibit 67 for a letter of Cecilio Apostol, a Filipino poet, complaining about the abuses of certain officials.

37 Cf. J. Taylor, Philippine Insurgent Records, Vol. IV, Exhibit 684.

An interesting case showed that the high officials of the Republic were determined to realize the trial provisions of the Bill of Rights. This case involved General Antonio Luna, one of the ablest military men of the Revolution. As Mabini, who was then president of the Cabinet, told Aguinaldo on March 6, 1899:

> Many complaints have been received here on account of the abuses committed by General Luna. It is said that he has lately published a decree in which he warned the people that those who disobey his orders shall be shot to death without summary trial. He ordered in Bocaue a Chinaman shot to death without summary trial . . . . To be shot to death without summary trial is a punishment which can be inflicted on soldiers, but a chief cannot enforce it in a civilized community . . . . [38]

The Bill of Rights was taken very seriously by the revolutionary leaders. It was the main thing which they could offer the Filipino people, in order that consent to the government could be preserved—for what were the Revolution's goals, if not the securing of certain rights believed to be prior to all government or law?

8. *The Role of the "Ilustrado" in the Revolution.* Although the Malolos Constitution was never put into full force due to the outbreak of hostilities between American and Filipino troops, it nevertheless demonstrated what the most educated segment of the population wanted as the form of their own government. Just how the educated segment was able to gain control of Congress and to command a greater say in governmental affairs (to the extent that it was able to promulgate a constitution which, in theory at least, lessened the powers of the very man who allowed them to constitute a congress) deserves some discussion.

In the first place, Aguinaldo had the loyalty of the bulk of the revolutionary soldiers. His leadership of the *Katipunan* after the Tejeros Conference was undisputed. Now, during the early days of the Revolution against Spain, many members of the educated class and of the small but rising middle-class may not have directly favored the upheaval; at all events they feared it. But when the Revolution showed signs of success, many of the *ilustrados* joined it—-motivated possibly by patriotic principles or ties of consanguinity.

[38] *Ibid.,* Exhibit 618.

But these men had no intention of being governed by the leaders of the masses. On the contrary, they were out to grasp the leadership of the Revolution to insure that no one but themselves would govern.[39] Yet the revolutionists welcomed these men, because Filipinos have always placed a high premium on education. Habit may have led them, too, to seek the advice of those men upon whom they had always reposed confidence.

When Aguinaldo became dictator after his return to the Philippines, it became clear to him that the support of the *ilustrados* was essential. There was a government and a system of administration that had to be run. It was important, too, to let the educated segment of the population belong to a movement that needed the support of the entire population. Mabini's primary aim in having a Revolutionary congress was to secure greater sanction for the leadership of a man who was already recognized by the masses. Thus, to Mabini's mind, the Revolutionary Congress was merely an advisory body, that is, it was created merely to give formal sanction to a *de facto* leadership. But once organized, and then having been consulted on governmental matters, Congress was not content in remaining a mere consultative body. On the contrary, it was determined to have a greater share in the government. The result was that Congress was able to go to the extent of promulgating a constitution intended to make the legislative the supreme force of the country. It is ironic that the Revolutionary Congress, a brain-child of Mabini, was the very body responsible for the downfall of his cabinet and probably the cause of his having left political office. With or without Congress and a constitution, Aguinaldo

[39] An interesting and important, but tentative, essay of the relations between the educated class and the masses in the Philippines is Teodoro Agoncillo's "The Filipino Intellectuals and the Revolution." This is found in *Philippine Social Sciences and Humanities Review*, XVII (June, 1953).

Agoncillo well demonstrated the aversion that Filipino intellectuals had towards revolution and how many of them decided to join the band wagon only when it showed signs of success. However, his tendency to identify the *"ilustrados"* with the "middle class" disregards the fact that membership of the former crossed economic lines. The *"ilustrados"* were essentially a social class. It would not have been difficult to localize this class as the educated Filipino could have been easily differentiated from the bulk of the population. It is to be expected, however, that most of the *"ilustrados"* would come from the economically better-off groups in the Philippines. It may be emphasized that the Propagandists and other *"ilustrados"* sympathetic to reforms either from Spain or the Revolution, came from the "lower middle-class" and not from the most opulent Filipino families.

would have been secure in the loyalty of the masses. But to have the support of the educated segment of the population and therefore part of the rising middle-class in the Philippines, he had to go a long way to please this group. However, whatever personal ambitions he may have had, it is quite probable that personally he did believe the Revolution would be better guided and, therefore, led to a successful conclusion with the advice of educated Filipinos.[40]

That the members of the Malolos Congress were sincere in their republican and constitutional programs may be safely assumed, for in many ways they were the products of the liberal ideas that had already spread in Europe by the end of the nineteenth century; but it is equally likely that the masses would have required a long time to grasp fully those republican ideas. Nor could they easily have thrown overboard habits of obedience that were inculcated in them by both Church and State during Spanish times. Democracy cannot be born overnight. Yet the fact that a larger proportion of the population was given the right to elect local officials (who in turn were able to elect provincial officials) induced in part of the general population a taste for certain democratic processes; a taste difficult to forget overnight.

[40] It was not with some admixture of hope and sarcasm that in one of the addresses of Aguinaldo in Malolos on September 15, 1898, he said: "There are educated men who do not wish the revolution to profit by their education, but who stand aside waiting for the end of the war, and this in spite of the fact they are intelligent people. This government has many detractors who say that it is an incapable one, and yet it is their duty to aid these ignorant men in their efforts for the success of our cause; they ought not to stand separate from us because we are like brothers to each other." Taylor, *Philippine Insurgent Records*, Vol. III, Exhibit 246. This message is interesting in that it referred to a small group of conservative well-to-do Filipinos in Manila who found it to their own material convenience to display a form of "neutralism."

Aguinaldo, like Andrés Bonifacio, assumed that wealthy Filipinos would support the Revolution—both as Filipinos and as persons desiring to get rid of foreign domination. With this assumption, they failed to be aware of the possibility that some Filipinos, on account of their economic interests, would fear any change of the *status quo*. In other words many rich Filipinos believed that the Revolution presented a danger to their economic interests. One can just imagine Bonifacio's feelings and surprise when wealthy Filipinos, not only refused to give monetary aid to the *Katipunan*, but were horrified at the revolutionary aims of the society. Aguinaldo showed bitterness when some of his "compatriots" were more interested in the security behind the ramparts of Intramuros, which was under American rule, than in proffering their services to their "own" Filipino government at Malolos. Here we see another of the divisive elements that plagued the Revolution.

In the light of these factors, John Taylor's assertion that in all probability the word "republic" was bound to disappear in the Philippines in any case displays an element of prejudice. One reason he gave was that the masses did not have an adequate conception of what it meant to be citizens of a republic. Further evidence adduced by Taylor was the manner in which the people addressed Aguinaldo in their letters and, also, their general attitude in dealing with governmental authorities.[41] In another part of his work, Taylor wrote with regard to the republican program of the Philippine government:

> Within these lines the men of greater intelligence dreamed of a government to be conducted for their exclusive benefit under the name of a republic. The great mass of the people who had gathered there knew nothing of a republic . . . . Many of them have lived for generation after generation upon the same land, and when not under the control of the friars, under the dominion of that class of natives who called themselves "ilustrados" (enlightened men), whose blood is, in almost every case, partly Spanish or partly Chinese. The supremacy of the friars was passing, and men of this class intended to be, in all things, the heirs to their domain.[42]

It is of the essence of a revolution that a group should attempt to seize by force the powers of government; and such a group need not, at least historically speaking, come from the masses. A revolution begun by the masses may, however, undergo a shift in leadership when a special group takes away the leadership from them. This is what actually happened in the case of the Philippine Revolution. Still, not all of the leaders were narrowly self-interested; there were some men in this special group who had the interest of all in mind—an attitude that required disinterestedness and an ability to dissociate oneself from the class or group of one's origin. The Philippines had men of this sort and Mabini may be considered as a paradigm. He firmly believed that if a democracy were to survive and remain strong, it must be based on active participation of all the people in the processes

---

[41] Cf. *Philippine Insurgent Records*, Vol. II, 73-74 LY. To a great extent, Taylor mistook the courtesy and stock phrases which social grace and Latin courtesy demanded in the matter of signatures, to signify obsequiousness on the part of the Filipinos. Such social convention need not be contradictory to one's democratic beliefs.

[42] *Ibid.*, Vol. I, 28 FZ.

of government. His electoral system was a step towards this end. Thus, even though initially the leadership of the Republic tended to become the monopoly of the *ilustrados,* their propaganda and increasingly large concessions to the democratic mood developed expectations of even greater concessions. Many people became conscious of being citizens of a Filipino Republic. Had the Americans not destroyed the Republic, this feeling would, in all probability, have continued to become more and more widely diffused among the people. Further demands for an increased participation in government would have been made. But, for the moment, at least, History was to take a different turn.

CHAPTER NINE: *Conclusions and Observations*

THE POLITICAL AND constitutional ideas of the Philippine Revolution originated from the social class in the Philippines historically known as the *ilustrados*. The members of this class, whose peculiar position in Filipino society sprang from the education and also the manner in which they were looked up to by the people to guide them and voice their aspirations, were the first to demand from Spain certain reforms. Among these was the recognition of those "rights" which belonged to the general stream of ideas of late eighteenth century European Liberalism. Within the decade before and up to 1896, a group of educated Filipinos in Spain known as the "propagandists," began a movement directed to exposing before Spanish officialdom and public, the need for the granting of political and social reforms to the Philippines. The "Propaganda Movement" may be viewed as a movement initially intended to gain for the educated segment of the Philippines (in particular those from the lower middle-class) a greater hand in the political control and the shaping of the destiny of their country. It may be suggested that most members of the opulent Filipino families were initially not averse to the continuance of the *status quo* under Spain.

The propagandists not only contended that they were voicing the actual aspirations of the people but, also, that they knew what was good for the people. All the instruments of mass communication were used: books, newspaper articles, pamphlets, oratory, and group gatherings. The continuous agitation and proddings of the propagandists at home and abroad made the masses more aware of the political and social inequalities prevalent in their country. Although generally inarticulate for more than three centuries of Spanish rule, they began to realize that their country belonged to them. The masses were stirred and gradually a popular leadership was born.

When it became clear that the Spanish government would not heed the demands of the propagandists, a revolution appeared as the sole alternative. The *Katipunan* may be considered a mass movement initially intended to achieve by force what the propagandists failed to accomplish by peaceful methods. As the *Katipunan* society took over the initiative in creating moral and political ideals in order to make the Filipino people more of a community, its membership grew to the extent of including a few *ilustrados* and Filipino priests. But the armed uprising in 1896 was practically the sole work of the *Katipunan*.

In the resurgence of the Revolution in 1898, when the Revolution showed signs of success and when American cooperation was believed to be contributory to consolidation of the revolutionists' gains, many of the *ilustrados* joined the Revolution. For these men, who considered themselves to be natural leaders in guiding their countrymen, would not easily be denied a share of a movement that showed signs of success. Essentially, the problem was transformed into the question of which social and economic class was going to control the country. Yet, the masses themselves, either by habit or by the felt need for guidance in an organization that had attained national proportions, were actually the very ones who invited the *ilustrados* to play a role in the Revolution. The influence of these *ilustrados* in the towns made their support indispensable for the success of the Revolution.

Because of the complexities of government and the necessity of dealing with foreign powers, the role of the *ilustrado* in the latter days of the Revolution assumed an important character. Thus all the constitutional ideas and abstract declarations of intention of the Revolution and therefore the relatively more sophisticated political ideas of the Revolution came from this group. With the disintegration of the Philippine Republic, many of the *ilustrados* abandoned what they thought had become a lost cause. The last few days of the Revolution witnessed a tenacious struggle personally led by a leader who directly sprang from the masses. It thus became a losing struggle that may be said to have been "politically" unguided. The political and constitutional principles of the Philippine Revolution came from a group including both educated men and mass leaders who were essentially voicing the general line of thinking laid down by the educated men.

The political thinkers of the Philippine Revolution were voicing demands and ideas that were current in the minds of contemporary Spanish liberals. These, is turn, were the ideas of the eighteenth century Enlightenment: belief in natural law and natural rights. This belief was secular because religion was dispensed with as a sanction for natural law. Another common element between the thinkers of the Enlightenment and the propagandists and the leaders of the *Katipunan* was the desire to reconstruct a new way of life and build a new society. The individuality of a person was emphasized, even though it was maintained that he had a definite position in society and that it was a duty for him to work for the welfare of all. To facilitate the building of a new way of life, legal and moral norms were held necessary. Believing that consent and not force was the basis for Authority, Filipino thinkers utilized the "compact theory." This theory also served as a justification for revolution. Nowhere is the influence of the Enlightenment more evident than in the belief man had great intellectual and moral potentialities. These were held to be conducive to Progress.

It may seem anachronistic to find in the Philippines during the last quarter of the nineteenth century, a set of ideas that had been voiced by French political thinkers a hundred and fifty years earlier. That the Enlightenment should affect the Philippines so long after the peak of its flowering, can only be understood in the light of the deliberate material, cultural, intellectual, and religious isolation of the Philippines. Events in the Philippines in the last quarter of the nineteenth century were analogous to what might have happened in Europe during the thirteenth century if the Enlightenment were suddenly thrust into it. The liberal ideas of the propagandists were not in any sense inferior or less sophisticated than those of their Spanish counterparts. The fact was that Spain in the last century was comparatively backward, when compared to the general trend of political ideas prevalent in the other countries of Western Europe.

Most Filipino political thinkers were greatly influenced by Spanish Masonry, since most of them were members of it. This is a possible source of many of the ideas of the Enlightenment that crept into the literature of Filipino political thinkers. But unlike French Masonry, which substituted Comte's positivism of the materialistic and mechanistic type for the spirit of the Enlightenment, Spanish and Filipino Masonry stuck to the Enlightenment and its republican tradition. In common with Spanish and French Masonry, Filipino Masonry was decidedly anti-clerical. In the context of Philippine history, "anti-clerical" was usually equivalent to "anti-Spanish friar." There was no manifest wave of resentment or antagonism towards the Filipino clergy during the Propaganda days and the beginning of the Revolution. On the contrary, both "anti-clericals" and Filipino priests were solidly antagonistic to the Spanish friars. But during the latter part of the Revolution, with a partial solution of the friar problem, possible sources of conflicts between the Filipino clergy and revolutionary leaders, sprang.

The ideas of the Filipino political thinkers from the time of the Propaganda Period up to the time of the promulgation of the Malolos Constitution provided the bulk of the political and constitutional ideas of the Revolution.

Man was created by God and endowed with certain intellectual and moral faculties. These had a natural propensity for good, and the situation where they were allowed to be developed, unhindered, was "freedom." It was principally by the development of the intellect and the enjoyment of virtue that man attained the good life. This was equivalent to stating that without freedom, the good life was not possible. Since man had a "natural right" to all those conditions that made intellectual development and virtue possible, freedom was a natural right. Whether natural rights were based directly on Nature or God was of no consequence, since God was conceived as the ultimate author of Nature and natural law. Freedom also implied the consonance of man's reason and action with the requirements of natural law. Rizal's concept of freedom was more complex than those of the other propagandists. The free individual was one who had actually developed himself both intellectually and morally and who opposed any tyranny that might have hindered this development. If need be, the free individual should be willing to give his life in opposition to this tyranny. Rizal believed that an increase of both intelligence and virtue implied an increase of freedom. To state that man had a right to "self-respect" and "dignity," only meant that both society and government had to recognize that man had natural rights.

On the subject of the necessity of government and of the nature of political obligation, and therefore revolution, it was Mabini who presented a detailed theory: society was primarily a collection of individuals gathered together for the mutual satisfaction of economic wants. The existence of individuals in society who appropriated for themselves the products of the labor of others, constituted a violation of the natural right to the products of one's labor and therefore a loss of his freedom. Thus the necessity of Authority or government. The coercive power of government was derived from the people and existed primarily to prevent a loss of freedom. As such government was conceived as subordinate to the well-being of the individual and constructed for maintaining harmonious relations in society. Consequently when the government, once come into power, took away freedom from men, that is, violated natural law, all political obligation to it automatically became nullified. This was one of Mabini's justifications for revolution. In defining revolution as a popular movement designed to overthrow a government that existed solely for the benefit of a special class in society, Mabini showed a general awareness of socialistic doctrines.

In Mabini's view, the Philippine Revolution had a Messianic element that was related to other peoples of the Malay race. The Revolution was intended to serve as a model for the social emancipation of those peoples who were racially linked to the Filipinos. As such, the Philippine Revolution may be understood as heralding the eventual emancipation of other Asian nations from the yoke of colonial domination.

The demand for both self-respect and dignity as understood by Rizal is significant in the light of the Philippine scene during the days before the Revolution. The Spanish colonial authorities at that time always considered themselves to be not only racially superior to the Filipinos, but had even questioned the capacity of the Filipino to attain the intellectual and moral heights claimed by the Spaniards. Opportunities of intentionally humiliating Filipinos were seldom missed. On the basis of the theory of natural rights, it was asserted by Filipino thinkers that the Spanish government and the Spanish friars were the agents that caused the Filipinos to be deprived of their freedom and natural rights. The propagandists were asking from the Spanish government that minimum number of rights which they believed properly belonged to man *qua* man. Among these, in the political sphere, was the right to freedom of speech, press, communication, association, religion and petition. Also, the propagandists attacked arbitrary arrest and arbitrary deportation or exile to other islands and they asked that the people be protected from both the abuses of the *guardia civil,* and the constant meddling into their everyday life by a *frailocracia.* More positively they sought increased participation in local government, more opportunities for education, and more control of the parishes by members of the Filipino clergy.

It was a daring step for the *Katipunan* to take when it resorted to force in order to recapture those rights believed to have been granted by Nature—when all other means were believed to have been futile. The *Katipunan* in maintaining that Spanish rule in the Philippines was historically based on an original "Blood Compact," presented a technique utilized for justifying a revolt against Spain. The justification was that not only did the Spanish government not fulfill the terms of the compact but actually violated it by its tyranny. Essentially, the *Katipunan* was presenting a plea for a government by consent. Thus the *Katipunan* continued the tradition of the propagandists who maintained that the Spanish government was not one of consent but of pure coercion. It was on this very issue that Rizal emphatically demanded that the Spanish government had therefore to be as "moral" as possible. Now, how a government could be moral without the recognition of the natural rights of Filipinos appeared to be a paradox. Such a paradox was dissolved by the demand of the propagandists for full "assimilation" by Spain. This would have made the Philippines a part of Spain.

The struggle for the recognition and securing of political rights assumed notable proportions as proved by the incorporation of a bill of rights in the several constitutional projects. And no document was more symptomatic of Filipino hopes and desires than the Malolos Constitution. The Bill of Rights of this constitution may be viewed as an attempt to legalize aspirations derived from certain philosophical convictions and decisions of Filipino intellectuals. Thus the chain between the propagandists and the fathers of the Malolos Constitution had been forged: what was primarily sought was the recognition of those rights which were believed essential to man's well-being and self-respect. From this point of view, the Philippine Revolution was part of that tradition which brought about those great political movements that shook France and the United States in the last quarter of the eighteenth century.

Noticeable in the peaceful struggle for the recognition of rights by the propagandists, in the legal formulation of rights at Malolos, and in the theoretical defenses of the Revolution was the all-pervading influence of the doctrine of natural law. It might be suggested that the doctrine took a form similar to that of the Enlightenment. Natural law was held to be immutable, universal, and a law of reason. It was independent of religion. It was prior to any legal norm and served as a model and corrective to positive law. It also determined the morality of human actions. All the claims for rights were based on natural law. Yet the manner in which the principle of natural law was assumed by Filipinos was not without a Scholastic flavor. This latter situation may have been due either to habits of language and thought acquired by training in Catholic schools and universities in the Philippines, or to a conscious desire not to break completely from certain cultural and religious patterns of the country. Consequently, the attempt to secularize the sanctions of rights and duties was not entirely divorced from the concept of God. But the Church, as a corporation or as a system of theological doctrines, was entirely left out as a sanction of moral law. That men in the Philippines could talk in terms of secular moral values or base these on God as conceived in a deistic fashion, and at the same time gain a lot of willing ears, demonstrates that the historic function of the Spanish Church in Filipino society was, if not questioned, actually dispensed with.

Nowhere is the assumption of natural law more evident than in the belief that for a revolution to be successful, the element of morality should be present both in its leaders and their followers. What morality here meant could not conceivably be different from the general patterns of moral behavior as understood in the Hebraic-Christian tradition—considering that the majority of Fili-

pinos were Christians. The historic process was also conceived
as part of God's plan. It was on this account that there was
the belief that if the protagonists of the Revolution did not act
in terms of what was required by natural law, in some way
or another, they would be punished—at least the Revolution would
fail. Consequently, the Revolution to some extent showed a conscious effort to avoid the bloody abuses of other revolutions.
This effort is meaningful only relative to the Filipino belief in a
moral order in the universe. However, this belief does not ex-
clude the other conscious attempts of Filipino leaders to convince foreign powers that they were not as culturally backward
as portrayed by their former colonial masters.

The Philippine Revolution was essentially an attempt to break
away from much that belonged to the past. The theory of natural
law and natural rights was not resorted to in order to fight for
a *status quo*. On the contrary, it was adhered to as a rallying
sign for the construction of a society whose characteristics were
dimly anticipated. A whole social and political system had to be
either abandoned or reconstructed "nearer to the heart's desire."

Within the political and social context of the Philippines, it
may be expected that ideas of Western import may acquire a
different meaning in use. The Bill of Rights of the Malolos Constitution presented to the people might have entailed in actual life
a certain variation from that originally intended by people who
were trained in the liberal tradition of Europe. Long-ingrained
habits of subservience and the calculated brutalization of the
people would not easily permit them to adapt themselves fully
with ease and familiarity to a new way of life. The short life
of the Philippine Republic does not allow an analysis of what
might have occurred in the application of the bill of rights, but
certain observations may be ventured: it is safe to assume that
Filipino political leaders, especially those at Malolos, believed that
regardless of whether or not certain laws were suitable to the educational level of the inhabitants or their actual social mores, they could
in time instill among the people certain new habits of thoughts
and develop in them a sense of expectation for certain future
situations provided for by legislation. After all, the very nature of the
Revolution demanded a radical change of social life.

The problem of Church and State is relevant to this discussion. Since for more than three centuries Filipinos were ruled by a sort of joint civil and ecclesiastical authority, and bearing in mind that the Church was an integral part of the daily life of the people, it might have been argued, as was done by some delegates to the Malolos Congress, that a unity of Church and State was the most "natural" thing for Filipino life; and that any form of legislation providing for a separation of Church and State would have done violence to their social mores and thereby cause a possible disruption in their everyday way of life. But other political leaders in the Malolos Congress argued that a system that had been tried for more than three centuries and which had produced so much suffering and dissension in the body politic, should give way to a radically different system. The mere fact that today the system of separation of Church and State in the Philippines appears to be working and that it has to some extent reduced the wave of anti-clericalism widely prevalent during the Revolution, shows that legislative activity may create a political and social situation entirely different from that existing before. However, during the Revolution, to prevent an abrupt departure from the past, the concept of a national Church which was to be Catholic steadily gained ground in the minds of political leaders.

The revolutionary fathers might have hoped that a new social system would be developed, provided they could also change old habits of obedience found among the Filipino people and instill new habits among them. Thus, the electoral laws of the Revolutionary government and the Republic were to be utilized to progressively extend democratic ideals and practices among a larger number of people. For not only was this the original intention of the laws, but people would not hesitate to have recourse to the means offered to them if in so doing they would achieve a greater control over their government. In any case, the Filipinos, having had an orientation in Spanish and Western ways and having been imbued by the Hebraic-Christian tradition, presented great potentialities for the ready acceptance of Western democratic ideas.

The Philippine political development showed a tendency towards a strong government. This was evident from the prohibition of secret societies and by actual attempts to encourage the formation of a national Church. The desire for a strong government represented the universal attitude of Filipinos looking forward to government as a tool to secure rights never before exercised for the last three hundred years. Yet government was limited in the sense that it had, by incorporation into the fundamental law of the land, to recognize the tenets of natural law demanding the inalienable rights of men. Since these rights were not found with the Filipinos before the Revolution, it was to be expected that a revolutionary government had to be a positive agent to guarantee these rights—hence a strong government. It is to be expected that a revolution leads to the strengthening of the State. The Philippine Revolution was no exception to this principle.

All parties in the Malolos Congress believed in strong government, but the problem was just which of the three divisions of the powers of government was to be strongest. Filipino tradition demanded a strong chief executive, provided that now such an executive was a Filipino. The cult of leadership was a prominent feature in the Philippine Revolution, where the masses looked forward to a strong leader to guide and lead them, and to be a symbol of those martial virtues that they held admirable. The desire for a strong executive on the part of the masses was neutralized by the demand for a strong legislative by the *ilustrados*. This did not mean that in principle these were devoid of a cult of the leader. It was suggested that if the actual leader of the masses during the Revolution was an *ilustrado,* the insistent demand for a strong legislative as against a weak or symbolic executive might not have taken the form it actually assumed. Contemporary events in the Philippines have shown that a Filipino legislative was not unwilling to grant greater governmental powers to certain dynamic leaders who were looked upon with unabashed awe and admiration. In the days of the Revolution, in spite of Aguinaldo's humble origin, he was always granted the courtesy due both his personality and the symbolic function of his office. The tradition of a strong government in the person of a strong executive may be partially due to the type of governmental system which the Filipinos were solely exposed to—a highly centralized government with a Spanish governor and captain-general who, formally, at least, was vested with strong executive powers.

The theory of the division of the powers of government was also shown to be, not a system of checks and balances, but rather one of a specialization of functions and origin of power. Since the legislative chose the chief executive, and in conjunction with this chose the chief justice of the Supreme Court, it stood above all the others in the hierarchial division of governmental powers. Since the doctrine of the supremacy of the legislative power was claimed to be based directly on the sanction of the people, unlike the other powers, the Malolos Constitution assumed as a postulate the theory of the supremacy of the people.

Whereas the attitudes of Filipino political leaders towards education and the moral uplift of the people were definite and did not present many variations, that attitude toward the future economic structure of the counry appeared to have been devoid of a definite and complex program. In all probability, the members of the *Katipunan* would have desired a kind of economic system that was communal in nature. This did not mean one in which everything was owned equally by all, but rather that the wealthy should share their good fortune with their less-fortuned brothers. It was a system that was primarily moral in character and probably close to the form of life of the early Christians. In practice, the *Katipunan* in its beginnings witnessed a type of relation among the members of the society that was characterized by mutual economic help. What the economic condition of the Philippines would have been if the doctrines of the *Katipunan* had prevailed may only be dimly guessed. It might have been expected that most of the *ilustrados* who came from the middle class might have looked with intense suspicion on the prospects of a future determined by the desires of the masses. In any case, both the Revolutionary government and the Republic perpetuated the Spanish system of taxation and form of property ownership. The lands taken from the Spanish monastic orders were not all distributed to the tenants or peasants who worked on them. Indeed, the government collected for itself what was formerly paid as *canon* of the friars. That there was an intention to give the land to those who could validate their claims to it, may not be doubted; but just how the distribution of land would take place and how the government would share in the control of agricultural properties, if and when the Revolution triumphed, cannot but be another guess.

If Western ideas assumed a less complex form in the Philippine scene, they were adequate both as an initial step and as a fertile source of ideas for political and social reconstruction. In a country where the bulk of the population was for many years isolated from any contact with both the Asian continent and the Reformation and other political movements in Europe, the ideas that were suddenly introduced were eagerly seized upon.

Although it may be asserted that, in general, the propagandists and the *katipuneros* had similar ends, their means differed. The "absolutists" like Mabini and the "constitutionalists" under Calderón's leadership, both intended to find means to control the possible abuses of the army and at the same time argued for a strong government. The proponents for either unity of Church and State or their separation, both intended to avoid the former particular Spanish system of unity of Church and State. All of these proponents believed, too, that it was essential to have some control of the Church by the State. That differences regarding the general aims of the Revolution were reduced to a minimum can be understood in the light of the times, of stress and war, which forced the political leaders to adopt, at least verbally, the same ends.

Since the Philippine Revolution never secured the full independence for the Philippines desired by its political leaders, it never witnessed the full application of those rights and liberties in the name of which it was launched. Had the Republic been allowed to exist, it may well be doubted whether the majority of the people would have immediately understood the full import of their "rights" and "duties," or the notion of a "republic." Yet the men who framed the Malolos Constitution believed that by raising the standard of education of the people, and by political indoctrination, the number of people who would understand these ideas would increase.

Yet the Philippine Revolution achieved many of the results intended by its protagonists. The mass movement it involved, the rise to prominence of a group of people able to demonstrate their political skills, and the infectious spread of the desire for independence, all contributed to a deep sense of nationalistic feeling and a social consciousness that became a permanent feature of the Philippine political scene after the Revolution. The Revolution was the school for the political education of Filipinos. It was thus possible to have an organized leadership that, by peaceful political methods, was in the end able to gain independence from the country that succeeded Spain in the Philippines. In dealing with the contemporary scene, it is not enough to consider the political principles of that country which made the final achievement of Philippine independence possible. It is also necessary to remember that the Filipino people and their leaders had taken up ideals and practices of self-government that permitted them ultimately to win independence. A people capable of producing such leaders as Burgos, Del Pilar, Rizal, Bonifacio, and Mabini proved that they deserved independence and had enough strength and vision of their own to achieve it.

Bibliography

Primary Sources

A. Books and Documents:

Agoncillo, Felipe. *To the American People*. Paris: Imprimerie et Librairie Centrales des Chemins de Fer, 1900.

Aguinaldo y Famy, Emilio. *Reseña Verídica de la Revolución Filipina*. Tarlak, Islas Filipinas: Imprenta Nacional, September 23, 1899. English versions are found in *Congressional Record* (1902), part vi, Volume 35, pp. 439-450; and *The Philippine Social Science Review,* Manila: University of the Philippines, Volume XIII, No. 2 (May, 1941), pp. 178-233.

Alejandrino, Jose. *La Senda del Sacrificio*. Manila: Loyal Press, 1933.

Ataviado, Juan. *The Philippine Revolution in the Bicol Region*. Manila: The Encal Press, 1953, Volume I. Original title: *Lucha y Libertad*.

Blair, Emma and James Robertson. *The Philippine Islands 1493-1898: Explorations by Early Navigators, Descriptions of the Islands and Their Peoples, Their History and Records of the Catholic Missions, as related in Contemporaneous Books and Manuscripts, Showing the Political, Economic, Commercial and Religious Conditions of Those Islands from Their Earliest Relations with European Nations to the Close of the Nineteenth Century.* Cleveland, Ohio: The Arthur Clark Company, 1907. Volume LII. This volume contains the following documents:

Internal Political Condition of the Philippines. Sinibaldo de Mas; Madrid, 1842.

The Philippines, 1860-1898; some documents and bibliographical notes. James A. LeRoy; Durango, Mexico, 1907.

Constitution of the Liga Filipina. José Rizal; Tondo, July 3, 1892. The Friar Memorial of 1898. Manuel Gutierrez, O.S.A. and others; Manila, April 21, 1898.

Blanco Erenas Riera y Polo, Ramon. *Memoria que al senado dirige el General . . . acerca de los ultimos sucesos ocurridos en la isla de Luzon.* Madrid: Establecimiento tipográfico de "El Liberal," 1897.

Calderón, Felipe G. *Mis Memorias Sobre la Revolución Filipina: Segunda Etape (1898 a 1901).* Manila: Imprenta de "El Renacimiento," 1907. An English version was published by Teodoro M. Kalaw under the title "The Memoirs of Felipe G. Calderón" in *The Philippine Review,* Manila, Volume IV, Nos. 6-7 (June-July, 1919) and No. 10 (October, 1919).

Columnas Volantes. Lipa. June 25, 1899, No. 13. A weekly newspaper.

Compilation of Philippine Insurgent Records: Telegraphic Correspondence of Emilio Aguinaldo, July 15, 1898 to February 28, 1899 (Annotated). Washington: War Department, Bureau of Insular Affairs, Government Printing Office, 1903.

Constitución de la Republica Filipina decretada por la Asamblea Nacional de Malolos en su solemne sesión de 21 de Enero de 1899. Madrid: 1899.

Correspondence Relating to the War with Spain: April 15, 1898-July 30, 1902. Washington: Government Printing Office, Volume II, 1902.

El Heraldo de la Revolución. A bi-weekly organ of the Philippine Revolutionary government. September 29, 1898 to January 22, 1899, Malolos.

Heraldo Filipino. A continuation of the above. It was the organ of the Philippine Republic. January 26, 1899 to March 10, 1899.

Indice Oficial. A continuation of the above. April 18, 1899 to May 13, 1899 (Numbers 1 to 7).

Gaceta de Filipinas. A continuation of the above. May 17, 1899 to October 14, 1899 (Numbers 1 to 18).

Facts about the Filipinos. A series of pamphlets issued by the Philippine Information Society in Boston, from May 1, 1901 to September 15, 1901.

Filipinas Ante Europa. A periodical edited by Isabelo de los Reyes in Spain, October 25, 1899 to June 10, 1901 (36 numbers).

El Defensor de Filipinas. A continuation of the above. July 1, 1901 to October 1, 1901 (4 numbers).

Foreman, John. *The Philippine Islands: A Political, Geographical, Ethnological, Social, and Commercial History of the Philippine Archipelago,* 3rd ed. New York: Charles Scribner's Sons, 1906.

Halstead, Murat. *The Story of the Philippines.* Chicago: Our Possessions Publishing Co., 1898.

Kalaw, Teodoro M. *La Constitución de Malolos.* Manila: Imprenta de la Vanguardia y Taliba, 1910.

————. *Planes Constitucionales Para Filipinos: Colección de textos constitucionales, antiguos y modernos.* Manila: Biblioteca Nacional de Filipinas, Bureau of Printing, 1934.

La Independencia. A daily edited by Antonio Luna. It was published in 1898 and 1899 and contains many important decrees of the Philippine government.

La Republica Filipina. A daily edited by Pedro Paterno and published in 1898 and 1899.

La Situación del País: Colección de artículos publicados por "La Voz Española" acerca de la insurrección tagala, sus causas y principales cuestiones que afectan á Filipinas. Manila: Imprenta de "Amigos del Pais," second edition, 1897.

La Solidaridad: Quincenario democrático. Published first in Barcelona and then Madrid from February 15, 1889 to November 15, 1895 (160 numbers). This was the principal organ of the "propagandists." It includes most of the articles of M. H. del Pilar and Rizal.

López-Jaena, Graciano. *Discursos y Articulos Varios.* Manila: Bureau of Printing, 1951.

Mabini, Apolinario. *La Revolución Filipina (con otros documentos de la Epoca).* Documentos de la Biblioteca Nacional. Manila: Bureau of Printing, 1931 (2 volumes). Contains most of the articles and extant letters of Mabini. Volume II contains his work *La Revolución Filipina,* which he wrote during his exile in Guam.

Paterno, Pedro. *El Pacto de Biyaknabato.* Manila: Imprenta "La Republica," 1910.

Philippine State Papers Nos. 1-38. Found in *The Philippine Social Science Review,* Nos. 1-17 (Volume III, 1931); Nos. 18-22 (Volume IV, 1932); Nos. 23-30 (Volume VI, 1934); and Nos. 31-38 (Volume VII, 1935). Contains documents relating to the

Pact of Biak-na-bato, official communications between Aguinaldo and American officers, Mabini's Constitutional Program and Decalogue, and a proclamation of the Hongkong Junta.

Plaridel, M. H. (Marcelo H. del Pilar). *La Soberanía Monacál en Filipinas: Apuntes sobre la funesta preponderencia del fraile en las islas así en lo político, como en lo económico y religioso.* Barcelona: Imp. de F. Fossas, 1888.

―――. *La Frailocracia Filipina.* Barcelona: Imp. de F. Fossas, 1889.

Ponce, Mariano. *Cartas Sobre La Revolución: (1897-1900).* Manila: Bureau of Printing, 1932.

Primo de Rivera, Fernando. *Memoria dirigida al senado por el Capitán General . . . acerca de sugestión en Filipinas.* Madrid: Imprenta lit. del Deposito de la Guerra, 1898.

"Public Instruction during the Revolutionary Regime," *The Philippine Social Science Review,* Volume XI, No. 4, Document Section (November, 1939).

Report of Major General E. S. Otis, U.S.V. on Military Operations and Civil Affairs in the Philippine Islands. Washington: Government Printing Office, 1899.

Report of Major General E. S. Otis (U.S. Army) September 1, 1899 to May 5, 1900. Washington: Government Printing Office, 1900.

Report of the Philippine Commission to the President, 1900. Washington: Government Printing Office, 1900 (4 volumes). This is the report of the Schurman Commission. It is also found in *Senate Document* No. 138, 56th Congress, 1st session (4 volumes). Volume I contains historical materials and an English version of the Malolos Constitution.

Retana y Gamboa, Wenceslao E. *Archivo del bibliófilo Filipino: recopilación de documentos históricos, científicos, literarios y políticos y estudios bibliográficos.* Madrid, 1895-1905 (5 volumes). Volumes III, IV, and V contain documents pertaining to the *Katipunan.*

―――. *Frailes y Clérigos.* Madrid: Libreria de Fernando Fe, 1890.

―――. *Los Frailes Filipinos.* Madrid: Imprenta de la Viuda de M. Minuesa de los Rios, 1898.

Rizal, José. *The Social Cancer*. Manila: Philippine Education Company, 1912. This is a translation of *Noli Me Tangere* by Charles Derbyshire.

————. *The Reign of Greed*. Manila: Philippine Education Company, 1912. This is a translation of *El Filibusterismo* by Charles Derbyshire.

————. *The Philippines a Century Hence (and other writings)*. Edited by Austin Craig. Manila: Philippine Education Company, 1912.

————. *Rizal's Political Writings*. Edited by Austin Craig. Manila: Oriental Commercial Company, 1933.

————. *Epistolario Rizalino*. Edited by Teodoro M. Kalaw. Manila: Bureau of Printing, 1930-1838 (5 volumes).

Sastron, Manuel. *La Insurrección en Filipinas y Guerra Hispano-Americana*. Madrid: Imprenta de la Sucesora de M. Minuesa de los Rios, 1901.

Senate Document No. 62 (parts i-iii), 55th Congress, 3rd session, 1898-1899. The first part contains the Treaty of Peace between Spain and the United States. The second part contains a great deal of American consular and army reports on the Philippine situation during the war with Spain.

————. No. 95, 55th Congress, 3rd session, 1898-1899. Contains reprints of various newspaper articles on the Philippines.

————. No. 66, 56th Congress, 1st session, 1899-1900. Contains the article "The Backwoods Filipino" by W. B. Wilcox (paymaster U.S.N.) and Leonard Sargent (Naval Cadet U.S.N.); and the "Memorial to Congress [United States]" by Felipe Buencamino.

————. No. 208 (parts i-iv), 56th Congress, 1st session, 1899-1900. Contains communications between the United States Executive Department and Aguinaldo. It also reproduces many of the official documents and proclamations of Aguinaldo and the revolutionary government.

————. No. 112, 56th Congress, 2nd session, 1900-1901. This is the *Report of the Taft Commission*.

————. No. 135, 56th Congress, 2nd session, 1900-1901. Contains papers relating to the exile of Mabini and other prominent Filipinos to the island of Guam.

————. No. 190, 56th Congress, 2nd session, 1900-1901. Deals with the problem of land held by religious orders in the Philippines. Contains the testimonies gathered by the Philippine Commission relating to Filipino attitudes towards the friars. Contains about 28 interviews with leading ecclesiastical authorities and prominent Filipinos.

————. No. 331 (parts i-iii), 57th Congress, 1st session, 1901-1902. Contains hearings before the Committee on the Philippines of the United States Senate.

St. Clair, Francis. *The Katipunan or the Rise and Fall of the Filipino Commune*. Manila: Amigos del Pais, 1902. The author's name is a pseudonym. Pages 13 to 35 contain part of the statement of Captain Olegario Diaz on the *Katipunan* (October 28, 1896) which is found in Retana's *Archivo*, Volume III, pp. 412-441.

Taylor, John Rogers Meigs. *Philippine Insurgent Records*. This consists of 5 volumes that are still in galley proof as the publication was suspended by Taft, then Secretary of War. It is the most extensive and valuable collection of its kind. It contains the English translation of about 1,562 revolutionary documents, A copy is found in the Library of Congress, Washington, D.C.

————. *Report on the Organization for the Administration of Civil Government Instituted by Emilio Aguinaldo and His Followers in the Philippine Archipelago*. Washington: Government Printing Office, 1903.

B. Articles:

Aglipay, Gregorio. "Independent Catholic Church in the Philippines," *The Independent*, Volume LV, No. 2865 (October 29, 1903).

Anderson, Thomas M. "Our Rule in the Philippines," *The North American Review*, Volume CLXX (February, 1900).

LeRoy, James A. "Apolinario Mabini on the Failure of the Philippine Revolution" (Document No. 2), *The American Historical Review*, Volume XI (1906).

Mabini, Apolinario. "A Filipino Appeal to the People of the United States," *The North American Review*, Volume CLXX (January, 1900).

Regidor, Antonio. "The Filipino Case Against the Friars," *The Independent,* Volume LIII (February 7, 1901).

Santos y Cristobal, Epifanio de los. "Emilio Jacinto," *The Philippine Review,* Volume III, No. 6 (June, 1918).

―――. "Andrés Bonifacio," *The Philippine Review,* Volume III, Nos. 1-2 (January-February, 1918).

―――. "Marcelo H. del Pilar (Plaridel)," *The Philippine Review,* Volume III, Nos. 10-12 (October-December, 1918).

Secondary Sources

A. Books:

Agoncillo, Teodoro A. *The Revolt of the Masses.* Quezon City: University of the Philippines, 1956.

Artigas y Cuerva, Manuel. *Andrés Bonifacio y el Katipunan: Reseña Historica Bio-Bibliográfia.* Manila: Imp. de "La Vanguardia," 1911.

―――. *Galeria de Filipinos Ilustres.* Manila: Imp. Casa Editora "Renacimiento," 1917.

Blount, James H. *The American Occupation of the Philippines.* New York and London: G. P. Putnam's Sons, 1913.

Castillo y Jimenez, José M. del. *El Katipunan o el Filibusterismo en Filipinas.* Madrid: Imp. del Asilo de Huerfanos del S. C. de Jesus, 1897.

Castillo y Kabangis, José Lopez del. *Malolos y sus Prohombres: Estudio Crítico Histórico.* Manila: Published by the author, 1950.

Craig, Austin. *Lineage, Life and Labors of José Rizal.* Manila: Philippine Education Company, 1913.

―――. *The Filipino's Fight for Freedom.* Manila: Oriental Commercial Company, Inc., 1933.

Fernandez, Alejandro M. *The Spanish Governor and Captain-General in the Philippines.* Thesis (M.A.), Cornell University, September, 1955.

Fernandez, Leandro H. *The Philippine Republic.* New York, 1926 (University of Columbia Studies in History, Economics and Public Law, Volume CXXII, No. 1).

Garcia-Barzanallana, Manuel. *La Masonización de Filipinas—Rizal y su obra.* Barcelona: Libreria y Tipografia Catolica, 1897.

Hayden, Joseph Ralston. *The Philippines: A Study in National Development*. New York: The Macmillan Company, 1950.

Kalaw, Maximo M. *The Development of Philippine Politics (1872-1920)*. Manila: Oriental Commercial Company, Inc., 1926.

————. *The Case for the Filipinos*. New York: The Century Co., 1916.

Kalaw, Teodoro M. *The Philippine Revolution*. Manila: Manila Book Co., 1925.

————. *La Masonería Filipina: Su Origen, Desarrollo y Vicisitudes hasta la Epoca Presente*. Manila: Bureau of Printing, 1920.

LeRoy, James A. *The Americans in the Philippines: A History of the Conquest and First Years of Occupation, with an Introductory Account of the Spanish Rule*. Boston and New York: Houghton Mifflin Co., The Riverside Press, 1914, 2 volumes.

————. *Philippine Life in Town and Country*. New York and London: G. P. Putnam's Sons, 1905.

Manuel, E. Arsenio. *A Portrait of Felipe G. Calderón: Father of the Malolos Constitution*. Manila: Bookman Inc., 1954.

————. *A Dictionary of Philippine Biography*, Vol. I. Manila: Filipiniana Publications, 1955.

Norton, M. M. *Builders of a Nation: A Series of Biographical Sketches*. Manila, 1914.

Palma, Rafael. *Apolinario Mabini: Estudio Biográfico*. Manila: Bureau of Printing, 1931.

————. *Biografía de Rizal*. Manila: Bureau of Printing, 1949.

Retana y Gamboa, Wenceslao E. *Vida y Escritos del Dr. José Rizal*. Madrid: Libreria General de Victoriano Suarez, 1907.

Reyes y Florentino, Isabelo de los. *Independencia y Revolución*. Madrid: Imp. y Lit. de J. Corrales, 1900.

————. *La Religion del "Katipunan."* Madrid, 1900.

————. *Catedra (Sermonario) de la Iglesia Filipina Independiente*. Edición oficial. May 25, 1932.

————. *La Sensacional memoria sobre la Revolución Filipina de 1896-1897*. Madrid: Tipolit. de J. Corrales, 1899.

Russell, Charles Edward, and E. B. Rodriguez. *The Hero of the Filipinos*. New York and London: The Century Co., 1923.

Russell, Henry. *Our War with Spain and Our War with the Filipinos: Their Causes, Incidents, and Results*. Connecticut: Hartford Publishing Co., 1899.

Sexton, William Thaddeus. *Soldiers in the Sun: An Adventure in Imperialism.* Harrisburg, Pa.: The Military Science Publishing Company, 1939.

Pardo de Tavera, T. H. "History of the Philippines," *Census of the Philippine Islands of 1903,* Volume I, Washington: United States Bureau of Census, 1905. This is an English version of the *Reseña Histórica de Filipinas desde su Descubrimiento hasta 1903.*

Van Meter, H. H. *The Truth about the Philippines, from Official Records and Authentic Sources.* Chicago: The Liberty League, 1900.

Wilcox, Marion. *Harper's History of the War in the Philippines.* New York: Harper and Brothers, 1900.

Wise, Francis H. *A History of the Philippine Independent Church* (M.A. thesis in History). Quezon City, University of the Philippines, 1954.

Zaide, Gregorio F. *History of the Katipunan.* Manila: Loyal Press, 1939.

————. *The Philippine Revolution.* Manila: Modern Book Co., 1954.

B. Articles:

Agoncillo, Teodoro A. "The Filipino Intellectuals and the Revolution." *Philippine Social Sciences and Humanities Review,* Volume XVII, No. 2 (June, 1953).

Bonsal, Stephen. "The Work of the Friars," *North American Review,* No. DLI (October, 1902).

Fabella, Gabriel F. "Church Administration in the Philippines 1581-1762," *The Philippine Social Science Review,* Volume IV, Nos. 3-4 (July-August, 1932).

Kalaw, Teodoro M. "The Constitutional Plan of the Philippine Revolution," *Philippine Law Journal,* Volume I, No. 5 (December, 1914).

————. "El Ejemplo de Mabini ante la Juventud Filipina," *The Philippine Review,* Volume I, No. 5 (May, 1916).

————. "Los Escritos de Mabini," *The Philippine Review,* Volume IV, No. 4 (April, 1919).

LeRoy, James A. "The Aglipayan Schism in the Philippines," *The Independent,* Volume LVI, No. 2891 (April 28, 1904).

————. "The Catholic Church in the Philippines," *The Independent,* Volume LVI, No. 2875 (January 7, 1904).

Malcolm, George A. "The Revolutionary Government," *The Philippine Review,* Volume I, Nos. 4-6 (April-June, 1915).

Parker, Donald D. "Church and State in the Philippines (1896-1906)," *The Philippine Social Science Review,* Volume X, No. 4 (November, 1938).

Rivera, Juan A. "The Aglipayan Movement," *Philippine Social Science Review,* Volume IX, No. 4 (December, 1937) to Volume X, No. 1 (February, 1938).

Shane, Charleson. "A Sketch of Catholicity in the Philippines," *The Catholic World,* Volume LXVII, No. 401 (August, 1898).

Veyra, Jaime C. de. "The Constitution of Biak-na-Bató," *Journal of the Philippine Historical Society,* Volume I, No. 1 (July, 1941).

Villanueva, Honesto A. "A Chapter of Filipino Diplomacy," *Philippine Social Sciences and Humanities Review,* Volume XVII, No. 2 (June, 1952).

————. "Diplomacy of the Spanish-American War," *Philippine Social Sciences and Humanities Review,* Volume XIV-XVI (June, 1949-1951).

Yabes, Leopoldo Y. "The Filipino Struggle for Political Emancipation," *A Republic Is Born* (Official Commemorative Volume on Independence Day, July 4, 1946), Manila, 1948, pp. 195-198.

General Bibliographies

Griffin, Appleton P. C. *List of Books on the Philippine Islands in the Library of Congress.* Washington: Government Printing Office, 1903.

Pardo de Tavera, T. H. *Biblióteca Filipina.* Washington: Government Printing Office, 1903.

Collections

Philippine Insurgent Records. Most of these documents were formerly in the National Archives in Washington, D.C. until they were transferred to the National Library, Manila in 1958. Translations of the most important documents are in John Rogers Meigs Taylor's *Philippine Insurgent Records,* 5 volumes.

Index